Death Thousand Clots!

By David Scott

ISBN: 978-1-326-22599-5

PublishNation, London

www.publishnation.co.uk

Preface

A good character is the best tombstone. Those who loved you and were helped by you will remember you when forget-me-nots have withered. Carve your name on hearts, not on marble. - Charles Spurgeon.

I dithered about publishing this book. After all, who is interested in what I have done in my lifetime? That got me thinking. I still dithered, but I continued writing and the more I wrote, the more convinced I became that some people would enjoy reading my musings.

And just to be contrary I started at the end.

Several people have asked me for advice when they have thought about writing a book. I have always told them to write for enjoyment – anything else is a bonus. After all, in this day and age self publishing is not difficult and relatively inexpensive if authors want to see their work in print.

I wrote my first book with the help of friends in 1987. The Title – *Once a Week is Enough* – was better than the content, but it did raise more than £1,000 for the Oesophageal Cancer Research Appeal at East Birmingham Hospital.

Nearly 20 years later I wrote my first novel – *The Standard Bearer* – set in an Essex town in the late 1970s. This was a much better effort and sold more than 700 copies. I wrote it on trains and while staying in hotels round the country to avoid boredom. It proved I could write more than a 400 word newspaper splash or a 5,000 word essay.

In the summer of 2013 I had a flash of inspiration while giving a talk to a Probus Club and set to work on a book titled *The Joys and Terrors of Public Speaking*. I wrote about my own experience of speaking to a multitude of audiences and invited newspaper editors, politicians, clergymen and others to contribute. Fifty three of them did and the resulting book, published in April 2014, made people laugh while offering some wise advice and informed tips to would-be speakers.

I did contemplate writing a follow up to *The Standard Bearer*, the ending of which I deliberately left open for such a possibility, but instead felt the need to put something down in writing about my life and family for my children and future generations of the Scott clan. At that stage I did not intend to publish whatever I wrote in book form, but thought a few photocopied and bound 'books' for a limited audience would be as far as I would go. I secretly hoped my children and grandchildren would get round to reading my life story at some stage of their own lives.

Is it vanity to want people to know what you have done and achieved? Perhaps! In my defence I can only state that quite a few people have told me I have led an interesting and sometimes colourful life.

The more I wrote, the more I realised there was a story worth telling.

The first few pages explain much of what follows. Discovering a family secret proved to be the answer to many questions and the key to my life.

I finally decided to publish again when my good friend and fellow author Mel Menzies told me: '*Don't hide your light under a bushel.*'

In later chapters I have indulged myself by writing about the present state of the regional newspaper industry. I hope people don't think I am an 'old fuddy duddy' when commenting on some of the dreadful mistakes which, I believe, will result in the death of many regional newspapers. I have been in a good position to observe and chart the sad decline of an industry which has given me a wonderful life.

I have not set out to settle any scores. At times I have left some names out to protect third parties who might have been embarrassed by what I have written.

I make no apologies for including my own personal testimony as someone who found God and His grace – eventually.

One chapter is an edited version of a chapter from *The Joys and Terrors of Public Speaking* for those who have not yet read that book. Feel free to skip it.

Finally, I have taken my own advice and enjoyed writing *Death by a Thousand Clots*! I hope you enjoy reading it just as much.

David Scott is the former editor of several regional newspapers and was Managing Director of a daily newspaper in Birmingham before setting up his own media consultancy and journalism training company.

He has trained more than 8,000 journalists and managers in the UK and abroad.

He lives in Torquay with his wife, Valerie, and has three grown-up children, none of whom now live at home.

He is an avid fan of Burnley Football Club, the New England Patriots and Boston Red Sox and spends as many warm summer days as possible watching Somerset cricket.

His other books include *Once a Week is Enough*, published in 1987, *The Standard Bearer*, published in 2005, and *The Joys and Terrors of Public Speaking* published in 2014.

This book is dedicated to my wife Valerie, daughter Georgina and sons Timothy and Robin with a heartfelt 'thank you' for enriching my life.

CHAPTER ONE

A MYSTERY IS SOLVED

Some people spread joy wherever they go; some people spread joy whenever they go – Oscar Wilde.

The telephone caller in early September 2010 was my sister, Sandra, who was still living in Barnoldswick on the Yorkshire/Lancashire border where I spent the majority of my school years. It was an invitation to meet her and husband John later in the month while they were enjoying a week's late summer holiday at a holiday caravan park in Exmouth. I thought it was a little surprising because they normally go to Fleetwood or Scarborough. The 300 mile drive to Devon was further than they had ventured for some time, but I readily agreed that my wife, Valerie, and I would join them on the Thursday for coffee and then lunch.

'*It's the Avon Holiday Camp,*' said my sister. '*You can't miss it. Just look up how to find it on Google.*' I struggled for several hours trying to find the place until I remembered most people in my home town drop their 'aitches'. She meant the Haven Holiday Camp.

Caravans have never really appealed to me. My idea of camping is a three star rather than a five star hotel. But my sister loves them so we duly turned up mid morning on the last day of the month for coffee, a chance to catch up on family news and a friendly, sunny day out. All went well until I excused myself to visit the toilet. When I came back Valerie was looking glum and my sister was crying. Whatever could have gone wrong in three minutes?

'*I have something to tell you and don't know how,*' was Sandra's opening remarks amid her tears. I immediately feared the worst and thought she had some life threatening illness. '*Your father wasn't your real father. I couldn't not tell you any longer,*' she blurted out amid more sobs. And so I began to unravel a mystery which in my 63rd year answered many questions.

1

I had suspected for more than 30 years there was a family mystery and something I did not know about my difficult childhood; some reason why I was treated the way I was. But I had never been able to pin down anything of substance and as I grew older and a little wiser I pushed all such questions to the back of my mind.

To the general surprise of the other three I smiled. It was as if someone had lifted a curtain and set me free. It explained a lot: the sneers; the lack of interest in my successful political and business career; the limited interest in his grandchildren; and the occasional violence. Ernest who brought me up and I had always called 'dad' was not my real father. It was such a simple, quick answer – a truly cathartic moment. Two and a half years after his death I knew the truth at last.

When I had managed to convince my sister I was fine with the news and not in the least upset she fleshed out the story she had come 300 miles to tell - the story she felt she could not hold onto any longer. My real father was actually a Polish pilot who joined the RAF during World War Two with whom my mother, Violet, had a brief affair in Blackpool at the end of 1946 and early 1947. When that ended she met a local lad just out of the army - Ernest. She probably didn't know until a few weeks after meeting him that she was already pregnant with me. How she managed to persuade him to marry her in late June 1947 - five and a bit months before I was born - will never be known. He must have considered himself very unlucky to have made her pregnant so quickly.

They had both suffered during the Second World War: my mother's first husband, Alan, died in a Japanese prisoner of war camp; my apparent father told lies about his age so he could enlist and saw untold horrors in Burma fighting the Japanese. I can imagine how distraught Ernest would have been when my mother told him she was pregnant. He did what he thought was the 'right thing' and married her when he was led to believe the child was his. It must have come as an awful shock when I arrived several months early in December at the start of the second coldest winter for 100 years! He never let on that he knew I was fathered by somebody else; I give him credit for that.

In my early twenties hints were dropped by Irene, my mother's sister, that things weren't quite what they seemed in 1947, but all she would say when I pressed her was that there were *'family doubts'*. Doubts about what were never explained. Irene was good at playing mind games and I was always too busy to raise the matter on the rare occasions my mother and I were alone. It made no difference because inwardly I knew from an early age I was 'different.' By then I had a sister and two brothers, but we had little in common. Sandra, Brian and Stephen had obvious facial similarities with my 'father.' I didn't and throughout my childhood I acted and behaved very differently to them. It wasn't that they did anything wrong, it was just that I was the odd one out. I didn't bond with any of them in the way normal brothers and sisters often do. They must have found me strange. Fortunately, time is a great healer and in later years the situation changed. Sandra and I have a close relationship we both value today.

When she finished the story she came all the way to Devon to tell me and had stopped crying I had an overwhelming sense of relief. It explained so much about my childhood and the troubled times I endured until I could make my own way in the world. Above all I now knew none of it was my fault. I hadn't do anything wrong apart from being conceived. I shall continue to call Ernest my father because whatever his shortcomings - and there were many - he did stand by my mother and bring me up. And when he died I received a quarter of his small estate. As to my real father, there was no way I could begin to trace him 63 years later and I have never tried. Of course, I don't feel Polish in any way. I am a proud Englishman despite my wife frequently calling me 'Scottski'.

The fact my father treated me differently, something I always knew and felt, is partially explained by his own difficult upbringing and history. However, it is not something I would wish on anyone else in the same circumstances. I was an unhappy child and many of my early memories are not good ones. In my ignorance I set out to prove myself to him. The problem was that the more I succeeded in life, the tougher it must have been for him.

It is comforting to know the real reason why he held such a grudge against me, but it doesn't excuse the treatment he meted out. He never praised me and never asked how I was doing even when I was making good progress, first at school and then in politics and at work. Until I knew the truth I put his behaviour down to the fact that because of me he had been forced into a marriage he didn't want; he had stupidly got my mother pregnant and he was determined to take out his anger on me as well as her. Another thought I held on to for many years was that as the eldest I saw the violence he dished out to my mother. I was their baby sitter on Saturday nights from around the age of nine. It was not unusual for the pair of them to have a row on the way home and my mother to suffer a black eye or worse. He was good with his fists and not afraid to use them in any alcohol-fuelled argument.

From my teens onwards I also offered too much back chat when silence would have served me better. I must have made him very unhappy every time he looked at me, doubly so when he had had too much to drink.

There were times when I felt his failure to be a real father to me more keenly than others. In my teens I played in two football cup finals and a cricket semi-final - all on the nearby Victory Park in Barnoldswick - but he never came to watch any of the matches. Other dads and some mums were on the touchlines cheering on their sons, but I never once had that experience. I trudged off on my own at the end of the games while my teammates shared their jubilation with their families. I was lucky if he even asked about the score when I got home! There were never any congratulatory words.

We were reconciled to some extent in later life because by then I refused to let him get to me. In his later years he did show some minor recognition of what I had achieved in life, but there was always a sarcastic edge to his comments and his cruel streak was never far from the surface. One Easter when Valerie and I visited he refused to put on the heating even though there was snow on the ground *because it isn't April yet*. Whenever we visited he spent most of the time telling me how well my brothers and sister were doing. I wasn't the only one who noticed! His lack of any real interest even extended to my three children – his grandchildren.

I didn't come to terms with the problems my parents must have encountered in the late 1940s until I was happily married with children of my own. They came out of the war determined to make up for lost time and in Blackpool they spent what money they had on beer and dancing. The Blackpool Tower ballroom was their favourite venue. Who could blame them for wanting to party as much as they could after six 'lost' years?

My mother was given £410 as compensation for her first husband's death. She also had money from the sale of a house, but blew it all within 18 months. She was never any good at handling money. When the money ran out, reality set in. She did not have it easy as a child: her father died when she was six and she watched as my grandmother dealt with a mob who stoned their house during the General Strike of 1926. She was not unintelligent and passed her 11 plus exam, but the money was not available for her to be sent to a grammar school. She worked in shops and then in the Lancashire cotton mills and got by on her friendly disposition rather than any sales or weaving abilities. Woolworths did not take kindly to her breaking up perfectly good biscuits when the broken biscuit section ran low! From all accounts her first marriage to Alan in 1941 was a happy if brief one. A few months after their wedding, Alan was sent to Singapore where he was captured by the Japanese and died in a prisoner of war camp. The war shattered her nerves and she took valium from 1945 until her death. Amazingly, doctors also told her to smoke heavily to help combat nerves; she was a heavy smoker for the rest of her life. She did well to live into her late eighties.

My father had a terrible childhood. His mother died when he was young and he had no proper job experience before he joined the army. He had to start from scratch when he was demobbed in 1946 so his later achievement in becoming a hard working engineer for Rolls Royce was very much to his credit. In his youth he was trained to kill people and little else.

When my mother and father married they had little money left after many months of drinking and dancing most nights. They rented a house 20 yards round the corner from my paternal grandfather and his second wife, Annie, in Thornton Cleveleys. My grandfather tended an allotment in his back garden while my grandmother spent most of her time in a kitchen which was also their bathroom. The bath had a wooden cover which served as a table when we all sat down to eat. He was gassed on the River Somme during the First World War - one of six brothers, all of whom survived that horrible war. Growing vegetables on his allotment was the only real work I ever saw my grandfather do. He never had a proper job.

I have only hazy memories of those early years. My grandmother was a jittery woman who believed God had given her a mission in life to dote on my lazy grandfather. She did everything for him. It made him even lazier. As far as he was concerned women were put on this earth simply to serve men! She was always short of money, but had a good if unrealistic heart. She would often give me a 'bacon buttie' and go without herself. I remember her as a kind, simple soul. My grandfather was a hard, difficult man who neglected my father during his childhood. He was a boxer of some repute and won a major championship in June 1910. I have in my possession the cup and belt he won. After the war he dragged my father round boxing booths and made him fight other youngsters for whatever coins were thrown into the ring.

When he remarried after the sudden death of my father's real mother both became keen Salvationists. My main memory of my grandmother is of her in her Salvation Army bonnet and uniform. She loved to sit in a chair praising The Lord when she wasn't serving food, drink or whatever my grandfather wanted. That suited my grandfather who did as little real work round the house as he could get away with. Apart from tending his allotment, he sat in a large armchair reading, sleeping or talking to a budgie called Joey. Unfortunately Joey learned to swear from him. It was quite embarrassing when they had visitors; my grandfather would cover the bird's cage with a blanket to keep him quiet.

My dad got a job on the railways in 1948 and soon my sister, Sandra, came along and then my brother, Brian. I was two and a half years old when he was called up to serve in Korea with the United Nations force led by the Americans. He was a reservist and was told it was going to be a 'police operation'. It was until the Yanks pressed on right through North Korea to the Chinese border and 'encouraged' a massive Communist army to send them running for their lives all the way back to South Korea. The horrors of war he saw for a second time never left him and made him a bitter man at times. I was too young to understand. In my teens I did not give him any credit for what he had suffered because the times he talked most about that war and what he had seen were when he had had too much to drink on a Saturday night. I always struggled on those occasions. He wrote his memoirs, but I have never read them. I am told they bring tears to the eyes of those who do read them. I never will. My sister has them for safe keeping.

A year after my father's return from Korea my brother Stephen was born and we moved into a house in Colne Road, Burnley, which we rented from my mother's Uncle Frank. It was a large house which gave us far more room but was very cold. There was no central heating in those days and if we lit a coal fire it was in one room only. My father got a job with the Towneley Fire Clay Company, but it wasn't well paid and there was little money left over by the time he had paid the rent and enjoyed a Saturday night out. Bath time once a fortnight was in a tub in front of the one fire. I suffered from chilblains, a painful inflammation of small blood vessels in my skin that occurred in response to sudden warming from cold temperatures, usually when I took off damp socks and warmed my feet by the fire. They caused itching, red patches, swelling and blistering on extremities, such as my toes, fingers, ears and nose. They were supposed to clear up within a few weeks, but I seemed to have them nearly all year round. The best approach to avoid developing them was to limit exposure to cold, dress warmly and cover exposed skin. There was never a chance my parents would do that.

In 1953 I started at my first school - Barden - about a mile away and at the top of a steep hill. I walked there and back on my own every day. I loved doing the beautiful handwriting with hoops and loops we were taught, but often felt very hungry. One of my better breakfasts was something called 'pobbies'; a bowl of bread, milk and sugar. My clothes were shabby compared with classmates of both sexes. I started playing football in the playground and found I had a knack of scoring lots of goals even at that early age. It was something both my son's 'inherited' in later life.

In an attempt to improve my status with my schoolmates I stole a bag of marbles from a shop near my home. When they were discovered I was given a sound thrashing by my father with a stick and hand over my backside. The only other occasion he imposed physical discipline for my misbehaviour came when I told a lie about the date of my birthday at Sunday School. I was sent to church for the first time when I was seven, just after my real birthday in December, and for several months I watched with envy as other children were given a bag of sweets and everyone sang *Happy Birthday*. A few months later I claimed my birthday was in July and duly got my bag of sweets and moment in the limelight. Unfortunately, a few weeks later my Sunday School teacher asked my mother what presents I had got on my birthday and the game was up. He hit me on numerous other occasions but these were always after a heavy drinking bout and more out of frustration at the constant reminder of who I was.

The first television programme I saw was the 1956 Cup Final between Manchester City and Birmingham at a neighbour's house. We didn't have a television of our own for another year but I did get to watch programmes like the Cisco Kid, Rag, Tag and Bobtail and Andy Pandy when I visited my aunty and uncle who lived the other side of Burnley.

We had summer holidays of a kind. They were courtesy of my grandparents in Thornton Cleveleys who somehow managed to cram us into their house for a week each year. My parents scraped together the rail fares but we had to walk right across Blackpool from the railway station to the bus station with our suitcases and bags to catch a bus to Thornton. The rest of the week we walked the three miles each way from Thornton to the beach at Cleveleys each day. I hated it. One year I caught chicken pox and had to stay indoors every day while the others went off to the seaside. I played in the back garden on my own with a cricket bat and ball.

The move to Barnoldswick 10 miles away on the Yorkshire /Lancashire border in 1958 didn't improve our lot as far as I was concerned, although my father now had his first good job at Rolls Royce and my mother found work running eight looms at a local mill. There never seemed enough food, even on Christmas Day when we had rare sight of real meat. It didn't make much difference because my mother usually managed to make a mess of any cooking.

We had an end of terrace house which was just as damp as our previous homes. The outside toilet produced an awful smell when the weather turned really cold because it froze solid; not even a kerosene lamp hung near to the water inflow pipe would unfreeze it. There was little hot water and certainly none in a morning so we all washed in cold water and went to school with little breakfast in our stomachs. I hate to think what might have happened if I had not got free school milk and a good free dinner. I didn't need an alarm clock to wake me; around 6.30 the next door neighbour used to smoke a couple of cigarettes while sat on her outside toilet. Her coughing woke up most people in our road.

Because I was the eldest I had the job of going to the corner shop to see if they would let us have some food 'on tick' - as it was called - until the end of the week when my mother would occasionally settle the bill. On numerous occasions I felt humiliated in front of neighbours when 'tick' was refused and I had to leave the shop empty-handed with the angry words of the shop owner ringing in my ears about the need to pay existing debts before asking for any more credit. It was the same when the rent man called and we all had to hide behind the sofa and pretend nobody was in. My mother was an awful cook and hopeless with what little money she was given.

Somebody once asked me: *'Did you feel poor?'* in the expectation that I would say I didn't know any better. Yes, I did feel poor; I did know my school mates were better clothed and fed; and I did notice they had a father who cared for them better than mine did.

Barnoldswick to my little mind seemed like a different country when I started at Rainhall Road Junior and Infant School. At least it was in a different county - being three miles over the border in Yorkshire and determined to stay that way for as long as it could. I was in the top class because the school had just got 'junior' status. I was among the first batch from the school to take the 11 plus and I also captained the school football team. The school had never won a match before I arrived, but my new friends and I did them proud because in two seasons we lost only once. Our first win was against the nearby Church School whom we beat 5-1. My little tubby neighbour Eddie Sutcliffe was our goalkeeper and he stopped nearly everything that came his way that day, while at the other end I scored twice.

I found the country dancing classes harder going though and was eventually dismissed from the mixed team for non attendance at several after-school sessions. I passed the 11 plus when I was only nine and a half but had to wait nearly two years for the move up to Skipton Grammar School. A lazy streak set in which academically I found hard to shake off for several years.

A year after the move to Barnoldswick I was climbing a wall which ran alongside our end-of-terrace home when a large pointed stone at the top came toppling down on me and sliced off the top of a finger on my left hand. It could easily have killed me. I managed to catch the severed part and ran home with it in my right hand. My mother took one look and fainted! Fortunately, I was quickly rushed to the general hospital in Burnley and they sewed it back on. The nerves were severed. For 30 years I had no feeling in the tip of the finger, but somehow the nerves eventually grew again. Although it left me with a deformed finger I now have its full use.

Even a 10-year old realised what a shock it was when almost an entire Manchester United team was wiped out in the 1958 Munich air crash, but that apart national events were never discussed in my presence. Anyway I was too busy playing football and cricket in the street where an older boy called Dick Lord taught me how to head a football properly. It hurt when I headed the lace part of the ball.

The things I saw and heard from an early age undoubtedly affected my attitude to both my parents. I loved my mother and cried with her when she broke down in frustration at the life she was leading. It has only been with the benefit of hindsight that I have been able to rationalise my feelings and try to come to terms with both what went on, and how I reacted. In addition to the way I was treated by my father several other factors played a part. First, there was my ability from an early age to mix and engage with older people through sport. From the age of 10 I was not home a lot and did not feel the need to join in family life to the same extent as my brothers and sister. Second, there was the part played by aunty (Irene) and her husband (Terry). Third, was the education I received at Skipton Grammar School and the subsequent friendships I formed with Barnoldswick lads Martin Newbold and Stephen Robinson. Martin had a subbuteo set which we set up in his dining room and played long matches. His mother fed us chocolate biscuits and orange drinks. We played golf on the small nine-hole Rolls Royce course during our school holidays because our fathers worked for the company and as such we had automatic membership. Stephen and I shared a love of cricket and football. Fourth, for reasons there is no way I could have understood at that time, I knew that not only did my dad not like me, but I didn't like him.

Irene and Terry made the biggest impact. They married just before my mother and father, but could not have any more children after my aunty had a stillborn child. It was a tragedy for them. They were more affluent than my parents - Irene was secretary to the chairman at Massey's Burnley brewery and Terry had a good sales job with several North West firms and eventually Guinness. My maternal grandmother, Ethel, lived with them in a smart well kept terraced house in Grenville Road, Burnley, not far from two large parks and a cricket ground. In my teens I walked to Turf Moor to watch Burnley play in the old First Division from their house in about 40 minutes - it was sometimes quicker than going by car. From about the age of seven they started taking my sister Sandra and I for weekend trips to Fleetwood or St Anne's and gradually these became more common. I stayed overnight at a weekend or during part of my school holidays. I was always keen to go because I enjoyed the car rides, the love I was shown and the better food. We would often go via the country route from Whalley and nearly always stop at the Miller Arms on the way back where I would be given a soft drink – a luxury at the time. After a couple of years Sandra lost interest, but I spent several weeks of my winter, spring and parts of summer school holidays with them.

I loved the seaside trips. Terry, Irene and my grandmother usually parked near the seafront at Fleetwood. They would hire three deck chairs and sit listening to the town brass band play all Sunday afternoon. I would sit on the grass. If I was lucky my aunty would take me to the slot machines for a while. When I was 12 they took me to the Scottish borders and I stayed in a hotel for the first time. Terry taught me how to handle the abundance of knives, forks and spoons at the dinner table and how to work from the outside in. They bought me my first suit for the occasion.

My grandmother, who showed me a lot of affection, was home all day. She and I would go for walks to a nearby park and in an afternoon play cards with Terry after he had done his admin work. Occasionally I would spend the day with him as he toured pubs and clubs in East Lancashire to check Guinness was being served at the correct temperature and the pipes were clean. He would draw off half a pint, get out his thermometer and either give the all clear or issue a warning. Three warnings would result in the drink being removed – a potentially fatal move for any Irish club. He did not drink the stuff so from around the age of 10 I developed quite a taste for draft Guinness, much to my aunty's displeasure when she had to put me to bed after I arrived back at the end of the day a bit worse for wear. My grandmother cleaned and cooked so that when Irene came home she had little to do.

When I was not in the local parks I would take a tennis ball and bash it against their backyard wall with my cricket bat, in the process learning how to deal with the different angles from which a ball could arrive. It helped me become a very good defensive batsmen a few years later.

Irene died in her early sixties after suffering with rheumatoid arthritis for many years. She and my mother didn't have much in common and in later years she became very bitter and sometimes downright nasty, but she and Terry taught me many good things and showered me with the attention I craved.

By the time I was 10 I was scorer for Barnoldswick Cricket Club's first eleven who played in the highly competitive Ribblesdale League. In those days all competitive amateur cricket was played only on Saturdays. When Barnoldswick tried to arrange a charity game one Sunday the Lord's Day Observance Society soon put a stop to that. My reward for keeping the score as immaculately as I could in the club's scorebook was a ham sandwich tea, a cake and a bottle of fizzy drink we called 'pop'. I loved Vimto and a drink called dandelion and burdock.

School holidays were one long game of cricket, football or golf with the occasional game of tennis inbetween during which - when I was home and not with my aunty and uncle - I had to take my mother's sandwich lunch to her at the mill because I was the eldest. My 'seniority' meant I also had responsibility for keeping my sister and two brothers out of trouble. I am sure nobody who has witnessed it has ever forgotten the combination of noise and cotton dust choking the air when they entered a cotton mill. I had to be careful when walking between the looms that the arms travelling back and forth did not break a limb. I learned to communicate in sign language because hearing yourself above the din of the looms was impossible. I don't think my mother was a very good weaver. The 'tackler' – a sort of quality control manager cum engineer - had to undo the knots which she let through and jammed her looms. I admired her for the hard work she put in while running a home, albeit not very well.

Once I started playing sport and then mixing among older sportsmen I drifted even further away from my brothers and sisters. None of them shared my academic or sporting interests. It was the start of a split which was only healed many years later. I felt I had nothing in common with them and they with me, and to make matters worse I hated being responsible for them while my parents were at work. Thankfully, the four of us get on much better in later life than we did in our early years.

Money was always tight. I did not receive any pocket money until I was 13. Some weeks my mother would cry because she had no money to buy food; I can remember consoling her and saying it didn't matter. My dad never gave her enough to feed the six of us and even when they became more prosperous he strictly controlled the amount of money he gave my mother for food and other essentials. He never changed; in later years when there was just the two of them he cut her monthly money if they went on holiday. She got her first washing machine when she was in her seventies, but only on the understanding she did not use it more than once a week. The first time she used it he read the electric meter before and after the wash.

When we moved in the early 1960s to a modern detached house on the outskirts of Barnoldswick the bedrooms were very small. Brian, Stephen and I shared two beds in a small bedroom which seemed permanently cold, even in summer. Those were the years when we really did have four seasons and during the winter we scraped ice off the inside of windows for days on end.

After passing my 11-plus exam I gained a place at the prestigious Ermysted's Skipton Grammar School which required my parents to make some considerable sacrifices given their parlous financial state - in those days any spare money went on a Saturday night out. I had no idea then how much it cost them, but the school insisted I wore a blue blazer with the school badge on its front pocket, short grey trousers, grey socks with flashes prominent under the turn back and the appropriate tie for one of six 'houses' we were assigned to. I was in Craven house, which basically was all the boys from Barnoldswick. We were expected to have both a black and white striped and a white rugby shirt and two pairs of shorts and full cricket gear. I felt I had entered a different world on my first day at Ermysted's in August 1959. The new intake had to assemble in the quad after which we were given some sort of induction tour. I was scared and felt very alone It was several weeks before I knew my way round the school and its labyrinth of corridors.

From the outset the school taught me the importance of doing my best for my 'house' in all sports. One of the biggest events was the annual cross country run which started at the top of the moors overlooking Skipton and always took place in January when we battled through snow and muddy fields back to the school. I came fifth out of 120 in my first year - first home from my house. I was fit then because I walked or ran everywhere I went. I also excelled at cricket and when the first school summer came round I was selected, along with my friend Martin Newbold, to represent the junior colts side mainly made up of boys two years older than Martin and I. In my first match against Giggleswick School, which we won by two runs, I top scored with 13 and took a diving catch at square leg to get rid of the opposition's star batsman. I can remember being surrounded by much older teammates who clapped me rather hard on the back. I was a slight figure weighing only around six stone. In the next match I hit 45 against Eshton Hall, a private school north of Gargrave.

The teachers who coached us would be jailed today for their methods. In the practice nets I was made to face the older fast bowlers. A master would stand by the side of the net with a stump in his hand and if I backed off from short pitched bowling the pointed end, which was usually driven into the ground, would be driven into my bum. The aim was to get me to play straight and get into line behind the ball - not back off. When I started playing a lot of club cricket this stood me in good stead and I was always difficult to get out if I decided to stick around and defend. In the return match against Giggleswick I was amazed to find I had been allotted a 'fag' who carried my cricket bag, laid out my gear and served me tea between innings.

It was a different story, though, in the winter terms. I did not enjoy the compulsory rugby. For a start we had to walk nearly two miles each way often in atrocious weather to the pitches at Sandylands on the edge of Skipton. By the time we got started I was cold and fed up, so I opted out in the third year and joined the cross country team. At least I was warmer! Much to my disappointment soccer was a taboo subject. If anyone started a game during the lunch break it was an automatic detention.

Unfortunately my sporting achievements were not matched in the classroom. I was lazy and did not do much homework which resulted at the end of my first nine months in finishing in the bottom 28 boys of my year. It would have been worse but for a good performance in history. Anybody who knows me today will not be surprised I was hopeless at art and woodwork. The coffee table I was supposed to make ended up as a stool because I could not get its legs level. This meant that when we were graded at the end of the summer term I was placed in the lowest C stream - the no hopers really. I did, however, get on well with all the masters for whom I had a lot of respect then and even more now; they found me easy going and no trouble, so I was allowed to have a relatively easy life. I did just about enough homework to avoid trouble.

There was a lot of bullying at the school and nothing like the pastoral care available today. The school had its own pool and until I learned to swim I was regularly dragged under the water by one boy who took great delight in trying to drown me. Even today I dream about drowning. I learned to swim in order to survive. The worst bullying was on the 25 minute train journey from Barnoldswick to

Skipton until Dr Beeching's axe closed the line in 1963. We were packed into old, dirty, closed carriages with no corridors. The older boys used to lift us onto the luggage racks and prod compass points into us, or thrash us with the leather belts used to pull down the windows. It got easier from my third year by which time most Barnoldswick boys went to Ermysted's by Laycock's bus. In the terrible winter of 1963 we got stuck in a snow drift and had to be pulled out by the emergency services.

Academically I started to get into my school work in a serious way in the summer of 1961 - my second at grammar school. Suddenly I went from 23rd out of a class of 27 to 10th thanks to coming second in history (shades of a future hobby beginning to develop) and third in maths. I was fortunate in that the standard of teaching was very high. There were no women teachers. Every master wore a black gown, had a perfect crease in his trousers and shining black shoes. Teachers in those days were far more valued and accorded more respect by both pupils and parents than they are today. In the autumn term (third year) I came top in history with 76% and moved up to sixth overall in the class. Despite another top in history, I slipped back to 11th next term and to end an erratic school year I came eighth in the summer term. By now the history top spot was all mine and my overall class position would have been very much higher but for woodwork and art and 38 absences through my yet to be understood migraine attacks which saw me visit the school nurse on many occasions. Every year the school measured and weighed me – when I was 14 and a half years old I was 5ft 1 tall and weighed 6stone 4lbs. No wonder I often felt ill!

The fourth year saw further improvement with an average place of sixth in a class of 30 and top place in all three terms in English language and history. I also made a big improvement in geography where I came fifth. My form master wrote ... ' *He is working hard and is a most useful member of the form'*. I was enjoying school and had every reason to believe that I would do moderately well in all my O Levels except French, which I never got to grips with. I dropped woodwork and art as soon as I could – or did they drop me?

During my summer holidays I went to work at Silentnight, the bed-making firm, which has its headquarters in Barnoldswick. For

16

five weeks I helped a man pick up planks of wood five feet long, place them in a machine, press a button and watch as two holes were drilled in either end. The planks were then stacked ready to be taken into the main factory. I realised that if I did not do well enough in my exams I might be doing something similar for the rest of my life. It was the motivation I needed.

I was never going to be sixth form or university material - only the top 10% went to university in those days - but I did hope to pass enough O Levels to get a reasonable job. I had thought of going into the travel industry, but fate dealt a tough blow that summer which set me back a year. I was playing cricket for the school second eleven; again in a team where the boys were much older. In early May I went to take a catch on the edge of the boundary and toppled off the pitch and down a steep slope. It was thought I had sprained my ankle; an x ray confirmed that initial opinion. But I hadn't, I had broken it and part of my right leg. I was in a lot of pain, but my father refused to accept something was wrong and continually told me I was being 'soft'. I struggled not to cry in front of him. He told me he had endured much worse when he was my age and lectured me on '*being a man.*' I got no sympathy when I was sick and pressed on for five weeks to the start of my O Levels.

Matters came to a head when I was sick in the middle of my geography paper - literally. The school could see something was wrong if my father couldn't. They took me to Skipton Hospital where the breaks were confirmed. My leg was slapped in plaster for six weeks because the strain of walking on the broken ankle had weakened it. I missed several of the exams, but still gained passes in history, geography and science. I never found out but I think the school had some stern words with my parents and I was allowed to stay on at school an extra year and take my O Levels again. I added passes in English Language, English Literature and maths, but it earned me another black mark from my father. Once my leg healed good food provided by my aunty and uncle, friends and while playing sport helped me put back the weight I had lost and regain full fitness.

The highlight of my week outside the cricket season was the Boys' Brigade nights held at St Andrew's Methodist Church in

Barnoldswick town centre. I joined when I was 12 and found myself mainly among other grammar school lads of all ages. I was placed in a squad of six under squad leader Stephen Robinson who made sure I turned up every Wednesday night with a sparkling uniform. Stephen became a life-long friend. The discipline I got in the Boys' Brigade stood me in good stead for the rest of my life and I only left when I was 17. Every week we were inspected for clean shoes, creases in trousers, polished badges and belts and brilliant white haversack/sashes across our chests. There was fierce competition to be squad of the month. After the inspection and marks we had a short service and sang *'Will your anchor hold in the storm of life'* the Boys' Brigade song. Then it was some first aid training and badge work, followed by PE and three-a-side football. On Friday nights we had band practice and games which also involved the Girls' Brigade. We had a joint band which proved more and more attractive as I got older and started to take an interest in girls.

Our company captains were Norman Hargreaves - an Earby chemist - and George Smith who worked at Rolls Royce. They gave us many hours of their time and I have nothing but total admiration now for what they did for me and the rest of the lads. Every Sunday morning at 9.50 we had our own Bible class and service. On the first Sunday of every month we paraded with the band round the town and attended the main church service. I found the latter dull and very boring, but we had to be there to get our marks. We marched round the town again after the service, bugles blasting out a variety of notes, just in case anyone was still asleep!

Every year some of us took part in the annual church concert when different church groups provided musical or other entertainment and those who played an instrument got the chance to play in front of a live audience. The minister used to sit at the edge of the stage and introduce each act. He brought the house down one year when he announced that John and Mabel, who had performed for the last dozen years, would not be appearing this time because John 'has *lost his knackers'*. Of course he meant maracas.

I worked hard to get my Boys' Brigade badges, much harder than I ever worked at school. We were a strong social group too and along with the girls we walked along the banks of the Leeds-Liverpool canal on a Sunday evening and listened to the top 20 on Radio Luxembourg. The girls supported us on a Saturday afternoon when we played football in the Burnley and District Boys' Brigade League. Norman managed to pack most of the team into his van when we played away. He came straight from closing his shop to take us to the matches. We won the league twice and also two cup finals, one of them 5-2 when I scored twice.

Most of my group left the Boys' Brigade at 16 but Stephen Robinson, who was an excellent cricketer and footballer, stayed on with me another year and it led to an amusing incident one Saturday. We played a Burnley Boys' Brigade team on the outskirts of Burnley and won 9-1. Both Stephen and I got four goals apiece. Instead of travelling back with the team we got Norman to drop us off the other side of Burnley at Towneley Park so we could watch Barnoldswick Park Rovers in an important match. Unfortunately, Towneley is a very large park and we could not find the game. We stood on the touchline of another match in our track suits trying to decide what to do 12 miles from home and with little money between us. We were spotted by one of the senior teams who were two players short so we were drafted in to play a second game that afternoon and we both scored twice in a 6-1 win. We then had the job in the gathering gloom of trying to make our way home which we did by walking all the way to Colne - about six miles - and then managing to thumb a lift to Barnoldswick. We were that fit then. Both Stephen and I were selected for an England Boys' Brigade football team which played a Northern Irish team. We drew 2-2.

During term time, until I was 16, I was not allowed out any nights but Wednesday and Friday unless I was sent to get a rare fish and chip supper for my parents. On one such occasion I was on my way back from the chip shop when I was surrounded by six secondary school boys with fishing rods. They began pushing and shoving. When it became more threatening I cracked a dish full of mushy peas on the head of one boy and dashed for home. My fitness paid off, but I got a tongue lashing and was sent straight to bed when my father found out where the mushy peas had gone.

There was constant rivalry in Barnoldswick between us grammar school lads and the secondary school boys and it came to a head one year when it was alleged three secondary pupils had been slashed with knives by grammar school boys. This was at a time when mods and rockers were making national newspaper headlines; grammar school boys were always regarded as mods and secondary boys as rockers. For two weeks I was not allowed out on my own and the police patrolled nearby when our bus returned from Skipton. Eventually the boys owned up that they had slashed themselves to cause trouble and things calmed down. The worst moment for me came on the mile walk from school over a canal bridge to the only bus stop in Skipton we were allowed to use. In those days private bus companies were not allowed to pick up passengers on bus routes run by the state owned bus companies, which meant we could not board anywhere near the school. A gang of secondary school pupils were waiting to bar our way and fights broke out. Fortunately, I was with a group of older boys who shepherded us across the bridge. When they came under attack they threw two of their assailants into the canal!

I started to take a greater interest in national events at grammar school even though Barnoldswick was - and still is - very much a backwater, off-the-beaten-track place which you only discover by chance if you wander off the main roads that connect Preston and Skipton on one side and Burnley and Skipton on the other, or travel along the Leeds-Liverpool canal.

A lot of people were scared about a possible nuclear attack by the Russians during the Cuban missile crisis of 1962; it even had us schoolboys worried for a few days. But we were all ears - and far more interested - whenever anyone talked about the Lady Chatterley's Lover trial and the sensational case involving War Minister John Profumo and call girl Christine Keeler. But like all stories they soon faded from the public gaze and for me the Ashes matches at Lords, Old Trafford and Headingley involving England and Australia were far more interesting. I had the good fortune to see Freddie Trueman and Brian Statham demolish one Australian innings during a Leeds Test when the school arranged a coach trip. I collected up bottles at the end and handed them in. It earned me a couple of shillings I spent on food.

CHAPTER TWO

FIRST JOB AND UPSET TEENS

"I didn't attend the funeral, but I sent a nice letter saying I approved of it."- Mark Twain.

The General Election of October 1964 proved to be one of those events the consequences of which I had no way of appreciating at the time. Skipton Grammar School held a mock election and one of my Barnoldswick friends, John Cockerill, was selected as the Liberal candidate. I offered to help his campaign and enjoyed it immensely. We received encouragement and help from the constituency's actual parliamentary candidate, Wilf Pickard, also from Barnoldswick and a member of the town's urban district council. John duly won - one of the few Liberal 'gains' at that election which swept out the Tories in the real thing and brought into power Harold Wilson and the Labour Party.

I volunteered to help on election day. We were given the day off because Ermysteds was a polling station. Wilfrid drove me to Hawes in the Yorkshire Dales at the northern end of one of the largest constituencies in England to take numbers as people went to vote at the local school. He dropped me off at 10am and said he would be back in two hours. Then he forgot all about me and only returned at 7pm after somebody raised the alarm about where I was. I had nothing to eat or drink all day apart from two glasses of water, but faithfully took down all the numbers of those who voted and displayed the colours by wearing a bright yellow rosette. The other parties did not bother showing the flag in Hawes. Wilfrid came third with 23% of the vote and I felt I had done my bit. More importantly, I enjoyed my first taste of political campaigning.

Soon after the election John Cockerill, myself, Wilfrid and his agent Jim Marshall met to discuss the possibility of forming a Young Liberal group in the town. Wilfrid and Jim offered us use of the sound but badly in need of repair Liberal Club in the centre of Barnoldswick as a base. Within a year we had 100 members and a thriving social and political organisation. The club was a solid building but run down. We set to work decorating all the rooms, created a snooker room with a full size table and pushed the rest of the snooker tables' slate tops together to form a stage in the large hall. Until then there was nowhere else in town where teenagers could meet apart from a Friday night youth club at the secondary school which was strictly out of bounds for grammar school lads who didn't want a beating.

Our timing was perfect. We were the first generation after the Second World War to benefit from new freedoms of both thought and action. Conscription into the armed forces had ended in December 1960 – thank goodness. The 'swinging 60s' were in full flow and in our small corner of Yorkshire we did our best to replicate what we could see happening in Liverpool and London. Because we had plenty of space at the club, five of our number formed their own pop group called *The Inmates* who took over one room and rehearsed there most days. After a few months they staged fortnightly Saturday night dances using the stage and props we had created. These dances were the highlight of the week for us teenagers and attracted hordes of girls to our organisation. *The Inmates* went on to be a popular group right across the North West and eventually appeared on Saturday night peak time television's *Opportunity Knocks* hosted by Hughie Green.

We didn't just play snooker and run dances though. Most of our group were ex grammar school lads and girls and over the next five years we shook up politics in Barnoldswick. We campaigned hard for more 'social amenities' and in particular for a swimming pool. It was a campaign which bore fruit after I left, but we set the ball rolling. We worked hard at election time and it paid off at the 1966 General Election when Wilfrid's vote went up – he relegated the Labour candidate to third place. A year later we worked even harder to get his father elected to the county council in a landslide win. The other parties had no answer. In the ensuing years the Liberals won most of the Barnoldswick Urban District Council seats which became vacant.

On Friday nights we held committee meetings and political discussions. These were serious affairs debating the major issues of the day. On several occasions we voiced our concerns about the then Russian government and particularly its treatment of dissidents. The secretary was often asked to write to the Kremlin and demand a reply. The following week the secretary would inform us that no reply had yet been received - there never would be. We didn't give up though. We continued to write to all and sundry. In those days the Young Liberals nationally were a radical, campaigning group who more than once upset the establishment, particularly when it came to attacking apartheid in South Africa. Peter Hain - a future Labour cabinet minister - was the Young Liberals' national leader; locally we had key activists like Tony Greaves, now Lord Greaves, and Gordon Lishman who went on to become Director General of Age Concern. Barnoldswick Young Liberals were much more parochial but still took national politics seriously. John Cockerill and I travelled to Hull in 1966 to help at a by-election and we also went to the Liberal party conference at Blackpool as official delegates.

In 1968 when French students rose in revolt in Paris I was nominated to show some solidarity and go and join them on the barricades. I took a few days holiday from my work as a junior reporter and set off to hitch-hike to France. My enthusiasm and revolutionary zeal ran out on the A1 at Newark at 2am with heavy rain pouring down my back. It was dark, nobody was stopping to give me a lift and I was wet, cold and hungry. I turned round, went back home and hid for three days. My report to the Friday night meeting the week after was glowing about my exploits in France!

Nine months after I helped launch Barnoldswick Young Liberals it was time for me to think about earning a living. My extra year at school was nearly over and my father was keen for me to start earning my keep. I have had more than my fair share of luck in life and none more so than when the time came to leave Skipton Grammar School. I was approached by the *Nelson Leader-Colne Times Series* of newspapers, producers of my home town paper the wonderfully named *Barnoldswick and Earby Times*, to see if I would be interested in becoming a trainee reporter. They had spotted my 'potential' because I had taken the trouble to give their local reporter,

Geoff Mattock, a number of stories from the Young Liberals, Boys' Brigade, cricket, football and other youth activities. Several had made the front page. Geoff was up for promotion to head office.

I attended an interview in Nelson with the intimidating Editor Noel Wild and soon after learned the job was mine. I was told I would serve an initial six month probationary period and if they liked me and I liked them I would then be indentured for three years - an old fashion apprenticeship which was legally binding and had to be signed by my parents. The pay was poor. My first week's wage came to £6 19 shillings, or £6.95 in today's money, of which I had to tip up £6 to my mother. My parents were not delirious about me becoming a trainee reporter because I earned about two thirds of what my sister was already earning in the mill and less than what my brother Brian would soon earn in the same job. As far as they were concerned it was my fault I had stayed on at school a year longer than they thought necessary and I had to do some financial catching up. There was no discussion with either of my parents about the career path I might follow. My dad was not interested in talking to me about what the future might hold and I was growing less inclined to share anything of importance with him. All I kept hearing was: *'You owe us'.*

I added to his general disapproval of me when I made it quite clear I had no intention at any time in my life of joining any of the armed forces. The other three took the opposite view and lived to regret it. Brian joined the army, but was home within a few months; Stephen joined the navy and lasted less than four weeks; Sandra toughed it out for quite a bit longer and probably got the most out of it.

The fact my pay would not rise by much until I was nearly 21 did not go down well and also meant my finances were perilous during my late teens. I had no money left by a Tuesday and borrowed from a senior reporter in Nelson if I wanted to eat. I could never afford to buy a round of drinks after a cricket match. I generally drank mild rather than bitter because it was cheaper, although I did develop a taste for a 'black and tan' made up of Mackeson and mild.

I managed to scrape together enough money over four years to have two very cheap foreign holidays. The first was to Lloret de Mar in Spain at the start of the holiday package abroad boom when I enjoyed my first flight - with Monarch Airlines - and discovered the pleasure of drinking cheap bacardi and cokes while lazing by a hotel pool. It was a lot warmer than any summer weather I had previously experienced on the edge of the Pennines. For my second trip abroad I hitch-hiked down to Harwich and then through Holland to join five other Young Liberal friends who were camping near the German border. I terminated that holiday early and hitch-hiked back on my own when two of the group damaged a car in Maastricht and had to pay a heavy fine. Hitch-hiking in those days was a common enough way of getting around.

Starting work was the start of a very unhappy period at home which ultimately led to a breach soon after my 21st birthday. I felt unloved, unwanted and unappreciated. I became cocky, opinionated and rebellious and felt a permanent need to prove myself, which must have tested the patience of many friends. It wasn't until I was in my early 30s that I calmed down and stopped boasting about any achievement – large or small. I hated being at home when my parents came in the worse for drink, usually after a night out at the Rolls Royce club - the best night-time venue in town at that time. When my father had a hangover I kept well out of sight.

Saturday nights and my parents' inevitable Sunday hangovers were the worst times for me. My mother's appalling cooking got even worse after a heavy night out; I cannot remember her managing a good Sunday lunch. Fortunately, I had a number of day-time 'safe havens' where I could go and stay with friends or simply have 'a brew' when things were at their worst. Stan Lawson, the local butcher and a cricketing friend, often looked after me when I needed someone to talk to and other friends like Wilf Pickard, Hilda Naylor, Stephen Robinson and Robert Boven plus those from the Boys' Brigade, Bethesda Baptist Church and the cricket club played an important part in keeping me safe and sane.

Robert became my best friend during this period. The son of Jewish parents Max and Lottie who had fled Hitler's Germany, he was full of life, drove like a maniac and befriended me at a key time for which I will always be grateful. He loved to tour the nightclubs in Burnley and Blackburn and I introduced him to one of his girlfriends.

We would end most of our evenings at a late night fish and chip shop in Brierfield where he would smoother his food with curry sauce.

After two weeks in my first real job learning what Geoff Mattock could teach me in such a short time, I was left to my own devices in Barnoldswick and Earby. I had four broadsheet pages a week to fill, somehow, one of them a sports page. In order to supply head office with all the material to fill each week's paper I had to make the most of whatever was happening. Every wedding made at least 12 paragraphs once I learned off by heart every question to ask, including the name of the most important person at any wedding outside the bride - the bride's mother. Most wedding reports even detailed what flowers the bridesmaids carried and always appeared in the paper the Friday after the actual wedding; unlike today when if they report weddings many local papers carry the pictures months after the actual day. Sometimes the couple get divorced in the meantime! I was told it was not unusual for the bride's parents to buy bundles of papers so they could cut out the wedding report and picture and send it to relatives far and wide in the days before photocopiers. It was my first lesson in what sold a local paper.

Every death also made a minimum of 12 paragraphs and I wrote about everything from whist drive results to pigeon racing winners. Inbetween I started to learn shorthand; a vital skill but one I struggled to master. I had no car. I walked and hitch-hiked everywhere and struggled to find a working telephone box to phone over my copy when the sub-editors needed a story to complete a page.

After the initial induction period and Geoff Mattock's transfer to the *Nelson Leader* I received little formal training of any sort. It was left to individual senior reporters and sub editors to look after us juniors. Most of my copy was re-written and while the subs did point out some errors, communication between them and me was always a problem. The same get-on-with-it-yourself attitude existed with regard to shorthand. Night school was difficult because the evenings I needed to be free I was generally sitting in a council chamber. There was no in-office shorthand training and apart from the mandatory two eight-week spells in college I never any received encouragement to grasp this basic skill.

I received little training in court reporting either. I had to pick up what knowledge I required from text books and learning on the job. I found local government much easier. A key part of my job involved reporting the affairs of two small, local councils. I learned how to battle my way through and understand every planning application and in the process to decipher local government jargon. Many journalists don't enjoy reporting on local government. A few, like me, turn the tables and become councillors, thus relieving the frustration they felt when they had to sit for hours on end listening to others pontificate without being able to contribute themselves.

Facilities offered to the press by the two councils varied, but were often poor, which was surprising considering the excellent coverage the *Barnoldswick and Earby Times* gave their affairs. There was not even a table to rest my notepad. I soon discovered councillors love playing to the gallery – some used to directly look at me before delivering their 'pearls of wisdom'. It was a shame members of the public rarely attended.

The now abolished Barnoldswick Urban District Council admitted me to its presence in July, 1965. I sat on an uncomfortable, old chair, beside the highly-experienced and respected Jack Heald from the rival *Craven Herald*. Jack had a 20-year start on me and seemed to know everybody and the background to everything that could possibly make a story before any meeting. There was a club atmosphere to the gatherings both during the meetings and in the pub afterwards; I was far too young to be considered a member. It was my first experience of who held power in my town and I looked up to those apparent wise men who appeared to have a wealth of knowledge at their fingertips. Today I see them for what they were – honest triers attempting to do their bit for the community, but full of their own self-importance.

Highlight of the civic year was the Mayor's Ball. It was an honour to get an invitation, never mind sit on the top table. However, tradition called for the local reporters - no matter how young - to hob nob with the cream of local "society". When Noel Wild declined the invitation citing a prior engagement, I took his place and wore an ill-fitting dinner suit I borrowed from a much older friend. In return I was expected to take down verbatim every word uttered by the speakers. It was a painful evening.

Despite my twice a week attendance at council meetings, I soon discovered the best stories were about people, not issues. Apart from reporting on the occasional row about new council offices, or whether to tarmac cobbled streets, I spent the bulk of my time writing about what people were doing, going to do or wanted others to do.

In small towns there are always a few people who are larger than life within their communities – extremely newsworthy, whatever they do. We call them 'characters.' Such a man was Dr. John Pickard who brightened up many a day with his eccentric approach to life. He could have been one of this country's top doctors in his younger days, but he enjoyed living in Barnoldswick; to all intents and purposes he was a typical small town doctor.   His patients, particularly the elderly, spoke highly of him, but as he grew older some of his more eccentric ways didn't always meet with approval. He was kindness itself with children, but he had a long-standing suspicion of anyone aged 20-50 who might be seeking a few easy days off work.   You couldn't get any sort of certificate out of Dr Pickard easily. A friend went to him for a medical required for a new job. When Dr. Pickard tested the man's hearing he took out a pocket watch and asked if he could hear it ticking. My friend couldn't hear a thing but didn't want to admit to a hearing problem, so he nodded his head. *"Amazing,"* said Dr. Pickard *"because I haven't been able to get it to run for six years"*.

Over the years I heard a legion of stories about Dr John, some true but many embellished by time and exaggeration. My favourite story is true. One day he was asked to call on a woman who was having trouble breast feeding her baby. When he arrived he did his usual trick of knocking on the door and walking straight in – a not uncommon practice in the north in those days, where everybody knew everybody else. He found a woman sat in front of the fire cuddling a baby. Without much ado he went straight up to her, unbuttoned her blouse and then proceeded to tell her: *"No wonder you are having trouble breast feeding, there's no milk there"*. The poor woman, mouth agog, managed to reply: *"It's not my baby, I'm just baby-sitting for a while*". It wouldn't have bothered Dr. John, who took his car down to the ambulance station to have it cleaned by the ambulance men "*when they had nothing to do*". He also had a motorbike. He never treated me for any ailment, but he did visit my sister. After he had seen her, he asked if he could leave by the front door to see another patient, having arrived at the back. My parents didn't object, until he proceeded to drag his motorbike through the house, leaving oil and mud on the carpets.

I only went to head office in Nelson on Wednesday afternoons and Thursdays; I worked from home the other days. Geoff Mattock would call every other day to collect my copy and pass it on. The *Nelson Leader* office up a narrow flight of stairs was cramped, dusty and noisy when everybody's typewriter was clattering away. Twelve of us shared one toilet on the same level which received the attention of a cleaner only very occasionally. Senior members of staff were housed on the second floor; plaster fell on those of us underneath when anyone walked on certain parts of its flimsy carpet. When the National Union of Journalists complained about the conditions in which we were working and came to have a meeting with Noel Wild some of us deliberately walked on the worst spots while the meeting was in progress to show how bad it was. It made no difference.

Barnoldswick had a part-time fire station. I had the job of following, on foot, the fire engine every time the siren sounded and the men raced to the station from all over town. I hated false alarms. Once I had just got in the bath after playing football - caked on mud nicely wet again - when the alarm went. I had to jump out, pull on a track suit and find out what was going on.

The fire station was just one of my daily calls. At 9am and 4pm each day I visited the town's police station. A burly sergeant would open the 'calls book' and tell me what had been happening. Unlike today when the police withhold most information unless they want publicity, there was very little I wasn't told about. I got on well with the desk sergeants. If there was anything they were not supposed to give me it was not unusual for them to make a trip to the toilet while I looked at the daily log. It helped that I played football for their midweek team if they were ever short of players.

Today my training would be regarded as rather unusual by the average regional newspaper journalist, to say the least. In addition to the police my daily round of calls included three undertakers, shopkeepers, vicars and 'people in the know' like pub landlords and hairdressers. Noel Wild once told me that people chat a lot when having their hair cut *'so find out what they are talking about'.* I also played dominoes in the Conservative Club on Thursday afternoons once the paper was put to bed and listened to the pensioners chat; they gave me a wealth of good stories. I had to go to Wednesday night bingo on several occasions.

Twice a month I went to the printing works in Burnley on a Thursday to see the paper to bed and learn how to read the metal type upside down when it was made up into broadsheet pages on 'the stone' – a long sturdy bench. As each working week progressed my stories were edited and sent to the printing works where they were set in type which was collected in long galleys in readiness for placing within the relevant pages. This enabled me to read how my stories would actually appear in the paper once I had learned how to read upside down. I didn't find it too difficult after a bit of practice. One of the first jobs the senior member of staff who accompanied me to the printing works had to do was work out how near we were to filling that particular issue by quickly measuring the type that was set. The trick was to have just enough stories left over just in case an advertisement didn't arrive in time, but not too many. That kept costs down.

One newspaper tried to ensure it didn't set more stories in type than it required by conducting regular measuring sessions each day. A senior manager would measure up all the galleys full of type with the aid of a 12 inch piece of string. If he had 150 string lengths, he knew he had enough to fill a certain number of pages, and if he added in the size of the pictures and the adverts, he could determine how much more the reporters had to write in order to fill that week's paper. This system worked well for many years until one day two mischievous printers cut an inch off his piece of string. That Wednesday night he went round all his galleys and proudly announced no more editorial copy was required, so the reporters stopped writing. When the pages were made up the next day all hell let loose because there were huge gaps which were hastily filled by any means possible. From that day on the piece of string was made redundant and more modern technology in the form of a ruler was introduced.

There was something about the old linotype machines and the entire hot metal process that I found intimidating. The machines were all powerful and the men who sat at them were gifted craftsmen. The same could be said for the men who made up the pages in their metal frames. They spaced out stories skilfully with the liberal use of small strips of lead and took great pride in the finished product. When computer setting of type was introduced to regional weekly newspapers the type became clearer and easier to read, but the product suffered from a lack of direct care as bits of under-glued paper slipped off pages.

A hot metal room in an old fashioned newspaper closely resembled working conditions in the weaving mills of that age. The linotypes were equally spaced out, leaving just enough room to dodge between them, and noise levels were high. There were strict union-enforced rules about who could touch what. Anyone who did not carry a union card risked causing an industrial dispute if they touched any of the metal type. I was familiar with the hot metal system only while working at the *Nelson Leader*. Its demise in the late sixties and early seventies reduced the craft element of the printing trade considerably. The old skills were no longer applicable. The only skills compositors required from then on were similar to those needed by someone who was good at jigsaws! What didn't change for just over a decade were the pay scales.

A few weeks into my life as a trainee reporter I had the worst job possible: reporting on my sister Wendy's death from leukemia. My mother fell pregnant eight years after my brother Stephen was born, much to everyone's surprise. Soon after Wendy's first birthday she became very ill and we were warned she would have a short life span. Drugs kept her alive for a while. Many people took this pretty blonde-haired girl to their heart and through the newspaper and my father's workmates at Rolls Royce they followed her short life with interest in the hope that a cure could be found. Her death, when she was just four, devastated my mother and father. They had turned to religion 18 months previous in the hope that God would intervene. My father became very involved with the Christadelphians, a group I still don't know much about today. They came to the house every week to pray and seemed nice people, but I didn't feel comfortable when they allowed my dad to preach some Sundays. I listened to one sermon and felt sick, but for once didn't let it show. How could this man treat me the way he did and yet stand in front of a congregation and preach about God's love and forgiveness? I knew too much about what went on at home to take seriously his sermons from a pulpit. Soon after Wendy's death they both stopped going to church and never returned. Everyone at my work was sympathetic, but I also had a job to do. Noel Wild made it clear I was expected to help put together the page one story, including an interview with my father.

I hadn't seen a dead body before joining the *Barnoldswick and Earby Times*. By the time I finished my training I had seen plenty. I was told by Noel that if invited I had to pay my respects when doing the dreaded 'death knock'. This meant going into any room where a body was laid out, looking in the coffin, bowing my head while mumbling what might appear to be some sort of prayer and remaining there for a couple of minutes. On one memorable occasion when a man died on his holidays I was joined by two neighbours. One commented: '*Eeeh, didn't his holiday do him good?*' He had a lovely tan.

On another occasion I forgot to ask a widow some important details about her cricketer husband and was sent back to get them from the man's only other surviving relative who didn't have a telephone. In those days there were no mobile phones. I walked two miles up a steep hill in a snow storm, knocked on the door and hoped she was in. I was cold and soaked through. I had already learned that when doing the 'death knock' you could expect several different reactions when you told people who you were and what you wanted: a few people told you to get lost; a few allowed you to question them in between their sobs; and the majority invited you in when you explained you wanted to do a tribute type story. The woman took one look at me, invited me in, poured me a glass of whisky and dried my coat in front of a blazing fire. Bliss! When I had finished I walked the two miles back into town. At least it was downhill!

After six months I had done enough to persuade the company it was worth offering me a full apprenticeship and my indentures were duly signed. This meant I was locked in to the one newspaper company for a further three years. I was sent to Harris College, Preston (now the University of Central Lancashire) to do the first of two eight week courses that were mandatory under the new National Council for the Training of Journalists training scheme the company belonged to. I attended law, local government and journalism lectures as well as doing more of the dreaded shorthand in order to try and get my speed up to 100 words a minute. The company paid for digs in Fulwood, Preston. I returned home each Friday night and travelled back early on a Monday morning by hitching a lift with a Silentnight lorry driver at 4.30am who took me to the M6 from where I walked in all weathers into Preston to catch a bus to the college. It was the first time I had been away from home outside staying with my aunty and uncle.

My first eight-week spell at Harris College was a disaster. I had to start from scratch with shorthand and struggled mightily. I spent a lot of time in the evenings trying to catch up, but only managed a dismal 40 words a minute by the end of the eight weeks. I now regard that as a minor miracle. At the end of the first course I returned to the office but there was no further training for another 12 months until I went back to college. This time I was expected to get 100 wpm. Somehow I got a certificate for 80 wpm and followed it up within a month – at my own expense – with the much sought-after 100 word certificate, given to me by a teacher who must have sympathised with my predicament.

Back on the job I was now expected to really compete with Jack Heald, my rival on the *Craven Herald*. Jack was a superb reporter-one of the best. He seemed to know everybody. I had a tough task just trying, and often failing, to keep up with him. I got the occasional scoop but didn't cover myself in too much glory in the next 12 months. Every Friday Noel Wild would call me into his office after reading the *Craven Herald* and ask me why I didn't have this story or that quote. I was often dismissed from what seemed to be his unworthy presence with the words '*make sure you do better next week*,' ringing in my ears. I tried that bit harder to compete with

Jack, but it was a hopeless task. He never knew how much I cursed him some days. However, we forged a friendship which lasted until his death in the summer of 2014.

In the 1960s local reporters were always expected to be heavily involved with their communities. After all, it was what had got me the job in the first place. When the *Barnoldswick and Earby Times* was asked to nominate someone to sit on the town's struggling Gala Committee, I was told to get on with it. At the second meeting they made me secretary when nobody else would do the job. I was 'up' for anything in those days and like to think I did a reasonable job in keeping the annual Gala going for a few more years. It gave me some useful contacts and also provided a few good stories that Jack didn't get. However, it also led to an embarrassing night when we chose the 1967 Gala Queen. The competition was run through our newspaper. Each week a different girl was featured in the paper. There was never any shortage of entrants. The final was held at a top local hotel when Noel Wild was one of the judges along with West Indian test cricketer Charlie Griffith. To cut a long story short the judges had too much to drink, they failed to add up their own marks correctly and we had to crown three girls within an hour when the marks were re-checked. It was not easy taking the crown off one girl late at night and giving it to another. There were fights afterwards among rival family supporters. It made a good story in next week's paper.

One job I did do well was the sports page. I helped set up the first Barnoldswick Darts League, which is still in existence today. This earned me promotion to head office after 18 months of general reporting where I covered local sport and Burnley football for the *Nelson Leader and Colne Times*. Unfortunately, the paper was banned from the Turf Moor press box because of a row between Noel Wild and Burnley chairman Bob Lord. I reported home games from the terraces – the paper would not pay for me to have a seat. The *Nelson Leader and Colne Times* weren't the only ones to fall foul of Bob Lord who ruled the football club with an iron fist. Other reporters banned for writing something the Burnley chairman didn't agree with formed a club which had its own tie. The '*Banned By Bob Club*' became quite famous for a few years. I didn't mind standing on the terraces, but enjoyed not having to queue to get into a ground when I could use the press box when Burnley played away. Bob Lord's ban extended to the players who were not allowed to speak to the press without his permission. This made it difficult to have any contact with them.

I didn't enjoy the travelling – mainly by bus. Noel Wild made little allowance for the time it took me to get from home to away games by public transport or supporters' buses. In 1968 Burnley met Swindon in the semi-final of the League Cup. It was a two-legged affair; Burnley lost the home leg 2-1. I travelled to Swindon on a supporters' coach for the return leg, leaving Nelson at noon on a Wednesday. It was a long journey and we arrived just before kick-off. Burnley won the second leg 2-1 to square matters. A quick cup of tea later I set off on the return journey which got me back to Nelson about 3.30am. I went straight to the office and typed up my report ahead of that morning's deadline. Noel had left a note on my typewriter which said that in view of the long journey and late working I didn't have to report again to the office until noon the same day!

I enjoyed rubbing shoulders with well known national newspaper reporters I held in some awe. It was not unusual for several of them not to watch much of the game. Instead, they would remain in a warm lounge and enjoy the liquid hospitality provided for the press at many First Division grounds. At the final whistle they would come to me for my notes about the game for which they would pay me and then do a few interviews of their own to pad out their reports. Some weeks the money I earned was nearly as much as I got in my Friday pay packet; it was more than welcome. I enjoyed the matches, although Burnley were no better than a mid-table team by now, unable to compete with the wages offered by the big city clubs. In one game I reported on they lost 7-0 to Manchester City at Maine Road - it could have been 20-0.

Apart from when I came to leave the *Nelson Leader*, I can only remember one angry exchange with Noel which left me feeling bitter. For a while I had the job of looking after old photographs submitted by readers and a favourite section in most weekly papers. It was a job fraught with dangers because the photos could be lost in the production process, damaged by copy carriers or, if returned by post, damaged in some other way. We used to carry a lot of these photographs, which were lent to us by trusting readers, and in 99% of cases everything was fine. It was my bad luck to lose one which was particularly important; it appeared in the paper the week I left the office to do my second eight-week block release course in Preston. I should have returned the photo the day before I left, but it didn't come back from the printers, although I was assured it was on its way. Two weeks later I was pulled out of a class to the telephone where I listened to my angry Editor tell me the photo was lost. I was ordered back to see him at his home in Nelson that night. I didn't have a car, but fortunately a fellow trainee was travelling back to Nelson and was prepared to give me a lift. The weather was awful as I walked up the steep hill to Noel's house. By the time I knocked on his front door rain was running down my neck and back. Noel made me stand on his doorstep for 15 minutes while he tore into me and I got wetter and wetter. Eventually, he dismissed me from his presence and I made my own way back to my friend. I never lost another photograph.

By now I had left the Boys' Brigade. When I was not reporting on local sport and Burnley FC I played football for Bethesda Baptist Church, who had a team in the Nelson and Colne League, and cricket, first for Thornton and then Barnoldswick. I started playing for Thornton while still at school. It is a beautiful village a few miles from Barnoldswick on the main road to Skipton. The small, compact cricket ground is in a valley at the bottom of a steep hill. There are not many grounds that can boast such wonderful panoramic views. It was a shame we didn't have one village lad in either Saturday team. I topped the second eleven batting averages in 1965 when we came second in the league. I got a telling off at school that summer when I chose to play in several vital club games rather than school matches. On the following Monday mornings I had to explain myself to the sports master; as far as he was concerned I did not have any right to decide for myself what I did on a Saturday afternoon until I left school that July.

I switched to playing for Barnoldswick in 1967 when they allowed me to play on and off for the third eleven. My reporting duties meant I was not available every week. Butcher Stan Lawson captained a young side. We rarely managed to score 100 runs between us. I had a golden summer in 1968 under his guidance topping both the club's batting and bowling averages and finishing second overall in the Craven League's bowling averages. At Keighley I recorded my best ever bowling figures of eight wickets for 11 runs when we skittled them out for 38. I always bowled at the wickets so if a batsman missed I bowled him. That day they missed a lot and I was just about unplayable.

Most of the wickets we played on were bowler friendly and at one ground - Embsay north of Skipton - you could not see what was happening if you fielded at fine leg because the ground dipped away steeply at one end. If the ball headed my way the rest of the team yelled to alert me! At Kildwick the home team had to take down the electric fencing before the game which preserved the square from the cows that roamed there all week. The rest of the ground was covered in cow pats; you learned never to attempt a diving catch!

Our home fixtures were played on Victory Park which was a wide open public space with a 'square' in the middle. The changing rooms were so small only half the team could get changed at any one time and some players chose to arrive in their whites. Somehow we managed to reach a cup semi-final which we lost by five wickets after we were bowled out for 58. By the time I came on to bowl our opponents had already scored 35 for the loss of only one wicket. I gave them something of a fright by quickly getting four batsmen out, but they held on to win. I have always wondered what would have had happened had I opened the bowling.

CHAPTER THREE

TIME TO GET OUT

If at first you don't succeed, don't try sky diving – unknown

I was deeply unhappy at home after starting work and determined to leave the Pendle area when my indentures were up in December 1968. I had no idea where I would go, but I knew I had to get away from my miserable home life and see whether I could make a go of it on my own. I endured a lot of inner torment for three long years, but never lost the inner drive and determination to move as quickly as my work and indentures would make possible.

I was prepared to go anywhere as long as it was more than a hundred miles from Barnoldswick, even though I had many friends there and was enjoying reporting on Burnley football.

Two events conspired to convince me that any move had to be as far away as possible. The first came in the summer of 1966 when the Young Liberals played a friendly rugby match against a team from Rolls Royce. I played on the wing and in going to catch the ball I dislocated a finger. When I got home my father was in a foul mood after a particularly heavy drinking session the night before. I must have said something that irked him because he grabbed the finger and yanked it. Pain shot through me and I flipped both mentally and physically. With tears streaming down my face I ran - as far as London. I hitch-hiked my way to the capital and ended up wandering the streets 300 miles away until I walked into a police station and asked for help.

It was a stupid thing to do, but I did many stupid things in haste at that time, most which I regretted. Phone calls were made and money was sent to get me back north on a bus, but mentally I was a wreck.

It was the lowest point of my life. I got no sympathy at home: my father said nothing; my mother didn't know what to do or say. From then on my father and I hardly exchanged a civil word for the next two years. I really hated him and he knew it. He hated me back. Neither of us could see it from the other's viewpoint.

Only a few hours after I returned to Barnoldswick friends stepped in to the breech and arranged for Dr Pickard, his wife and son Wilfrid to take me in for two weeks while I recovered. I never discovered who told them what had happened, but they were wonderful; feeding me and repairing some of the damage, both physical and mental I had suffered. They gave me strength building broths and allowed me to talk about how I felt. They listened but did not pass judgement. For the first few days I lay asleep each afternoon on a couch in their garden. One evening while still staying with the Pickards I made up my mind to quit Barnoldswick. It seemed the only answer.

When I went back to work Noel Wild could easily have sacked me. I feared I would lose my job, but while he wasn't all that sympathetic to my personal problems because it wasn't in his nature, he allowed me to make a full recovery before putting me under any sort of pressure. I lost a lot of weight, but returned to work with a fierce determination to grin and bear whatever was happening at home and, in secret, plan a better future.

The second key event occurred on Christmas Eve the following year when my mother and father went on a heavy drinking binge which ended up with them four miles from home at 2am on Christmas Day. They turned right out of a pub instead of left and ended up in Earby. They had no idea where they were. Their slanging match was heard by, of all people, Jack Heald from the *Craven Herald* who got up and drove them home. I felt humiliated. Jack brushed it off as 'just *one of those things*' when we next met. That didn't stop me feeling acutely embarrassed.

Throughout 1968 I concentrated on passing my journalism exams, playing a lot of football and cricket and rarely being at home. My work was ideal cover for me being out so much because I did have evening meetings to attend. When I wasn't working I was either at the Liberal Club or visiting whoever would have me for a few hours.

I didn't know where Maldon was until November 1968. I had to look at a map to find it when I replied to an advertisement in *UK Press Gazette* for a sports editor for the *Maldon and Burnham*

Standard. Eventually I found it - a small dot on the east coast of Essex 320 miles from Barnoldswick and just about as far away as I could travel without going abroad. I sent off a letter of application more in hope than anything else because the time was fast approaching when my indenture would come to an end. A burning inner desire to move as quickly as I could kept me going some days. I didn't say anything at home about a potential move which led to a fierce backlash later. I instinctively knew that if I revealed what I intended to do life would become even more unbearable and I would be pressured into re-thinking my plan well before I even applied for any job. The bottom line was that my weekly contribution to the family budget would be missed and as far as my parents were concerned I had not yet paid my dues. The only people who knew of my determination to get away were my aunty and uncle and a few close friends.

Within a week of sending off my application I was invited to Colchester, head office for a group of newspapers of which the *Maldon and Burnham Standard* is one of their titles. The Editor was Bob Russell - later to become Colchester's Liberal Democrat MP. He and the company's owner, Harvey Benham, wanted to see me as soon as possible. I had to borrow the money for the train fare from my uncle. He took me to Nelson railway station to catch the 5am train to London after I made an excuse at home to stay with him and my aunty the night before. I took the Tube from Euston to Liverpool Street and then on to Colchester where I underwent a two hour interview, after which Bob drove me to Maldon to take my first look at the town and its High Street newspaper office. Bob then drove me to Chelmsford to catch the 5pm train back north. I arrived in Nelson at 1am the following morning and stayed another night with my aunty and uncle before going into work a few hours later.

I had no idea how well I had performed at my interview, but on the way back north I knew I would take the job if it was offered. I didn't have to wait long as a formal letter arrived within four days offering me the position on an enhanced salary with other perks such as free driving lessons and a week's salary as a Christmas bonus. Those were the days when some company's valued the people who worked for them and showed it in a positive way. There was only one condition I found a bit strange – my office would also be home to a pram for the Editor's children. He and his family lived in a flat above the office.

I wrote to Noel Wild giving a month's notice, but said nothing at home. Noel summoned me to his office and gave me an almighty rollicking for wanting to leave, and didn't speak to me again while I still worked for the company. He had done the same with others who had left so I knew it was not really personal. I was flattered he tried to keep me. He even tried to delay my move because technically I still had a few days to go before my indenture ran out, but he was never going to succeed. We met at an office reunion in later years, made up and managed to laugh about what had happened, but it wasn't funny at the time. A rollicking from Noel when he was sober was bad enough, but one after lunch when he had drunk more in three hours than I managed in a week was not something anyone would want to experience more than once in a lifetime.

How to tell everyone in Barnoldswick was my next task; I knew it wouldn't go down well. That was an understatement! I was never allowed to forget the extra year I had spent at grammar school and the 'making up' I was required to do. I knew the money I was now removing from the family's income would be the main factor. And so it proved.

There always seemed a touch of the dramatic to my life in those days and this was such an occasion. My 21st birthday fell four days after I accepted the Maldon job so I chose that as the perfect opportunity to inform family and friends what I was up to. I arranged, and paid for, my own party. I hired Barnoldswick Cricket Club's lounge and bar for the night. The Inmates agreed to play for free and other friends arranged some food. When it came to say 'thank you' and deliver a speech, I dropped my 'bombshell'. It went down like the proverbial lead balloon with my mother and father. They seethed while friends offered their congratulations. Many years later at a reunion with several of the people who were there that night I was quite taken aback when one of them told me: '*You do know, don't you, that we have followed your career since you left? You were the one who got away.*' It appeared that anyone who moved more than 20 miles from Barnoldswick except to go to university was held in some awe!

The next day I got the family reaction I expected; anger was followed by the cold shoulder. I was never asked if it was a good career move or even why I was going so far away. Instead I was made fully aware that I had not yet paid my dues for my early life and school years. Christmas 1968 was bleak, but I didn't mind because I spent most of it out with friends or working. I had arrangements to make including finding accommodation, which fortunately didn't prove difficult once an advertisement went into my new paper. From several replies I selected Mr and Mrs Moss, of 34 St Giles' Crescent, Maldon, who seemed a friendly couple prepared to offer me a new home and two meals a day weekdays and three at weekends for the princely sum of £6 a week. *'We should be having the money you are paying someone else,'* said my dad.

On the first Sunday in January 1969 I left Barnoldswick early in the afternoon to travel again to Maldon. I didn't leave with the best wishes of the family ringing in my ears. My dad absented himself, while my mother managed to hold back her tears. Good fortune was on my side, however, because Wilf Pickard and his girlfriend, Sheila, were travelling back to their London home that same weekend after an extended Christmas/New Year break visiting his parents. He generously offered to give me a lift, although he too had no idea where Maldon was. After journeying down the M1 and navigating London's North Circular road we headed down the A12 past Chelmsford until soon after midnight we discovered we were in Maldon. Two hundred yards up the road I spotted a sign which read St Giles' Crescent and I had found my new home. Nobody could have guessed that in 10 years' time I would become the town's youngest ever Mayor!

I started work the next morning and ran into immediate trouble because I had never written a headline or designed a page before. I was a writer. I did not know my sans serif from my serif, yet within two days I had to produce three pages of sports copy fully prepared for the Colchester printers. My predecessor had departed the previous Thursday without leaving a note about anything and no material had been prepared in advance. I had to see numerous callers all wanting my precious time, seek advice on what was important and what wasn't and decide what would go where on each page. It was a nightmare, but somehow I got enough material to the printers that first week and there I met the man who got me out of trouble: his name was Dick Mead. He was an old fashioned printer, a true craftsman, who had learned his trade and knew how to handle rookies like me. Dick had been sorting out the *Maldon and Burnham Standard's* sports page for several years. He took me under his wing from day one. I was to learn a lot from him and others in those first months.

I loved Maldon and its townsfolk from the start, but that didn't stop me experiencing real loneliness for the first time. I had never been away from home except for the two eight week terms I spent at Harris College doing my journalism exams. Even then I had gone home at weekends. This was totally different. Mr and Mrs Moss did their best to make me feel at home. Mrs Moss was a good cook and treated me like a son. I enjoyed staying with them, but my inner turmoil was not helped by the hostile reception I encountered whenever I telephoned home.

I went back to Barnoldswick in late February for a four day stay and it unsettled me even more. The journey was an adventure on its own: bus to Chelmsford, train to London, round on the Tube to Victoria and then the 10.30pm overnight bus to Colne, which arrived at 6am the next day. From there it was another bus to Barnoldswick. It was a journey I was to do a number of times - until I passed my driving test two years' later. I got to know a couple of the bus drivers very well.

My fellow passengers and I from London to Colne could have made up the League of Nations; the majority were West Indians or Asians travelling to meet their families. On one trip the driver and I were the only white faces! It didn't bother me. I spent most of the journey standing at the front talking to the driver. When we stopped for a break, toilets and something to eat on the M1 he and I would go to a special area reserved for drivers and enjoy a slap-up breakfast around 2am. I talked for England on those trips!

It didn't take me long to make friends in Maldon. The Sports Editor of any weekly newspaper is always likely to get to know a lot of people if he likes his job, and I had boundless enthusiasm. On top of that I was soon playing football and then cricket for local sides. The first pub I wandered into in Maldon High Street was the Chequers - now a bank. Mine host was Albert Wright, a jocular, hearty character ideally suited to running a 1970s pub. He was the self-appointed manager of the pub's Sunday football team who played in the Chelmsford Sunday League. I played centre forward for them until the end of the season and scored a dozen goals. I spent three or four nights a week in the Chequers where most of the chat centred round sport and forged strong friendships with Alan Everard, Keith Searle, Tony Hawkins and many others. They struggled to understand my very broad northern accent and often ribbed me when I pronounced a word differently to what they were used to.

I soon made the acquaintance of Dave Lomas, a Burnham on Crouch school teacher, who provided acres of copy from the Dengie Hundred Minor Football League and the Burnham Table Tennis League. He came into my office on my second day and from then on was one of my best friends. He was a dream contact for any Sports Editor because his copy was lively, factual and well written. All I had to do was headline it and send it to the printers. And because I gave his material ample space in the newspaper, a bond was forged which lasted until his untimely death.

In later years he proved a popular choice as my daughter's godfather. On most Saturday afternoons between 1980 and when he died in July 2011 he would call from different locations in the UK and sometimes the world, always to discuss sport. He neglected his health after he left Burnham for a teaching post in Croydon, but that didn't stop him earning a well deserved Lifetime in Sport Achievement award from Sir Bobby Charlton. Former England Test cricketers Mark Butcher and Michael Carberry were just two of the sportsmen David taught and encouraged while they were youngsters. He died far too young from a variety of illnesses brought on by a poor diet and lifestyle. I travelled to Croydon and back by train on the same day to attend his funeral and was glad I was given the opportunity by his family to speak about what he had meant to me. I still miss him.

Dave and I were touchline colleagues at Maldon Town on Saturday afternoons, who in those days played in the semi-professional Eastern Counties League. Between us we made a few 'bob' on the side sending match reports to two Saturday night sports papers and a variety of East Anglian daily and weekly papers. Maldon Town played in the more senior league than neighbours Heybridge Swifts which meant they got more in-depth coverage, much to the chagrin of several future friends. Ironically the Swifts attracted treble the support for their games in first the Border League and then the Essex Senior League.

There was only one telephone in Maldon Town's clubhouse; Dave and I had to agree the times we needed it to phone through our copy midway through each half, at half-time and the end. Maldon were near the bottom of the table all the time I covered their games. I went to a few away matches at distant places I had never heard of like March, Chatteris and Histon when the team, manager, physio, press and supporters half filled a 48 seater bus.

I had my moment 'in the sun' one Sunday when Maldon Town travelled to Newmarket. Two players travelling by car were in an accident and the word was they wouldn't make the game. There were no substitutes in those days. Maldon manager Peter Gordon, who knew I played Sunday morning football, urgently summoned me to the dressing room from the press box to ask if I had any football boots with me? 'Err, *sorry I don't carry them round just in case I might get a call-up,*' I replied. Undeterred, he asked the size of my feet and within a few minutes came back with a pair of boots that fitted. There was still a problem, though. I had agreed to telephone copy through to various papers throughout the match. Peter solved that one when he said: '*Tell the ref what you need to do and just slip off when you have to.*' Fortunately, I had to disappear only once during the first half, much to the amusement of the opposing full-back. Maldon had the last laugh because somehow we won 2-1. I hardly got a kick, but I kept one member of the opposition occupied. I was not asked to play again for the first team but did turn out for Maldon Reserves occasionally, which probably said everything you need to know about my performance that day at Newmarket. There was one interesting follow-up. The *Cambridge Evening News* report of the match was by-lined ... By our man IN the match. A nice touch. I wish I had kept the cutting.

The *Maldon and Burnham Standard* will always have a place in my heart, although today it is not the paper it was when I joined in January 1969. It sells about a third the number of copies it used to. Over the years this small weekly newspaper has been the starting point for several notable journalistic careers with the *Daily Mail's* American correspondent Bill Langley and gossip columnist Richard Kay (who had a close friendship with Diana, Princess of Wales and succeeded Nigel Dempster) the most famous. They worked on the paper soon after I left, but I got to know them well. The *Standard*, situated slap bang in the middle of the High Street, where all local newspapers should be, was one of six newspapers in a stable privately owned by the much loved Harvey Benham and a few other shareholders. The *Essex County Standard* based in Colchester was the company's flagship with other titles in Clacton, Harwich, Braintree and Witham. Today the *Maldon and Burnham Standard's* two reporters operate out of Braintree and the old office is a fabric shop

Bob Russell was Editor for a couple of years before leaving to become a press officer with the Post Office. He later turned his mind to national politics, first as a Labour candidate, then a Social Democrat and finally as a successful Liberal Democrat MP. When I arrived in Maldon Bob, his wife Audrey and their children lived in the flat above the office. Sir Bob, as he is now after being knighted in 2012, and I got on well from the start. He gave me a lot of encouragement. If classified advertising fell short some weeks, he offered me the extra space for all the sports reports I was struggling to get into the paper. My efforts produced more and more match reports from club secretaries keen to feature in the *Standard*'s sports pages

There was a very good reporting team too. Brian Samuel, Kelvin Brown - later to be Ford's top press officer - Stuart Harris, Jill Roberts and Maryta Pankiewicz covered everything that moved in Maldon and district; every parish council meeting had a *Standard* reporter present. One young reporter who did not make a successful career in journalism was Steve Nice. He used to moan: '*Not making enough bread at this game, man'*. Eventually he left and the next thing we heard he had set up a pop group. He made far more money in a week than the rest of us earned in a year because that band was Cockney Rebel and Steve Nice became better known as Steve Harley.

Our photographer was Rodger Tamblyn who produced some smashing pictures. Fifteen years later I was to employ him in Birmingham. The team also included Barbara Land, who later became a top national travel writer. Barbara switched from being our front office receptionist to reporting when Maryta was promoted to head office in Colchester. Tragically, she collapsed and died while only in her forties.

In addition to the journalists we had our own circulation rep, Jack Eves, who along with his parents, Arthur and Anne, became another good friend. The Eves lived in Heybridge and treated me as another son. I didn't know it then but they were to help me through some difficult yet formative years. Jack had the job of keeping the newsagents happy and ensuring they were well stocked with the *Standard* until Monday at least; the paper came out on a Thursday. He collected the returns and looked after the newsagents' accounts. He loved to tell fanciful stories about his exploits which we all took in good heart because we knew they were harmless. Soon after I joined the *Standard* a story appeared in *Press Gazette* which revealed we were the youngest editorial team in the country.

In my second week as the *Standard*'s sports editor I had a visit from Brian Riedling who was the *East Anglian Daily Times'* man covering Maldon and district. More importantly from my viewpoint, he was a stalwart of Maldon Strollers Cricket Club and was keen to sign me up for the coming season ahead of the other club in the town, Old Maldonians. Many years later the two clubs rightly combined to become Maldon Cricket Club, but in those days there was fierce rivalry. Both teams played on a ground situated next to Maldon promenade. I had had an excellent season in 1968 playing for Barnoldswick and expected to carry my form with me, but it didn't turn out that way, for the first season at least. In my first match I was bowled for a duck by a full toss I tried to dispatch into the nearby lake and struggled with the bat thereafter, although I took a few wickets with my slow medium pacers. I made up for that poor first season in future years, but I had a bad dip in confidence, not helped by the lack of real competition. There were no league matches, everything was 'friendly' except when we played Old Maldonians.

Emotionally I was still in turmoil. I had several bouts of deep depression despite everyone in Maldon being so friendly. Matters came to a head in June 1969 when I went home for another weekend visit and fell out with my parents big time. I should have known that at some stage my dad's anger would boil over. It was just a matter of time. They went out for their usual Saturday night drinking session at the Rolls Royce Club and came back the worse for wear. If I had been more mature I would have ridden some of the provocation I suffered, but I reacted and it ended up with my dad and I at each other's throats - literally. I stormed out and went to stay with my aunty and uncle in Barrowford. I went back for my clothes the next day and didn't see my parents again for six years. Ironically, although there were several hiccups along the way, it was the making of me.

I returned to Maldon after that upsetting weekend and from then on whenever I went back to Barnoldswick I stayed with my best friend Robert and his parents. Mr and Mrs Boven were wonderful to me at that time. It helped that they knew the background to all that had occurred - my parents' reputation for heavy drinking and violent outbursts was public knowledge. I was grateful they could see the consequences for me of my parents enjoying a lively night out. They took me under their wing and treated me like a member of the family. I thoroughly enjoyed staying in their beautiful house up a private drive. Robert and I went out on Friday and Saturday nights to clubs in Blackburn, Southport and Manchester looking for 'talent'. We rarely found it! Or it rarely found us! How he didn't kill me during that time I don't know, because he drove like a maniac at speeds approaching 100mph. All I do know is that he was, and still is, a great guy who stood by me when I needed such a friend. I owe him and his parents a huge debt which I partly repaid when I helped get him and his future wife together some years later.

Back in Maldon I struggled to come to terms with what had happened with my parents and in October it led to me making a rash decision to leave and return north when offered a job on a daily newspaper. It was promotion, but a bad move when what I really needed was some stability in my life. I landed a sports writers/subbing job on the *Sheffield Morning Telegraph* upon the departure of a man who went into radio. I don't think anything was heard of him again. His name? John Motson. Of course, he went on to have a brilliant television career. It was a good job, a step up to a daily newspaper on more money but I hated Sheffield and I hated the hours; I worked from 4pm to around midnight.

The newspaper found me accommodation in a house with three male students, but it was awful. I took one look at the unwashed sheets, a sink filled with dirty plates and a filthy lounge and fled. I ended up that first night in a strange city renting one bedroom in somebody's house with no television and no cooking facilities. I suffered two nights on my own and then moved across the city to take up lodgings with Mrs Doreen Rhodes, a former shopkeeper/cafe owner who had been one of the church and Boys' Brigade helpers several years previously in Barnoldswick. Her two boys, Stephen and Malcolm, and I were friends and in the same Boys' Brigade football team. All three of us had been at grammar school at the same time. I telephoned in the hope she would know somebody who would offer me lodgings. Instead she told me she had a spare room and I was welcome to have it and use of her house on an estate on the edge of the city. She worked all day so I rarely saw her, but yet again somebody had come to my aid at a time when I was feeling alone and desperate. I wasn't to know it but they were the second worst few months of my life. They would have been a lot worse if Mrs Rhodes had not helped me get through them.

When I left the *Telegraph*'s city centre office around midnight after completing my daily shift I had to catch a bus and then walk more than a mile in all weathers to my new digs. At least once a week I was stopped by the police who wanted to take a look in my bag and satisfy themselves I wasn't a burglar who didn't have a car. Working in Sheffield with a talented team of experienced journalists, however, did have some benefits. One of the other sub editors was a kindly man in his 40s called Benny Hill who took a shine to me. He knew I was a novice. He took me on one side and said: '*Do you want to learn what sub-editing is really about?'* When I said I did, he gave me lessons in page design and subbing while we waited most evenings for football or rugby matches to finish. The chief sub editor, Mike Marsh, had me round for lunch some days and tried his best to make me feel at home. But I was lonely and when I had to work on New Year's Eve I felt so alone and unwanted. There I was, 22 years old, spending New Year's Eve with a piece of metal in my hand banging on a stone table to bring in the New Year with a group of printers! Little did I know that things were about to get much, much better.

Two days later the unexpected happened. In my absence Bob Russell had left the *Maldon and Burnham Standard* and was succeeded by Peter Laurie. My replacement as Sports Editor had not lasted long. Peter rang to see how I was and to find out whether I would be interested in having my old job back. I couldn't get back to Maldon quick enough. I cannot begin to explain the relief I felt as I stood on Sheffield railway station one Saturday morning three weeks later waiting for the trains that would take me first to London and then onwards to the Essex coast. My old digs with Mrs Moss were still vacant too, although I wasn't to know that she had less than a year to live because she had cancer.

When I walked into the S*tandard*'s office the following Monday morning it was as though I had never been away. But something had changed for the better in the four months I had been in Sheffield: I now knew how much I really liked Maldon, its people and the *Standard*. The Sheffield nightmare made me realise how lucky I was to be back. I threw myself into my work with extra enthusiasm and continued to improve the sports pages.

Peter Laurie was a tough Scotsman who was one of the finest Editors I ever worked for. For several years until the Scots rampaged round Wembley he and I watched the annual England v Scotland football match on his television; his support for his native country bordered on the fanatical on such occasions. I don't think anyone who worked for Peter found him easy, but good journalists respected him and I for one knew that he always strived to produce the best possible paper in any one week. He gave me a hard time on several occasions but it kept me sharp and I learned a lot. Peter built on the

50

work done by Bob Russell and the paper's circulation grew each month. It peaked during his editorship. A few years later he was rightly promoted to Editor-in-Chief of the whole group.

The Chequers found me a place in their team again and I continued to regularly score goals. The Strollers were also glad to have me back when the new cricket season started in mid April, despite my poor performances the previous summer. This time I was far more successful and I accepted an invitation to play for the Warren club when the Strollers didn't have a game.

I appeared to have found some stability in my life, but in February 1971 Mrs Moss died. I weighed less than nine stone when I first arrived on her doorstep, vastly underweight for someone 5ft 11 inches tall, but her excellent cooking and the general better quality of life in Maldon saw me reach 10 stone within a year. After her funeral I walked down the High Street and to the end of the sea wall beside the River Blackwater. I found a spot on my own and cried. Hers was the first adult death to touch me personally. It was a new feeling.

There was no way I could continue to stay with Mr Moss and his daughter so I advertised again in my own paper and after sifting through several replies selected Mrs Lilian Burfoot to be my next landlady. She was in her late sixties, had recently been widowed and said she would take me on for three months to see how it went. I stayed nearly eight years. My aunty told me to always look at how clean the cooker was in any home where I intended to eat - Mrs Burfoot's was spotless.

I like to think I became the son she never had. She had a two bedroomed old people's bungalow in Heybridge, two miles down the hill from Maldon High Street. I installed a telephone which she welcomed and in return for my weekly payment she fed me even better food that Mrs Moss, and gave me a comfortable secure home the like of which I had not experienced up to then, except when staying with my aunty and uncle. She said that because she had to cook for me, she enjoyed a meal herself. I am sure that having me around the house extended her life. I gave her a feeling of security; she gave me a comfortable, warm, homely environment. I still felt a constant need to prove myself, but I wasn't living on my nerves any longer.

I was desperate to have a car and be more mobile, but it took me three attempts to pass my driving test. I was very nervous on each occasion, but just about held it together the third time. My first cars were all cheap and in constant need of repair. I had little spare money and was fortunate that Clive Church, who I met through the Liberals, ran his own garage and came out on numerous occasions to do makeshift repairs or get me started in a morning. I had a Ford Cortina and then a Ford Corsair with column gear change, both of which were built like tanks. Eventually I progressed to a powerful 1275cc Mini which I really enjoyed driving. Insensitively, as far as my parents were concerned, I also had a Japanese car at one stage.

Once I started driving I stopped drinking any alcohol, sticking to orange juice or cola. A few friends used to rib me but one by one they were breathalysed and lost their licences. One night I went to a fancy dress party dressed as Andy Pandy with Luby Loo sat next to me in the car. On the way home around 1am we were stopped by police after an accident blocked the road. A policeman came down the queue of cars to tell us there would be a short delay. His face was a picture when I wound down the window; thank goodness I had not been drinking!

I made myself known to Maldon Liberals soon after arriving in the town. There were a few stalwarts and a vibrant group of Young Liberals, but Maldon and district had never been fertile Liberal ground and there was no record of consistent campaigning. Maldon was, and still is, a staunchly Conservative town apart from one district full of social housing and the suburb of Heybridge, both of which regularly returned Labour councillors for many years after the Second World War. Even these areas nowadays have Conservative councillors.

In 1969 the Parliamentary constituency covered a massive geographical area stretching from Burnham on Crouch in the south to Finchingfield on the Suffolk border. At the time it was geographically one of the largest in the country. Although it was named Maldon it contained two larger towns to the north in Braintree and Witham. I was soon invited onto the constituency's main committee – there wasn't much competition! There was little political activity or organisation outside Maldon itself.

My personal problems plus attempts to establish a newspaper career meant any campaigning was restricted. At the June 1970 General Election I helped the likeable but largely ineffective Parliamentary candidate, Roderic Beale, who lived in south London. I soon discovered he had less money than I had because his wife controlled the purse strings. I never saw him buy anyone a drink! The election was a disaster for new Liberal leader Jeremy Thorpe. The party was reduced to six MPs. Roderic lost his (our) deposit because he polled less than 10% - money local Liberals could ill afford to lose. It was only the hard work put in by the Young Liberals that gave the campaign any sort of impetus. After the election a national review of Parliamentary boundaries hived off Braintree and Witham plus their surrounding villages into a new constituency.

I am sure Maldon Liberals would have gone out of existence but for the youngsters, myself and a few more senior people, the most prominent of which were Pat and Beryl Manaton and an ageing Norman Smith. The Manatons tried their best to help me settle in Essex. On my 22nd birthday they arranged a surprise party at their home. It was such a surprise I wasn't invited. They expected me to call in, as I did most days. When I got to their front door I heard a lot of people enjoying themselves. I thought they had visitors or it was a family event so I went home.

Between us we kept some sort of Liberal organisation going. Beryl and I thrice stood as candidates in elections for Maldon Borough Council before it was abolished by the 1972 Local Government Act which came into force in 1974. In those days there were no wards - the whole of the town voted at every election. I got 17% the first time I stood and then 22%, but that fell back to 13%. All three elections were won by the Conservatives. Each time we managed to deliver a leaflet to just about every home, but outside that we had little organisation. I canvassed on my own most nights, full of misplaced, youthful optimism. Nationally the party was still in the doldrums. However the next time I tried to get on Maldon Council I lost by ONE vote. But I am getting ahead of myself.

The Young Liberals were a great bunch. There was a hard core of about 20 who were politically active with a few social hangers on who fancied some of the girls. Their leaders were Stewart Rayment, who became a councillor himself in Tower Hamlets in the 1980s, his sister Linda, Tudor Nicholls, Dulcie Finch and Andrew Good, who became a Maldon councillor in years to come. They met most Friday nights in a rundown building at the bottom of Market Hill near the River Blackwater and debated the great issues of the day, just like Barnoldswick Young Liberals. They scared the stuffy Tories. Long haired, sandal wearing, noisy youngsters had not been seen in Maldon politics before. I fielded more than one complaint from older members of the establishment about the Young Liberals' exuberant yet harmless behaviour. When I went canvassing with them the other parties tended to keep well out of sight. It suited me.

Some of the Young Liberal political debates were lively. It was not unusual for the secretary to be asked to write a letter of protest to whoever was in the firing line, be it Tory Premier Edward Heath or the Russian president - again as in Barnoldswick. After the debates it was time for loud music, the waving of incense, some alcohol and a general fun time. They were youngsters who cared about the society they were growing up in. I admired them.

The highlight of their social year was either a float at Maldon Carnival, which had everyone in hysterics, or their annual Wimbledon tea at the home of Tudor's parents. During the latter we sat on deck chairs in a beautiful garden eating scones smothered in jam and cream, talking politics and discussing how we would change the world if we got the chance. In the background the previous day's men's final was relayed over a loudspeaker system set up in the Nicholls' garden. The rights and wrongs of an incomes policy were often drowned out by the roar of the crowd and a shout of '40 love'. I went to five or six of these events and every one was held in glorious sunshine. As far as I was concerned, the sun really did shine on the righteous

The Liberal Party's fortunes revived in early 1972 with a series of Parliamentary by-election victories and the problems Ted Heath's Tory government encountered. This coincided with agreement over the new boundaries which would come into force at the next General Election due by mid 1975 at the latest. Roderic Beale was re-selected unopposed as the Liberal candidate for the Maldon seat while the new Braintree constituency began the search for its own Parliamentary candidate.

In the meantime I had at last found a campaign Maldon Liberals could get their teeth into and make an impact; it also elevated me into a serious political figure in the town. I became one of the leaders behind a vociferous campaign to stop Essex County Council building an inner ring road round Maldon town centre. The need was for a by-pass to take away the heavy traffic which was shaking Maldon's ancient town centre buildings because there was no alternative route for it to take. An all-party anti-ring road committee was formed and my training in pavement politics in Barnoldswick was at last put to good use. The committee was strictly politically neutral and contained some heavyweight local figures, but when it came to the campaigning side I had the field to myself. We had some good talkers, but the do-ers were the people who made things happen.

Essex County Council's bizarre plan - even by their standards of the time - to create an inner ring road round Maldon town centre united the town and split the Tories. Everybody was agreed that something had to be done to take away the large amount of heavy traffic from Maldon High Street and the notorious Market Hill area, but an inner ring road was not the answer; the locals knew it, but County Hall didn't. What was needed, and what eventually came about, was a by-pass to relieve the town of the traffic that didn't want to go anywhere near the High Street. There was cross party support for a campaign against what was widely perceived as the cheaper but ineffective ring road plan. This left local Conservatives with a dilemma because it was their colleagues at County Hall who were pushing ahead with it.

I was elected as the anti-ring road committee's publicity officer, which in effect meant it was me who spoke on behalf of everyone in the town. We invited all 30 members of the county planning committee and the local MP to a Sunday walk round the ring road route to see for themselves why it was not the answer to Maldon's traffic problems. Only one of them turned up. Maldon's MP, who lived near Colchester, made it clear he was not interested. He stood down a few months later. More than 200 people then attended a public meeting when more forthright action was agreed. This included an '*if they won't come to us we will go to them campaign'* which I instigated whereby one Sunday young torch bearers left Maldon carrying a letter outlining the main arguments against a ring road. They travelled across Essex to the homes of key county councillors on the planning and highways committees. About a mile from each home the torch bearer got out of their car, ran the last stage, knocked on the door, left the letter and ran back to their vehicle in what the local media said showed the strength of feeling and *'the spirit of Maldon'*. And just to make sure it all went with a bang the visits took place on November 5. I always had an eye for a good headline!!

The establishment were shocked into a re-think. Essex County Council said it had never met such stiff opposition to any of its plans and within two months back-tracked on the ring road plan. It was to be many years before the by-pass was built, but it was an important victory. From a personal viewpoint I had not only worked with many of the leading figures in Maldon, but they now took me seriously. I was viewed as a man of action who could make things happen. I had made some useful allies.

There was never a chance of a Liberal breakthrough in Maldon until the town and its suburb of Heybridge were split into different and smaller wards in 1974 following the 1972 Local Government Act, which abolished urban and rural councils in favour of larger district councils. Until then it was a straight battle between the Conservatives and Labour candidates for places on the soon to be abolished Maldon Borough Council, with the former guaranteed to win most seats. Often the result depended on what was happening nationally rather than locally. The council still had aldermen - again all Conservatives.

I and other Liberal candidates such as Norman Smith and Pat and Beryl Manaton were no more than irritants to the other two parties until the Liberal Party's fortunes improved in late 1972. The national Liberal Party slowly began to realise that the only way it could have any hope of winning more Parliamentary seats was by building up grassroots support and campaigning at a very local level on issues which affected people on a daily basis, like their dustbins not being emptied or cracked pavements. The Liberals also believed in informing people what was going on in their community through regular newsletters called *Focus* - a far cry from the traditional leaflets only produced at election time. The Young Liberals were also keen to try and improve the campaigning methods of the party. They were strong advocates of working hard between elections. It was dubbed 'community politics' by the media and it worked. At the time it was a major shift in political campaigning. An unpopular Tory government under Ted Heath and the creation of wards which elected up to three councillors each gave the Liberals an outside chance of winning some seats. It was one I was to eventually take in dramatic fashion.

CHAPTER FOUR

SPORTING TIMES

If it looks like a duck, swims like a duck, and quacks like a duck, then it probably is a duck – James Riley

My love of playing football and cricket peaked during my early years in Maldon. I later lived to regret giving up playing both sports when politics took over and my workload became heavier and heavier in my late twenties.

After my cricketing success with both Thornton and Barnoldswick I looked forward to the 1969 cricket season with Maldon Strollers, who still played most of their games on the town's Promenade cricket field. We used to get a reasonable sprinkling of spectators because of the cricket ground's close proximity to the river and bathing lake. There was only one competitive league in Essex at that time and the Strollers were not good enough to be in it - every match was a 'friendly'.

After I was out for that embarrassing 'duck' in my first match I scored just 94 runs in 10 innings with a top score of 23. I took four catches but didn't get enough chances to bowl that first season. When I was brought on I did quite well, but I found it frustrating to be relegated to the outfield for most of an opponent's innings. I don't know whether the growing crisis with my parents affected my game, but it certainly didn't help. I went back to Barnoldswick once every five weeks and more often than not matches due to be played on one of the weekends when I was available for selection were rained off. I never felt I got going all summer, and my confidence suffered.

By the time I returned to Maldon from my brief stint at the *Sheffield Morning Telegraph* at the end of January 1970 I was ready to play football again and re-signed for The Chequers. The team was made up of several excellent players who also played for Maldon Town or Heybridge Swifts - Maldon's two premier Saturday sides - and a mix of men who only played on a Sunday, either because of their work or family reasons. I, of course, did a lot of reporting on Saturdays so Sunday football was the only playing route available to me outside the occasional Saturday game for Maldon Town Reserves or as a guest player for Mundon Vics. Second time round I got off to a far better start than I had with the cricket and scored for Chequers within 30 seconds of my debut in a 5-1 win over Tiptree Monarchs. In the last two months of that season I scored 11 goals.

I couldn't wait for the 1970 cricket season and again turned out for the Strollers on a Saturday and a new club, The Warren based at the nearby village of Woodham Walter, on Sundays. My first game for the latter saw us bowled out for 49 of which I scored 25 on a dreadful wicket at Galleywood! We lost by nine wickets. The Warren players were a happy-go-lucky bunch who didn't take their cricket too seriously. I enjoyed their company on and off the field. The Warren had more faith in my slow to medium pace bowling than the Strollers and I repaid it. I took 3-26 against Old Libertians in a high scoring game and in the return draw against Galleywood took 6-35 in 14 overs only a day after taking 5-43 for the Strollers at Corringham, where I went into bat at number four and was stumped for the only time in my career. I didn't normally give my wicket away cheaply.

We played on some dodgy wickets away from Maldon Promenade best summed up by the game at Shalford when we bowled them out for 57 and lost by five runs. The ball either reared up into your face or shot along the ground. I top scored with 14 and to my mind it was as good as any 50 I scored. In the return I scored 21 as we rattled up 174-4 declared, Dave Gozzett hitting a rare century in our form of cricket when teams batted for a little over two hours a time. Shalford hung on at 133-8 for a draw; I took 2-17 off eight overs and held two catches.

The weather was wonderful that summer and the after-match revelries were just what I needed. Playing cricket helped me to settle down into a better lifestyle after the upheavals and upsets of the previous year. The social side was just as pleasant as the actual games; after every match both sides would retire to the nearest hostelry for several pints - often more than that. The Strollers' home was the Borough Arms in Wantz Road while The Warren players went to a village pub in Woodham Walter.

My rich vein of form continued into September with some impressive performances which banished memories of that 'duck' the previous year. I was a regular on the team sheet whenever I was available, although I had to miss three weeks when I strained my back playing for the Warren against an invitation eleven. We were bowled out for 67 on a dodgy wicket (Scott out for six) but we had our opponents rocking at 40-6. I opened the bowling and claimed 3-13 in 14 overs, five of them maidens. Unfortunately, the last over I bowled came after I had been taken off for a breather and then brought back too quickly without any sort of warm up. I tried to bowl a faster yorker and my back went. It was very painful. After resting I came back to take 6-47 against Maidstone, five of my victims clean bowled, and then score 31 not out in a team total of only 43 while guesting for Bentalls against my own club, the Strollers. The season ended with u quick 32 not out and two wickets in a win on a visit to Hollesley Bay in Suffolk. I took 27 wickets for The Warren that season which only cost eight runs apiece and more than 30 for the Strollers at a cost of little more. They are the sort of bowling figures any cricketer would love to have today on the better wickets.

I never got into any sort of trouble on the football pitch. I was never booked, probably because tackling was not one of the better aspects of my game. But it was a different story on the cricket field where I was far more aggressive. I also received more injuries while playing cricket including the broken leg referred to earlier while at school, a broken ankle the following year which mended much quicker, along with a broken finger, a damaged back and numerous cuts. I have no idea why I used to get so worked up and intense playing cricket, but I did and on one occasion at Tillingham I had to make a hasty exit through the back door of the pavilion when several members of the opposition wanted to have words with me after a game we won by one run. My colleagues suggested it might be better for my health if I hopped over a fence and ran across a neighbouring field so they could pick me up down a lane and drive me home.

During the summer of 1970 I was instrumental in setting up the Maldon district's first Sunday football league in conjunction with

Barry Goodey, Chris Wellsted and Ian Glass who came to see me at the *Maldon and Burnham Standard*. Until then any Maldon teams like the Chequers had to play in the Chelmsford League which involved quite a bit of travelling and was costly. I gave the idea lots of coverage in the *Standard's* sports pages and played an organisational role behind the scenes. It was a pro-active role I have always encouraged on any newspaper where I have worked; reporters should be involved with their local communities. By the time the cricket season was over and the local soccer season was ready to kick-off 12 pub and village sides were ready for the first matches. The league was to be a huge success for 25 years, growing to three divisions.

Barry, Chris and Ian formed a team called Sunshine City after trawling the Australian football pools list for a suitable name for their Maldon based side and I opted to play for them. Our name summed us up that first season - bright and cheerful. We were a mixture of reasonable players, one very good one in midfield and some hopeless cases who often had us in fits of laughter when they tried to head the ball. Unfortunately, one of the hopeless cases was the local hairdresser who was our goalkeeper.

Somehow we finished runners-up to Hanningfield in the two cup competitions and third in the league. I ended up the league's top goalscorer in all competitions with 44 – scoring four goals away to Marriages and five in the return at home; another four against Eastern National followed by four successive hat-tricks. Golden days indeed! We had one player, Ralph, who always drank too much on a Saturday night. We used to warn him not to head the ball. He would forget and be knocked stone cold. We stretched him out on the touchline in all weathers while the trainer brought him round!

By the end of the season a host of new teams wanted to join and a second division was formed. I was persuaded to move to Fambridge United based at the Cups pub where I was now a regular in their darts team. The second division was of a much poorer standard compared with the first and was more chaotic than I expected. In December I was approached to join one of the top first division teams run by Maldon butcher Nobby Stubbings and I transferred to Ulting Villa. There was no transfer fee! They needed a goalscorer and I fitted the bill. By now there were more good players in the First Division than fun players and standards were quite high. Most of my teammates were fit enough to play both Saturday and Sunday football. It was a shame, but inevitable, that in ensuing seasons the league lost its original aim of giving people who worked on a Saturday a chance to play football.

I repaid Ulting Villa's faith in my goalscoring abilities. They were a very good side and created lots of chances. I wasn't a skilful player - far from it - but I had the happy knack of knocking in goals from close range and with my head, although by now I was struggling to see the ball when I took off my glasses. I never tried contact lenses; they were in their early stages of development for sportsmen. I watched too many players who did try to wear them scramble around in the mud in a desperate attempt to find them when they popped out. I scored twice on my Ulting Villa debut and a hat-trick a week later which took us to the top of the table. I quickly justified Nobby's faith in me. Ulting Villa clinched the championship with a game to spare after suffering only two defeats all season.

On the first Sunday in May we met old foes Hanningfield in the Sunday Cup final on Maldon Town's ground in front of a 700 strong crowd. I had never been on the winning side against them the previous season, partly because they had a good centre half built like a brick toilet who enjoyed kicking me up in the air every time I got the ball, and did it with a smile on his face. Off the field he was a gentle giant, but on it he enjoyed roughing up anyone who came his way. I had my revenge. This time we triumphed 2-1 and I got the winning goal. Our manager, Dennis Hutchings, told me beforehand that Hanningfield's goalkeeper would spill the ball at least once if our midfield players shot from distance; I was to always follow up and be on hand to unnerve him. Sure enough he did just that after 15 minutes, and when he spilled the ball I popped the rebound into the net.

No sooner had the football season finished than I was playing cricket again. I was also busy involving myself with the ring road campaign which heralded the start of a hectic few years. This restricted the number of games I was available. I told the Strollers I could not turn out regularly for them and they, quite rightly, said they would given selection preference to players who were more regularly available. I scored 54 out of a team score of 109 all out for Maldon works side Sadds as a guest player and played several more games for them and other teams who needed a last minute replacement for anyone who was ill or injured. My best and most headline-grabbing performance came for the Strollers against their biggest local rivals - Old Maldonians. We bowled them out for 83 on a difficult wicket. Back in the dressing room nobody wanted to open the batting so I volunteered and scored 45 not out as we won by eight wickets. It is a good job I did because I managed to run out our top run getter and skipper Dave Gozzett. Old Maldonians had a very good bowling attack that mixed pace with rarely seen – at that level - leg break bowling. I combined stout defence with some lusty leg side hitting and the Strollers had their first victory in six years over their deadly rivals.

The 1972/73 football season was my last really competitive one. I was only 25 but my eye sight was deteriorating and I played some games by instinct. I did not train as such - keeping fit by the number of games I played. I scored four second half goals for Ulting Villa against my former team Fambridge after a dreadful first half performance in a 6-2 win. Villa went on to win another league title, but dropped me for the cup final, which they also won.

When the 1973 cricket season came round I had just been selected as Braintree's prospective Parliamentary Liberal candidate and most of my time was spent organising what had been a derelict constituency from the Liberal viewpoint. I managed yet another game on the dreadful Shalford pitch, which we won by three wickets; I was top scorer with 39 and took 3-12 when they batted. I must have liked playing them because in the return on Maldon Promenade I scored 53 and shared an 87 run fourth wicket partnership with fellow journalist John Perfect which took us from 28-3 to 115-4. A week later I took 5-5 as Sadds beat Chelmsford Nomads and then scored 41 as they beat Latchingdon. A knock of 44 against White Notley, when I was run out - a rare occurrence - was the end of my season. A year later I made the occasional guest appearance for Sadds scoring 28 not out in a low scoring win against Latchingdon, took 3-5 against Old Maldonians and scored 30 not out for a President's XI against Hatfield Peverel. It was the last time I played a competitive match. From 1973 onwards sport took a back seat as both work and my political ambitions gobbled up most of my time.

At the *Standard* I was promoted to Deputy Editor eight months after my return from Sheffield. Under Peter Laurie's guidance I learned a lot about how to run a successful weekly newspaper. We worked long hours - often well after midnight most Tuesdays when reporters would attend council meetings and then return to the office to file their copy. Circulation rose impressively and we were all proud of our work.

One week I attended a parish council meeting at Tillingham, a remote village in the Dengie Hundred. There was no village hall, just the one pub capable of hosting a meeting. I arrived to find a furious debate in progress about who could use the room. Apparently the parish council meeting clashed with the annual dominos final. Both parties felt they should take precedence, but eventually a true English rural compromise was reached: the parish council met at one end of the table and dominos were played at the other end.

For me money, or the lack of it, was still a problem. It was the quest for more money which led me to make an awful mistake. I left the *Standard* a year after becoming Deputy Editor to run Maldon's main sports shop just a few yards up the High Street. It was typical of the poor pay on offer in the regional press that I could earn much more managing a small sports shop than I could as a Deputy Editor. I knew I had done wrong the first week I got behind the counter, but the need for extra cash outweighed commonsense. I hated the work and did not get on with the shop's owner who had been all sweetness and light at the interview, but soon turned out to be somebody I did not like. A lot of the business came from anglers and I knew little about that sport. Keeping maggots in perfect condition each week was also not to my liking! I lasted four months after which we agreed to part company when I asked for a day off to help with local government elections and the shop owner refused. I took it anyway and found myself out of work.

I had already done some freelance work for the *Essex Chronicle* at Chelmsford and after contacting them they offered me a part-time job in their sports department covering senior football and Essex cricket as well as loads of amateur sport. Sports Editor was Bernard Webber who enjoyed reporting on Colchester United and Essex cricket but did not have much time for minor sports. My co sports writer was Martin Rogers who owned the King's Lynn speedway franchise. Martin was a gifted writer who could knock out 800 words in rapid fashion. At that time he was an avid supporter of Chelmsford City who came close on several occasions to being elected to the Football League. Martin's fanatical support got the better of him one Monday night when City conceded a last minute goal and lost a vital match. Suddenly the press box door at the back of the main stand opened and Martin's typewriter went bouncing down the steps. Martin liked fast cars and drove them at incredible speeds without any apparent damage to himself or anyone else.

The money I got from the Essex Chronicle hardly covered my outgoings but along with other freelance work enabled me to give more time to my main aim at that time - to fight the next General Election. My political activities in Maldon caught the eye of the few Liberals in the newly created Braintree Parliamentary constituency. They needed a candidate and after a couple of meetings with them I was selected. They had no councillors and little organisation, but the people they did have were enthusiastic hard workers. Their leader was John Ross, who along with his wife Dianna became a life-long friend.

The national Liberal Party thought Braintree was a lost cause and that we would lose our deposit. They didn't exactly write us off, but they didn't give us any backing either. There was never an offer to send a heavyweight political speaker to any of our events. Two years later they changed their minds and thought the seat was winnable, but that only came about after a lot of hard work. John, Dianna and the others set about building a team round me. We fought several council by-elections and John won a seat on Braintree Council. He was soon joined by another Liberal. We managed to put together good political organisations in Braintree, part of Witham, Coggeshall and some of the villages; above all we had a lot of fun. We had to raise the money we needed for leaflets and campaigning so there were plenty of fund raising events and socials; these drew in new people.

Nationally there was also a Liberal recovery as Ted Heath's Conservative government ran into more and more trouble. I attended a few events where I met senior members of the party including leader Jeremy Thorpe, Cyril Smith and later Clement Freud. Thorpe was charismatic and charming, but not a supporter of the grassroots campaigns I and other former Young Liberals were running. I was unaware of the cloud which hung over him because of his homosexual links which ultimately led to his demise and a high profile trial at the Old Bailey. Smith was a larger than life character in more ways than one. Again, there was no way I, or anyone else, could know he had a history of sexually abusing young boys, but when I met him I felt there was something not quite right. Freud was strange from the outset and the least likeable. On one occasion I had the job of 'meeting and greeting' him prior to a Liberal candidates' gathering. When he arrived I guided him towards the hall and gently tugged his arm to show him the way. He rounded on me and said: *'Nobody should ever touch me.'* He must have got that from watching royalty!

My two opponents in Braintree Tony Newton (Con) and Keith Kyle (Lab) didn't take me too seriously at first. Tony was straight out of the Tory party's research department; Keith was a well known television journalist. They had a major advantage over me when it came to national politics, but I knew how to campaign at grassroots level and to get good coverage in local newspapers. *Braintree and Witham Times* Editor John Savage was a canny news man. He soon recognised I was capable of giving him a lot of readable stories to get his teeth into. In an 18 month period I went to war on a complacent establishment, knocked on thousands of doors, found out what ordinary people were thinking and campaigned non-stop across a wide area. I was rarely out of the news.

Why was I such a staunch Liberal at that time? Part of it was my natural empathy with any underdog, plus the political grounding I had in Barnoldswick. As far as I could ascertain Britain was falling behind in the world and the two main parties didn't seem to represent ordinary people: the Tories were tied to big business, while Labour was in hock to the unions. It is hard for many people to understand nowadays how the big unions abused their power in the 1970s and brought the country to its knees. The union barons fought hard on behalf of their individual members but the rest of the working class, including the elderly and infirm, did not matter. I also passionately believed in the rights of the individual as opposed to the state and have never been a supporter of centralisation. I excelled in helping people on a day-to-day basis with their everyday problems and running local campaigns against the establishment. My feelings then and now are best summed up by something Lloyd George said: '*I believe in a radical but non socialist economy and society.*'

The General Election was scheduled for late 1974 or early 1975, but national events including a miners' strike and the state of the economy conspired to bring it forward to a Thursday at the end of February 1974; it was too early if I had any hope of winning. In those days I had great self confidence. I felt I could achieve anything with enough hard work. I think that was infectious when it came to building the Braintree team. I spent all my spare time in the constituency building up an effective election fighting machine from scratch. A lively social side combined with local campaigning produced more and more members. We held jumble sales, Christmas fayres, parties and a host of other events. John and Dianna Ross and many others were just as passionate as I was and by the autumn of 1973 we had at least 100 people willing to put in a lot of work to get me elected to Parliament.

In December 1973 the country was plunged into a three day working week to preserve fuel when the miners' strike began to take effect. At the beginning of the following February Prime Minister Heath called an election to find an answer to the question '*Who runs the country?*' and was duly told '*not you*'. Harold Wilson and Labour returned to power with no overall majority.

The three and a half week election campaign in Braintree was a round of daytime/afternoon/evening canvassing and a novel idea I introduced of an evening phone-in when anyone could call with a question. There were no public meetings where the candidates met voters. In the last few days my personal energy tank ran on empty and I was very tired. I didn't pace myself, did not have proper meals and my inexperienced but hard working team who had never fought a major General Election before had no idea how to control my schedule. Some days I was out canvassing and meeting people from 10am to 8pm and then going back to do the phone-in before kipping down on a mattress on my agent's lounge floor. My mind was too active for me to get any good sleep. I did not have the time to travel back and forth from Heybridge where I could have taken a break.

The election count was not until the morning after polling day by which time I knew that while the Liberals had polled six million votes nationally, they had failed to gain more than eight seats on top of the six they already held. And so it proved - so near, yet so far. Tony Newton won the Braintree seat with 20,000 votes, Keith Kyle got 18,000 and I got 15,000 - 27% of the vote. Not bad for a seat where the Liberals were marked down as deposit losers!

The BBC filmed the run-up to the election for 12 months and it made an interesting documentary many months later which, unfortunately, I never recorded. I got on well with both Tony and Keith. Whenever we met we always exchanged a few pleasantries. There was nothing nasty or personal about the campaign, in marked contrast to what I was to experience 30 years later in Torbay.

The election drained me emotionally, physically and financially, although the *Chronicle* generously paid me for the three weeks I had off. We came so close from nowhere. Both my opponents admitted they never expected me to get so many votes, but I had not won and I felt the loss keenly. I have never liked losing. Sometimes while playing sport I had been ungracious in defeat; but not on this occasion.

The following week I returned to my part-time sports reporter's job at the *Essex Chronicle*. I was earning just enough at the *Chronicle* to pay my accommodation and car costs, but it was time for me to face up to the fact that I needed a full-time job. To make matters worse Braintree Liberals pressed me for a quick decision as to whether I was prepared to be their candidate again, because it was obvious the Labour government would call a second election later in the year. I was in no fit state to think rationally about my political future. I needed a rest. It wasn't forthcoming. The Liberal Party now viewed Braintree as highly winnable and pressed me to make a quick decision.

I faced a stark choice - politics or newspapers. Wisely, I chose the latter and never regretted it. My successor in Braintree was one of the party's top brains, Richard Holme, who went on to become Lord Holme and an advisor to future leader Paddy Ashdown. He polled 3,000 fewer votes in the October General Election. Since then no Liberal or Liberal Democrat candidate in Braintree has come anywhere near matching that February 1974 result.

CHAPTER FIVE

MY FIRST EDITORSHIP

"Thank you for sending me a copy of your book; I'll waste no time reading it."- Moses Hadas.

I went straight back to the *Essex Chronicle* to report on Essex cricket and Colchester United football. When I told the company I wanted to be considered for any full-time job that became vacant they soon found me one as their first editorial training officer. I had the job of guiding five new trainees through their first few weeks in journalism. One of them was Alan Geere who went on to edit several regional newspapers. A few months later I was appointed production editor in addition to my training duties to ensure the smooth flow of pages from all the newspapers prepared and printed at Chelmsford.

I had to tip toe my way through a minefield of industrial relations problems posed by the print unions. There were three main unions in the one production area at Chelmsford. Not only did they each fight their own battles with the company, but they also jealously guarded their 'differentials' between each other. The main print union, the NGA, felt its members were worth 20% more than the other two unions' members; if we settled with one union the other two had to have their increases too.

It was anarchy that came to an end in the mid 1980s when new technology, Rupert Murdoch and Eddie Shah destroyed their power. Most regional newspaper production staff lost not only their perks but their careers. They were led over a cliff by their union masters. Some of them were skilled craftsmen who worked hard and thought they had a job for life. They deserved a better fate. Only a small minority were militant, but they had far too much power for far too long.

Out of the blue at the beginning of 1975 I was given my third promotion in 12 months when I was appointed Editor of the company's paper in East London, the *Romford Observer*. This was the climax of an extraordinary few years since leaving Barnoldswick. I was thrilled to get my first Editorship despite being warned the company intended to close the paper within a year because it had not been a commercial success following its launch 18 months earlier. When the *Observer*'s first Editor left rather suddenly for what he thought was a more stable job, the *Essex Chronicle's* management must have been tempted to close it there and then because it faced stiff and long established competition from three other weekly papers in town, including the all-powerful *Romford Recorder* selling 40,000 copies a week compared to the *Observer*'s 5,500.

Fortunately for me the company did not want to lose too much face by closing it too soon, making the entire workforce redundant. I was told to get valuable experience as an Editor and then see what the company could offer me upon my guaranteed return to Chelmsford.

It was not an easy task because the journalists wanted the paper's popular Deputy Editor, John Hill, to take over; they did not know me. I was fortunate that John soon forgot his disappointment and helped me not only settle in to my new role, but ultimately to save his job and those of the rest of the team. I was Editor for nearly four years, not one, and the *Observer* survived until the late 1990s. The rest of the staff never knew the paper was under constant threat of closure in the first 12 months of my Editorship. I soon got a good response from them and was delighted when the closure threat was lifted in 1977.

I never fancied living in Romford or any of its neighbouring towns within the London borough of Havering. I continued to enjoy life in Heybridge 45 miles away and travel up every day, often leaving home around 6.45am to beat the worst of the traffic and get round the bottleneck that is Gallows Corner on the A12. Editors did not get a company car in those days – it was another three years before they were introduced by the *Chronicle* group – but I was allowed ten gallons of free fuel from the company pump at Chelmsford after an accountant worked out the extra distance I would have to travel to work.

I started off with a staff consisting of a deputy, a sub-editor, three reporters and two photographers. The paper's growth meant I was allowed to recruit another junior and one senior reporter. I was surprised when recruitment proved to be a difficult task. There were more jobs available than reporters to fill them. A far cry from today! A train ride into London, where jobs were plentiful and the financial pickings much greater, were more attractive. After a heavy advertising campaign I managed to assemble a list of potential reporters, most of whom came ill-prepared for their interviews. It proved impossible to recruit a suitable male trainee so I ended up with an office staffed mainly by female reporters.

The women interviewed far better than the men. They made an effort to dress smartly, conversed better and showed signs they had done some homework about what the job entailed. Several potential male trainee reporters didn't bother to wear a tie, had dirty shoes and gave the impression they only wanted to become a journalist because they couldn't think of anything better to do.

At one set of interviews I rejected three potential trainees on the trot – two of whom didn't get beyond the initial pleasantries. One turned up on jeans and jumper and made it clear he did not feel how he dressed was important. He said he was a good writer and while his ultimate aim was to work in television, he was prepared to "slum it" while he got some initial training. He might have been the best writer available, but there was no way he would have got the stories in the first place. What he, and countless other job-seekers, didn't understand was that first impressions do count and can make the difference between getting a story or coming away empty handed. If someone turns up on a doorstep and looks as though he is in need of a good wash, few people are going to trust him or let him into their home. Quite often that initial reaction to a reporter's appearance and manner can be decisive. And if the story happens to be one where the interviewee has to be persuaded to release information then a white shirt, a tie and a decent haircut can make all the difference.

The second person I rejected came into the interview chewing gum. I took the opportunity to ask whether he had ever received any sort of tuition at school aimed at preparing him for a job interview; he claimed he had, but felt the "true person" ought to be revealed at an interview. I thanked him for his honesty and for not wasting my time to the point where I needed to conduct a formal interview. He left soon after muttering about the state of the office furniture.

The third potential trainee to be rejected the same day failed because of a common fault – lack of self projection and an inability to communicate with the interviewer. I have always believed that if a potential journalist cannot talk about himself at an interview, he stands little chance of being able to extract information from other people. When interviewing I have always tried to get people to spend five or ten minutes talking about their life, background, aspirations, etc., in the belief that by talking about things which are familiar, it helps to calm any initial interview nerves.

Over the years my interviews were an ordeal for some people who didn't always manage to do themselves justice, but when they were competing with a number of others they needed to sell themselves if they were to stand any change of getting a job. That didn't mean they had to be too aggressive or too knowledgeable, but reporters on papers I edited had to be good communicators and show an ability to find stories and feel easy with different types of people, in addition to possessing the necessary writing skills. Of course, they had to have certain basic qualifications to get an interview in the first place, but the person who passes A-level English doesn't necessarily make a good journalist.

When interviewing I looked for a variety of qualities in a trainee journalist: I tried to judge whether they would fit into my team – an important point in a small office; I needed to be assured the trainee would last the training course, which was expensive and time consuming; I tried to gauge whether they would get on well with members of the public and gain their confidence; finally, I looked for an orderly mind able to get events in perspective and transfer them into a story on paper.

Eventually, I did find some good people, but it was hard work. The ones I chose were worth the effort because they turned out to be excellent reporters. I never let on they were by far the best of a very bad bunch.

Part of their induction training concentrated on the proper use of that indispensible part of a reporter's life, the telephone. When used in an effective way, it is an excellent tool, but in the wrong hands it can do as much harm as good. Not enough time is spent training young reporters how to use a telephone properly and how to project an image of themselves to the person they are talking to. If an interview is conducted over the telephone, an aggressive or too casual approach can result in the loss of a story. The golden rules are never to keep someone waiting, to be as polite and charming as possible without going over the top, and to always explain who you are and what you want.

Inexperienced reporters need to be watched carefully when taking stories over the telephone. It is too easy for their minds – and eyes – to be distracted so they end up not checking all the facts, miss key elements of the story, fail to check the spelling of names, or don't recap what they have been told. I had to laugh one day, though, when I caught a young female reporter screaming down the telephone: *"Is that the Havering Hard of Hearing Club?"*!

The *Romford Observer's* editorial department suffered from a familiar problem – a bored receptionist/telephonist who handled all initial contacts with the public before calls got through to the journalists or advertising staff. I found out how badly she answered the telephone when I called in one day. When others told me they had similar experiences, I didn't hesitate in replacing her when she started to argue with me.

It has always baffled me how little newspaper companies are prepared to spend when it comes to their own marketing. They exhort others to spend massive amounts on advertising but rarely practice what they preach. The *Romford Observer* promotional budget for a newspaper less than two years old was £0, which presented something of a problem when I wanted to run a Miss Observer contest. After much pleading I was given £120 to pay for a finals night at a grotty venue in Upminster. By then I had whittled 40 entrants down to 12. They paraded round a cold hall in front of 150 hardy souls who paid £1 each for the privilege. I booked the hall, arranged the judges, had the tickets printed, got the prizes, sorted out a bar and even did a spell on the door.

Romford, however, was a great news patch and the *Observer* had some talented journalists. Charlie Whebell, Chris Stratford and Gill

74

Humphrey (now Powell) were as talented a team as one could hope for on a local newspaper and in addition to John Hill I had an eagle-eyed sub-editor in Patrick Faulkner. I made a number of mistakes, but each one appeared to strengthen my reputation with the editorial team. One of them paid me a compliment when he said I had '*guts*'. There were times I went where angels might fear to tread, but a lot of it was naive impetuosity backed by an eager team.

One of the best stories I ever handled landed the paper with a big libel bill in 1976. The first female deaconess of an Anglican church in Essex was sacked. She came to see me after we broke the story and revealed she was having a lesbian affair with the wife of a top London policeman. We ran another story and a long interview with the two women during which the wife said her marriage was a sham and she would soon be divorced, leaving her husband free to continue his affair with a London secretary. The policeman sued for libel. Unfortunately his wife was not regarded by our solicitors as a credible witness and we ended up paying him quite a bit in damages and costs. I made plenty of other mistakes, but none as costly as that one.

During this period our office was twice burgled and then four policemen searched my secretary's Hornchurch home with a warrant obtained by the Met. I was furious and made an official complaint which resulted in a visit by two plain clothes detectives who gave me the option of pursuing the complaint or leaving it with them because they were investigating the said policeman for 'other activities'. They made it clear I could expect some favours if I dropped the complaint. I believe they were Special Branch. I didn't hear anything for six months until *Private Eye* and the national press broke the story that the policeman had been suspended, and ultimately sacked, for helping his House of Commons secretary and girlfriend arrange parties where Iron Curtain diplomats, MPs, policemen and others met. I still have the page from *Private Eye* headed *'Anne of a thousand lays.'* The ex deaconess and wife moved to Gorleston in Norfolk where they ran a whelk stall for many years. They sent me a Christmas card.

I ran into big trouble with the race relations brigade, which exposed my inexperience in the Editor's chair, when Idi Amin kicked out thousands of Ugandan Asians, some of whom were offered temporary accommodation by Havering Council in a large property earmarked for development as an old people's complex. From the outset the council made it clear the Ugandan Asians would be moved to other accommodation when it could be arranged, but when the time came they said they were enjoying life where they were and did not want to be split up. It was virtually impossible to tell who was related to whom. They claimed they were one big happy family and wanted to remain under one roof rather than take up the council's offer of a number of houses in the borough. Feelings ran high for several weeks, culminating in a public meeting during which several people said they would '*burn them out*' if they didn't move'. I used those words in a headline and was attacked by left-wing commentators in the national media and local Labour politicians. The council refused to budge and the Asians eventually moved out so the old people's complex could be built. It was a tough lesson.

Circulation increased by 55% in the four years under my Editorship to more than 8,500. It still wasn't enough to deliver the advertising revenue the company wanted, so just before I left the *Observer* became one of the first weekly paid-for titles to turn free with a circulation in excess of 30,000.

During the winter of 1977/78 I had plenty of fun and continued to learn a lot when I had to bring out the newspaper virtually on my own when regional journalists went on a nine-week national strike in an attempt to improve their pay – a claim I felt had much to commend it but which was never going to be agreed. The only help I had for nearly two months was a sports editor, who was not in the National Union of Journalists, who was banned by the Chelmsford print unions from doing anything but his normal job. Such was their power in those days! I did get several readers to write stories for the paper and one turned in such good copy I wished I could have employed him when the strike ended. He was 82 years old! The *Observer* itself was not picketed; the NUJ concentrated its efforts on the *Romford Recorder* and the *Essex Chronicle's* head office and printing works. The print unions refused to support the journalists, but some printing staff provided them with regular tea, coffee and soup until University of Essex students manning the picket line one day intimidated a milkman in his float who was stopped from delivering his daily pints. From then on the journalists had to bring their own tea and coffee.

I ran the gauntlet of the strikers' picket line at Chelmsford every Tuesday afternoon when I went to 'put the paper to bed'. It became more aggressive as the strike went on with no sign of the newspaper owners backing down. At the outset most abuse was light-hearted. The pickets usually asked me to stop my car while they outlined why they were there. There was the mandatory request for me not to enter. I would listen and then drive on. Inevitably, as the strike dragged on, attitudes hardened and serious attempts were made to physically stop me entering the Chelmsford office with pickets thumping their fists on my car roof.

That was nothing compared to what happened one Thursday night when the NUJ put in their biggest effort in an attempt to stop the lorries and vans carrying the *Essex Chronicle* from leaving the site. Hundreds of pickets gathered at the only two exits – in itself not an illegal act at that time. Trades unionists and left wing students from all over Essex turned up in a show of solidarity along with two policemen who were there to ensure that nobody got hurt. Everything was peaceful for two hours but when the pickets attempted to drag a lorry driver out of his cab police reinforcements were called in. Unknown to the pickets a squad of police in unmarked vehicles was parked just round the corner. They burst on the scene and pulled out the ring leaders in no time, bundling them into the back of their vans. The pickets had been unlucky enough to be hit by the Essex Police Special Support Group which was operational at nearby Stansted Airport to deal with potential terrorist attacks. It was all over in less than five minutes and within a further 10 minutes most of the pickets had dispersed. There was no repeat the next week.

Most of my staff didn't want to strike and as the cold set in and it snowed they became a sorry lot, only too glad to return to work at the end of January having gained nothing and in the process having lost money most of them couldn't afford. Old routines were quickly restored. Ironically, the *Observer* put on sales during the strike. The National Union of Journalists has never called a national strike since.

When the strike ended the *Chronicle*'s Managing Director, John Saxton, paid for Valerie and I to have a week's holiday in Tunisia by way of a 'thank you' so I could *'recharge my batteries'*. That wouldn't happen today.

Next door to our office was a snooker hall run by Barry Hearn, today a leading boxing and snooker promoter. John Hill and I would play there some lunch-times. It was not unusual to see a large crowd gathered round another table in the hall watching a young Steve Davis take on all-comers at £5 a time. There were some rough characters in that hall most days; John and I kept to ourselves.

We had more than our fair share of murders and violent crime to report - some weeks it was hard to find the 'good' news - but I wasn't sorry though to leave in March 1979 when I moved back to the Chelmsford office to become John Saxton's Assistant Managing Director. John Hill was appointed Editor.

I was still estranged from my family when I became the *Observer*'s Editor, but that did not stop me making several trips a year north to stay with Robert Boven and his parents. Robert and I went on several foreign holidays to Spain and Italy until one year when we went to Rimini and he met his future wife, Michelle, on day two. It was love at first sight. For the rest of our holiday I had no choice but to tag along. When they both got back to England they planned to get married a year later, but Michelle called it off a month before the big day. She married another man a few years after, but this proved a mistake and they were divorced. Several years later I played cupid and arranged for Robert to meet up with her again. I was his best man and delighted for him, even if I found the ceremony at a Jewish synagogue in Manchester rather different from what I was used to.

In just over six years between leaving Barnoldswick in January 1969 and the spring of 1975 I made great career strides and, importantly from my viewpoint, I did it on my own without any help from home. It must have irritated my father who I suspect expected me to come back with my tail between my legs at some stage. What must have made it even worse were people telling him how well I was doing because Jack Heald was always keen to write stories for the *Craven Herald* about my political and newspaper exploits.

It wasn't until my grandfather died in 1975 that reconciliation of a sorts was possible. My grandmother asked if I would attend the funeral in Darwen, which obviously meant I would meet up with everyone in the family again. For several days I was undecided about whether to go, but in the end decided to make the trip. My father was grateful, while my mother was overjoyed; from then on relations slowly improved. I had matured a lot in the years I had been away. I now felt confident about my own abilities and knew I could handle the situation without falling out with anyone. I learned to laugh off anything that was said or I saw because I knew I had a life of my own 300 miles away. I rarely showed any emotion when a provocative comment was made, only allowing a faint smile to cross my face when something was said which in the past would have made me retaliate.

During my time as their Editor in Romford the *Essex Chronicle*'s management made it clear they would not view it kindly if I pursued my interest and involvement in national politics. Not unreasonably, they wanted to be sure I was going to be around for a while. However they had no objection to any political involvement at a purely local level in Heybridge where I still lived in a bungalow with Mrs Burfoot. There was no conflict with my work because Maldon is in Essex and Romford in a London borough. They might as well be on two different planets.

Early in 1975 after a short break away from politics I began to build up the Heybridge branch which already had some strong support from people like Pat and Mick Mead, Bill and Pam Fletcher and Clive and Judith Church. Within a few months we had a 10-strong local committee and managed a three monthly delivery to every home of a FOCUS newsletter which we eventually had professionally printed at Tollesbury - when we could afford it. We ran dances, jumble sales and a Christmas fayre to boost funds. I look back on that period as the happiest time of my political career. During one of the regular jumble sales I sold 'right handed tea cups' to a lady as a joke. She took me seriously and asked if we had any left handed ones, so I went under the counter and turned the handles round for her.

We had a lot of fun and team spirit was high when it came to the May 1976 Maldon Council elections. Labour held all three seats in Heybridge, but we felt we had a chance because apart from one well known councillor they had neglected the ward. Bill, Pat and I were the three candidates. The Conservatives were riding high in the national opinion polls and their candidates took all three seats. I lost by ONE VOTE to the third placed Conservative after two recounts. I cannot begin to describe how I felt after losing by that single vote. We had worked so hard and managed to relegate Labour into third place at a time when Liberal fortunes nationally were not good. What made it all the more galling was the number of people who came up to me AFTER the election to say they now wished they had voted! In particular I was annoyed with one couple whom I knew had not voted. I had helped them get land next to their bungalow cleared of rubbish and other items which had been dumped there. When I next met them I asked why they had not bothered to go and vote and was told: *'We never vote. We are Jehovah's Witnesses and leave everything in God's hands.'* It was a statement I remembered a year later when their dustbins had not been emptied for two weeks. When they asked me to help I told them to pray a bit harder. It was a churlish comment which I don't recall with any pleasure now, but I was very annoyed with them at the time. It was a reflection of how I still feel about people who cannot be bothered to take a few minutes to vote.

In the meantime I didn't sulk and give up. Maldon Council only held elections every four years so I was livid when I discovered one of the three successful Tories had moved to live in London only a few weeks after being elected. Heybridge Conservatives had the cheek to say they knew when they selected him to fight the election he would be moving. They could see nothing wrong in that. Everyone else could. I was determined not to let them get away with it for four years and took every opportunity to remind the public when he failed to turn up for meetings or deal with local issues. The Press had a field day. I think the Tories hoped I would eventually go away, but I didn't. On top of the newspaper coverage our FOCUS newsletters kept the issue in the public domain. By now we could deliver to every home in Heybridge within a week. I organised a small army of deliverers who delivered to their own and neighbouring roads. Not only did we keep up the pressure but we showed how effective we could be in highlighting and then getting improvements for a part of Maldon which had been sadly neglected for many years. There was no shortage of issues we could take up and when we started to get results more and more people started to come to us with their problems and sign up as members. It was time consuming, but often very rewarding.

Eventually the Tories cracked. Their missing councillor resigned at Christmas 1976 and a by-election was called for March. I campaigned on my record of getting things done and the simple slogan that every vote really did count. We left nothing to chance and on the day ran one of the best polling day organisations I was ever involved with. The election count was the same night and I romped home with 981 votes to Labour's 277 and the Conservative's 273 on a 54% turnout - a very high figure for a by-election and 20% up on the previous May. My two Jehovah's Witnesses still didn't vote! It was one of life's better moments at the count when the returning officer chose to pile up and count my votes on their own because there were so many. The look on the face of the man I had already clashed with on several occasions and was to do battle with over and over again in the coming years, Tory Councillor Rodney Bass, was worth all the pain I had suffered the previous May. He left before the result was declared - a worse loser than me. Battle lines were drawn.

I was under no illusions about what I had taken on. I was the only Liberal on a 30 member council which was dominated by 21 Conservatives along with six Independents, two of whom voted Conservative in national elections. Several Tories and a number of council officers were masons. There were two Labour councillors, Gerry Hughes and Eric Bannister, who represented the council housing area in Maldon. My first meeting was the monthly full council meeting when I was welcomed by the leader, Councillor Lister Bass, father of my 'enemy' Rodney. Two other members of the Bass family were also on the council - Rodney's brother Henry and brother-in-law Tony Peel. Bass senior always treated me with respect. However, after his initial welcome, he said: *'Don't think you will get anything done because nobody will second any proposal you make.'* It was a gauntlet I picked up with some relish.

Heybridge in the 1970s was Maldon's poor neighbour. It had a large number of council houses with few facilities for the locals. Its prettiest part was - and still is - Heybridge Basin on the River Blackwater, a yachting centre for those who can afford it. There were a few shops, but no local doctors or chemists. People had to either catch a bus or drive into Maldon and use one of the expensive car parks if they wanted to buy the most basic of items.

Heybridge Swifts Football Club provided the major social outlet on and off the field. I built up my political support there over the years. I often popped in for a drink on Friday nights and played cards with club chairman Mick Gibson and others. I attended their home games most Saturday afternoons. It was not unusual for me to be dealing with a council problem on somebody's behalf while standing on the touchline watching the football. My council work kept me busy most evenings and at weekends, hence the decision to stop playing competitive sport.

I won't bore you with all the campaigns I ran over the next three years, but I made a start in improving the lot of Heybridge residents and above all got the area some recognition after many years of neglect. I was able to encourage and get started the first youth club, get money to improve the village hall, have signs erected on the boundaries - before that nobody could find Heybridge - and began the work which led to a doctors' surgery and chemists opening after I left. I also dealt with the many little problems people had with the council and took an interest in the well-being of others across the Maldon district. In council meetings I lost more battles than I won because the Tories used their big majority to reject many of my plans but the occasional success made up for it. I also saw at firsthand how the masons worked together in the council chamber. On several occasions the council took what I believed were bad decisions, influenced by leading masons both inside and outside the council chamber.

It did not take long for me to attract allies: Independent councillors Patricia Herrmann and Beryl Board along with Conservative Roy Pipe resented the heavy-handed, domineering tactics of Rodney Bass and together we formed a formidable debating team in council meetings. The two Labour councillors also joined in and between us we had some fun - decisions were no longer simply nodded through. We had some thumping good debates which often ended with Rodney Bass glaring at me or throwing a sarcastic comment my way. The more times he did, the more I goaded him. It was still galling, however, to be told by some Tories after a meeting: '*You were right, but of course we couldn't vote with you.*'

The lively meetings were music to the ears of local newspapermen who had got used to sitting through boring rubber stamp debates; council coverage in the *Maldon and Burnham Standard* during this time was immense. I have two scrap books full of newspaper stories from the period. We caught the establishment off guard and they responded in typical fashion with a ban on council officers speaking to anyone in the media unless comments were vetted by the council leadership. It was a clear sign they were rattled and did not know how to effectively respond.

What they couldn't do was shut me up because whatever I wanted to speak about always got a seconder from one of the rebels; it meant the matter had to be debated. I also pulled another trick on them by researching what they had said they would do in their election leaflets, but hadn't, and then proposing the more sensible local items I found. When they voted en bloc against what I proposed, I tipped off the Press and the Tories were made to look silly. After a while of open warfare they began to treat me with a bit more respect and commonsense generally prevailed.

I was never impolite and only lost my temper on one occasion. Gradually some of the more sensible Tories began to seek my opinion, especially on planning matters. In 1977 I was appointed vice-chairman of the local planning committee under the chairmanship of Cyril Dowsett, one of the more elderly Tories. He and I found we had much in common and in a short time we became friends. I had the good sense to listen to him and learned a lot. After I left Maldon he died a horrible death when he fell asleep in front of his open lounge fire. He toppled into it and died of his injuries.

The mid to late 1970s were not a great time for the Liberal Party nationally after their high expectations during the two 1974 General

Elections. The Tories removed Ted Heath as their leader and elected Margaret Thatcher. Labour's Harold Wilson remained Prime Minister for two years before he suddenly resigned and was replaced by Jim Callaghan. The country's standing in the world was low and it took an International Monetary Fund bailout to stall an economic crisis. As a nation we were living well beyond our means, inflation was rampant and the unions looked to be in total control of government policy.

It should have been an opportunity for Liberalism to capture the public's imagination, but Jeremy Thorpe was literally in the dock. He was forced to resign as Liberal Party leader by his fellow MPs and in 1979 stood trial accused of conspiring to get an alleged former male lover killed by a hit man. Although he was acquitted it cost him his political career. I met Thorpe a couple of times and liked him and his wife, Marion.

His successor was Scottish MP David Steel who somehow managed to keep the party together. I did some work at the House of Commons for him along with Chelmsford councillor and parliamentary candidate Stuart Mole. Stuart and I produced a newspaper paid for by the Rowntree Trust extolling the advantages of the Lib-Lab pact which kept the Labour government in power for a further two years after it lost its majority. More than 12 million copies were printed and distributed round the country. I went to the Commons to meet Steel and he later wrote thanking me for my efforts.

CHAPTER SIX

MARRIAGE AND AMERICA

I chose my wife, as she did her wedding dress, for qualities that would wear well – Oliver Goldsmith

I did not have the time to develop anything serious with the girlfriends I had in my twenties. A couple of them hinted at a more permanent arrangement, but most relationships lasted only a few months, mainly because I was wrapped up in my council work and had a demanding job as an Editor. Several 'girls' got fed up with me; in hindsight I don't think I was great marriage material even though my financial woes were behind me and I could afford a relatively new car. I was happy to take some of my female friends to social events and dinners connected with my work or council duties, but I never allowed anyone to get really close and generally the girls who lasted the longest were the ones prepared to be friends rather than partners.

I was content to have a good night out most Saturdays at the Cups where mine hosts were David and Eve Jack. They knew how to run a good 1970s pub - it was packed most weekends. David was intelligent and sharp-eyed. He told one man who played cards with the rest of us never to return when he only bought one half pint all night. Eve was a buxom landlady with a great sense of humour who always put on a good buffet when we had a home darts match. I never heard her say one swear word, but she was full of sexual innuendo. The men loved it. The Cups was the perfect place for sporting chat any night of the week and the pub's Sunday football team had a couple of successful seasons in the Maldon League.

One female friendship I valued more than any other was with Pat Astin, a former pupil at Skipton Girls' Grammar School. Pat and I first met at a Skipton church event in 1965. She and I used to see each other off and on until I moved to Maldon. On my visits north in 1969 I went to tea at her mother's home before the long overnight trip back to Essex. On one memorable occasion she managed to send all the goodies on her mother's cake stand flying. A year later she moved to London. We used to meet up some Saturdays, enjoy walks through the city and visit museums and other places of interest. Neither of us had any money, but that didn't matter. They were fun days and we formed a friendship which is still on-going. Those days in London still give me a warm feeling.

Pat married a social worker, also called David. When she told me she was getting married I experienced one of the few times in my life when I felt jealous. I met David a couple of times, but didn't like him from the outset. At first I thought I was the problem. But the more I saw of him and heard from Pat what he was like, the more I realised he was a lazy social worker with a big ego who enjoyed mental bullying. They lived in Preston, had a family and all seemed well for a while. When we met up during this period Pat tried to hide her true feelings until one visit when it was obvious their relationship was not a happy one. She was far too good for him and once she realised just how unhappy she was and he would not change they were divorced. She is now happily married to Roger, whose company I do enjoy.

My life changed in early September 1977 when one of my 'girlfriends' Marcia Lawrence took me back to her home in Braintree to have coffee one evening with her parents and sister, Amanda. Also present that night was Valerie - Amanda's best friend. I was instantly attracted. Mrs Lawrence said later she knew right away something was going to happen between us.

A few days later Valerie telephoned me at Romford and we arranged to go out for a drink. We decided to try and find a pub somewhere off the beaten track in the Essex countryside where we could be on our own and not be interrupted by anyone wanting to talk about politics, sport or newspapers. But when we walked through the door one of my senior colleagues from the *Essex Chronicle* and his girlfriend were sat near the bar. That didn't deter us, though, and we continued to see each other two or three times a week.

It was the most time I had ever spent with anyone; I was obviously smitten. In late October we went off to the Lake District for a few days holiday and I proposed. Valerie turned me down, saying it was far too soon. I have never been good at handling rejection - probably a legacy of my upbringing in Barnoldswick and rows with my parents - and I took it badly. Very badly. I saw no point in continuing the holiday. We drove back to Essex in virtual silence apart from some crying by Valerie. It was a long seven hours and I behaved disgracefully. I always do when hurt. I dropped Valerie off at her home in Braintree and continued on to Heybridge. Two hours later the telephone rang; Valerie said she would say 'yes' if we officially got engaged at Christmas. I couldn't see any reason to hang around, but agreed.

From the outset I got on well with Valerie's mother and father, Ann and Ken, and soon met the rest of the family, who welcomed me warmly. I had a good rapport with her Aunty Phil and Uncle Jack and Aunty Pam and Uncle Robert. They soon made me feel like a member of a proper family. Valerie and I spent every bit of spare time in each other's company. I bought her an engagement ring at a Chelmsford jewellers. Afterwards I sat on a park bench to recover from the shock of its cost!

We set a wedding date for the following June and began looking for our first home in Heybridge. Friends could not believe what I had done; several even wondered if Valerie was pregnant. I had no doubts about who I wanted as my wife and was determined not to let her go. Why Valerie? I don't think anyone can truly express in words that wonderful feeling of knowing that you have met the person you truly want to love. From the outset I liked her bubbly character, infectious smile and get-up-and-go attitude to life. On top of that she was - and still is - very attractive. It was the best decision of my life.

Valerie and I started house hunting in Heybridge on New Year's Day 1978. Mortgage interest rates were around the 10% mark which meant we would not have much money left each month if we wanted to buy somewhere decent. I wonder what today's young couples would make of paying such a high interest rate? Two years later mortgage interest rates peaked at a record 17% - a mind boggling figure which created havoc with many family finances. It was not unusual for people to receive a letter outlining a new payment every couple of months. Within a few weeks we found an empty modern detached house in Wood Road on the edge of Heybridge. It had been reclaimed by a building society when the family who owned it had not kept up their payments. It was in a bad state inside; every room needed repairs and decoration. We had one scare when the building society tried at the 11th hour to up the price from the £14,000 we had agreed (gazumping), but our solicitor warned them off. He let it be known I was in the media with enough contacts to bring some bad publicity their way.

We got the keys at Easter and set to work on making it as homely as possible with the help of Valerie's parents. They travelled from Braintree every weekend to first of all give the house a good clean and then slap on some paint. Ann was an expert bonfire maker. We spent every pound we had on cleaning materials and magnolia paint, but my attempts at putting up coving were a dismal failure. The stuff would not stick and fell down within a few hours. Thankfully, Heybridge Swifts chairman Mick Gibson and two of his company's workmen came one Saturday and did the job professionally.

Valerie and I were married at Chelmsford Register Office and had our marriage blessed at All Saints Church in Maldon High Street at 4pm on June 3 in the same church where George Washington's great, great grandfather is buried. The sun shone on us all day during what proved to be a very wet summer. The reception was held at Maldon Town's clubhouse following which we left the next day for a week's honeymoon in Loders, Dorset, in a cottage given to us for a week by Valerie's friend Shael's mother and father. The World Cup started on our wedding day. I rigged up a television in one of the clubhouse changing rooms so the guys could watch Scotland lose 3-1 to Peru. I was less fortunate on honeymoon because television reception was poor in Loders and most games were late at night. I watched a few through what Valerie described as a 'snowstorm'.

My family travelled down from Yorkshire for the wedding but not my aunty and uncle. I never found out why they did not come, but in my heart I felt my aunty did not like Valerie. She was already showing signs of the serious illness which killed her a few years later. Her sharp tongue could reduce people to tears so it was probably for the best that she declined the invitation. She did come to Maldon for a weekend visit a few months later, but she and Terry got up in the middle of the Saturday night and drove back to Lancashire while Valerie and I were fast asleep. We woke up to find a short note saying they had gone. She never gave me an explanation for her extraordinary behaviour. If actions speak louder than words, she made her point!

There was one twist to our wedding though which came to light several months later. My Grandma Scott sent some money for us via my father. We were relying on such gifts coming in on the day because we had little money of our own after all the work we had done on our new home, having heavily committed what little savings we had to the deposit on the detached house and its repair. My dad handed over £15. When we next saw my grandmother several months later on a trip north she asked what we had bought with the £30 she sent! I thought her memory was faulty until I challenged my father who said he had taken some of it for petrol money because I had decided to get married so far away. He also made his point!

Once back from honeymoon it was time to think about my chances of re-election the following May. My by-election success had been a rare victory for the Liberal party during the mid 1970s. It didn't look promising because Margaret Thatcher and a rejuvenated Tory Party were in the ascendancy. The fight to retain my seat would take place on the same day as the 1979 General Election. The Tories were odds-on to win after a disastrous 'winter of discontent' for Labour which saw numerous public sector strikes by militant unions which left dustbins unemptied and the dead unburied. The Liberals broke off their pact with Labour 12 months before the election was due, but the party's opinion poll ratings were always in single figures with dire predictions they would lose all their MPs and possibly many of their councillors. I gave up any hope of becoming an MP to concentrate on retaining my Heybridge seat on Maldon Council. It was the right decision. I knew the Tories were desperate to see the back of me.

By now I had help build up a formidable political organisation in Heybridge. I knew that in order to progress the work I had started I needed to be joined by other Liberal councillors. A review of council ward boundaries split Heybridge into two wards - east and west. Heybridge East would select one councillor and Heybridge West two. I opted to fight the latter ward. Andrew Good was selected as my running mate. In Heybridge East Mrs Lesley Bermingham was our candidate. The Tories confidently expected their sitting councillor, who was also head of the council's finance committee, to easily hold that seat. I told Lesley she probably wouldn't win but would gain some valuable experience which might enable her to win in four years' time. I could not have been more wrong. Despite the Tories nationally sweeping to power and ousting Jim Callaghan's Labour government, we won all three Heybridge seats. I polled 1,088 votes and Andrew 977; the two Tories got 230 and 184; the Labour candidates – they had held the seats only five years previously - got 134 and 130. Lesley got 630 votes in her ward to the over-confident Tory's 340 and Labour's 114. I now had two hard working colleagues to back me up and that one vote defeat seemed a long time ago. The 1979 result was total vindication for several years' hard work. Both Andrew and Lesley became excellent hard working councillors; Andrew was full of ideas and some years later became chief executive of a Suffolk council.

One of the first meetings we had to attend was to elect a Maldon Mayor. Because of the town's historical links only the seven Maldon and three Heybridge councillors could elect the Mayor. The district council made up of 30 councillors elected a chairman, but in Maldon and Heybridge it was the Mayor who had the ceremonial role. The Tories had held the Mayoralty for many years, but the recent election had changed the arithmetic. Now there were three Liberal councillors, two Labour and five Tories, although the out-going Mayor had a casting vote so theoretically the Tories could still command a majority. At the meeting the Tories duly proposed and seconded their nomination. Without any warning one of the Labour councillors, with whom I had worked successfully over the previous three years, proposed me. Andrew Good seconded the motion so there had to be a secret ballot. Surprisingly, it didn't end up as a 5-5 tie, at which point the Tory chairman would have used his casting vote, but a 7-3 vote in my favour. Both the Labour councillors and two of the Tories voted for me. I was stunned. I had thought in private discussions with Valerie that I might become Deputy Mayor at some stage in the next few years because Heybridge was due to have one of its councillors recognised, but to be Mayor so soon was a dream come true ten years after first arriving in the town and not knowing a soul. Aged 31, I was Maldon's youngest ever Mayor and it sent a few shock waves through the town's establishment.

It was also quite a shock for Valerie. We had been married less than a year and although she supported me in everything I did, she had no real interest in politics or newspapers. Overnight she was thrust into the limelight and for somebody who did not enjoy being 'on public view' it was daunting. She made a popular and superb Mayoress, despite the unease she felt on numerous occasions. There was also the financial cost to consider because the Mayoral allowance was small. It was not easy for a newly married couple, but we managed. It was a year we would never forget for many reasons.

My boss at the *Essex Chronicle*, John Saxton, was also supportive. He gave me as much time off as I needed and told me it was an honour for the company to have a civic head on the staff. Fortunately, most of the Mayoral duties were in an evening or at weekend; in all I attended 255 functions during the year. The first major event was the annual Mayor-making ceremony at Maldon's ancient Moot Hall in the High Street followed by a civic reception in the Jubilee Hall. It enabled me to invite the many friends who had helped me reach this position and say *'thank you'*. Valerie's family also came and were very proud of her.

There were many highlights during the next 12 months but one was extra special and came about because of my interest in history. Links with Malden in Massachusetts had been allowed to lapse. I decided to try and revive them and boost tourism in the process. There are strong historical ties between the two towns: at All Saints' Church there is a Washington Memorial Window and George Washington's second-in-command General Gates came from Maldon. The American Malden - spelt differently but still named after its English counterpart - is on the edge of Boston. I wrote to its then Mayor, Jim Conway, to suggest links be restored and said Valerie and I would be prepared to visit if he would welcome us. I got an enthusiastic reply and the trip was set for mid to late September 1979.

The Americans threw themselves into the trip with great enthusiasm and formed a committee of local businessmen to plan and arrange it. They also raised a lot of money in the belief that Valerie and I would be keen to stay in a Boston hotel. I made another good decision when I said we would prefer to stay with a typical American family. There were several volunteers to host us during our 13 day visit but eventually it was decided our main hosts would be Don and Gail MacCuish who had a large home and four children. Little did we know then that Don and Gail would become our best friends! We spent seven days with the MacCuish family, three with another local family and three with an organising committee member and her daughter on Cape Cod.

I was determined to make it a working as well as a pleasurable trip, and for it not to cost the Maldon ratepayers a penny. I did not want anybody to be able to say we were just on a jolly at somebody else's expense. Twenty five years later it was that decision which made me so bitter about the antics of Torbay Liberal Democrats and their money-grabbing when they won power. That story is for later.

The cheapest flights to Boston in those days were those run by Freddie Laker. We booked - and paid for out of our own pockets - our seats and tried to gather together as many items about Maldon to take with us as we could carry. We had special Maldon sweaters made with a picture of a sailing barge on the front and we carried a host of small gifts and books. The *Maldon and Burnham Standard* and the *Essex Chronicle* gave the trip excellent coverage before and after and also provided some of the gifts.

A week before we were due to fly out the telephone rang at 2am. At first I ignored it, thinking it was a wrong number, but when it rang again I went down to the lounge while still naked to find one of Boston's major radio stations on line along with Mayor Conway. We proceeded to have a 20 minute chat about the two towns and politics while I got colder and colder. It was quite surreal. Finally the call came to an end with the radio station wishing me *'bon voyage'* and playing Rule Britannia down the line from 3,000 miles away. You couldn't have made it up.

It should have been a wake up call as to what to expect when we arrived in America. Valerie had been before - spending three months travelling round on a Greyhound bus with a girlfriend - but it was my first trip. Nothing though could prepare us for what happened once we were on our way.

We should have known something was up about an hour out of Boston's Logan Airport when a stewardess asked if *'we were Mr and Mrs Scott?'* She said special arrangements had been made for us to get off first as there was a small welcoming party awaiting us. True, the initial party when we landed was small - the Mayor, his wife, a councillor and the MacCuishes. We were ushered into a room normally used to frisk suspected smugglers and I agreed to put on my Mayoral robes and chain to humour the Americans. It was the only occasion I have never had to undergo a passport or immigration check when visiting America. When we came out of the room we were met by a flash of photographers' light bulbs and a school band striking up the two national anthems. There seemed to be flags everywhere. Various people surged forward to 'press the flesh' including distant relatives I had never met before who lived in Foxboro south of Boston. Valerie and I didn't know what had hit us.

When we got out of the airport we were taken in convoy to the MacCuishes home in the largest car either of us had ever seen which had the Union flag front and back alongside the Stars and Stripes. It also had plates attached to the side informing all and sundry who we were. It didn't take long for me to realise this was a one-off and I should make the most of it.

Both of us were very tired but any thoughts of rest were soon put aside when we reached Malden and found Don and Gail's house full of people enjoying a drinks and buffet party to welcome us. We struggled to bed at 4am English time.

The next morning we got our first tour of the MacCuish home and met their four children - Karen, Eddie, Debbie and Eric. It was obvious from day one that we would get on well with Don and Gail. They made the trip a memorable one - Valerie in particular proved to be a popular guest. I wasn't the stuffy Englishman they had feared they might get, but I did have a job to do and was less relaxed and more formal than Valerie.

After a few hours sleep we headed out to meet the people of Malden. Apparently we had seen only half the band at the airport. That first morning we got the full works with cheerleaders and drum majorettes at the front as we paraded through the town to the Town Hall to be formally met by Jim Conway and the town council. A large crowd turned up, some of whom were former residents of Essex, England. There were speeches and an exchange of civic gifts before we were whisked off to a civic lunch where there were more speeches and more gifts.

At least we were able to relax with Don and Gail and their children when we got back to their home after each day's engagements. The swimming pool at the back of their house was a bonus after a day of meetings. We ate well and from the outset I loved American food.

I had a busy schedule most days with visits to factories, schools, the local evening newspaper, the council, a baseball league dinner and various meetings with Mayor Conway. I made 10 major speeches. Everything we did was covered extensively by the newspaper including Valerie going shopping in Boston! We made several trips into Boston and met with the Governor of Massachusetts in the State House, senators and congressmen. I was made an honorary deputy sheriff and an honorary Boston fire chief. The fire department even put on a special fire fighting display on the River Charles to show what they could do. We were given so many books and gifts we had to get an extra suitcase to carry them all.

There were two hilarious moments as well. The Pope was visiting Boston at the same time and as we drove through the city our convoy obviously attracted attention with flags fluttering. People stopped to take our picture as we drove past and I perfected the 'royal wave' to acknowledge them. I wonder who they thought they had snapped when they had their films developed? The story about standing naked behind a curtain at 2am in our home lounge while doing a live radio programme caused much amusement and got back to the radio station. The presenter, the wonderfully named Larry Glick, sent me a couple of large t-shirts 'to cover my embarrassment' and we had another live chat one evening.

In the middle of what was an exhausting but enjoyable trip we had a three-day break from official engagements with a visit to Cape Cod as the guest one of the organising committee, Joan Wheeler, and her daughter. It was the first time I had ever been given a full lobster – they didn't have such food in Barnoldswick where tripe and onions was more to the liking of locals! When we returned to Malden we stayed with another family who looked after us for three days, but we didn't strike up the same rapport or friendship. We were glad that the last few days before our return to England were spent back with the MacCuish family.

On the first Sunday we were taken to Foxboro - about 50 miles from Malden - to see an American football game. Off we went in a large camper van and assorted cars to the stadium. We parked in the stadium's giant car park two hours before kick-off and enjoyed a bar-b-q before the game. The Americans thought nothing of it - after all that is what everyone does, don't they? It was an uncovered stadium, but who needs any covering when the temperature is in the 80s? I loved the atmosphere and occasion. The New England Patriots beat the San Diego Chargers 31-27 and I have been a Patriots fan ever since. This was just before American football became popular in the UK so I had a head start in understanding the finer points. Valerie was bored to tears.

The following Sunday we attended the local church and I gave an address. It was packed to overflowing and afterwards the minister asked if Valerie and I would line up with him to shake hands with people as they left and answer any questions. People did not know how to react to my robes and the badges on the Mayoral chain containing the names of past Mayors going back to 1690. Two elderly ladies curtseyed when it was their turn and we got lots of comments like *'do you know my Aunty Mabel in Bristol?'* It is incredible how many Americans think we in the UK have such a small population everyone knows everyone else!

One of the committee members, Earl Browne, had a private six-seater plane. He flew Valerie and I plus Don and Gail up the coast to Maine where we stopped off for a drink and then flew on to his home in New Hampshire where we had dinner before flying back. On the way home he allowed me to take the controls for 15 minutes while he turned to chat to Valerie, which gave everyone a bit of a shock.

After two hectic weeks it was time to say goodbye but Logan Airport at Boston was fog bound; it looked as though we were going to miss our connecting flight from New York to England at a time when I needed to get back for work and Mayoral engagements in Maldon. Don and Gail showed what wonderful people they are by driving us 250 miles to New York so we could catch our flight. A friendship which lasts to this day was firmly cemented.

During the time I was in Malden the evening newspaper owner, David Brickman, kept dropping hints about wanting me to work for him. He kept up the pressure upon my return and this resulted in me flying out in early January 1980 to have further talks with him and his team. I also spoke to other newspaper men in Massachusetts, but there was nothing that really interested me and nothing that I felt was better than the management job I had with the *Essex Chronicle* which I had begun the previous summer after leaving the *Romford Observer*. I stayed with Don and Gail again and experienced for the first time what temperatures of minus 20c were like. I also caught a nasty bug which laid me low for a week upon my return.

I had been home a few weeks when Valerie and I received terrible news - Don and Gail's beautiful daughter Karen, aged 16, had been killed in an accident while coming home from an evening event in a friend's van. It was later proved the van was faulty. Don and Gail received several million dollars compensation from Volkswagen, but nothing could compensate for the loss of their daughter and it haunted them for years. We immediately invited them to England to have a holiday with us.

Between early November and late March I had to plunge into a round of Mayoral events with the dinner season in full flow. I enjoyed the old people's ones the best because they were friendly, less formal and more easy going. Valerie joked that I got 101% of the old people's votes in Heybridge. One dinner I could not attend until late one Saturday evening was the one run by the Cups, my regular pub, to celebrate their football and darts successes. I had already accepted another dinner invitation for that night, but told the Cups organisers I would try and get to their event, being held near Colchester, later in the evening. When Valerie and I turned up around 11pm the whole room stood up to give us an ovation I have never forgotten.

There were many other highlights during the year including a full programme of visits on Christmas day and the annual London cabbies day on Maldon Promenade for disabled children from the East End when more than 70 black cabs came down the A12 for a day of games, food and fun. I had the job of giving each disabled child a 50 pence piece - it was lovely to see their smiles.

Carnival day on the first Saturday in August was also a big day out. I was blessed with a gloriously sunny day. Tradition insists the Mayor stops the afternoon carnival procession outside the Moot Hall in Maldon High Street, offers a glass of sherry to the two leading horse riders and then allows the procession to pass after he has given the carnival queen a kiss. In my haste I managed to knock some of the flowers off her float with my robe. Another tradition is that the Mayor and his guests watch all the floats pass by from the Moot Hall balcony before going down to the main arena for the afternoon's entertainment. I had 12 special guests who I entertained to dinner at a local hotel before we all returned to the Promenade around 9pm for an excellent fireworks display by the River Blackwater to round off the day's events. Alas, the fireworks display is no more because of stupid health and safety regulations.

The most humorous moment during the Mayoral year came when the town's Plume Library re-opened after renovation. The Lord Lieutenant was invited and because he was there the organisers felt they ought to hire a toastmaster to introduce everyone and run the proceedings. It was way over the top. Unfortunately, when his big moment came and he asked for silence he brought his gavel down on the new glass counter and it shattered into lots of pieces. I managed to keep a straight face - just.

Towards the end of my year in office I took various parties round my Mayoral 'home', the Moot Hall, an ancient building in the middle of the High street that used to house the town's court and dungeons. I wanted to open up the building to the public; as far as I was concerned it belonged to them. From the easily accessible roof there are spectacular views across the River Blackwater. It is a shame more people have not been inside. I also visited every local school and welcomed visitors from Malden who had been encouraged to come following my visit to the United States.

I had the job of welcoming the Deputy Prime Minister Willie Whitelaw to the town, sent a telegram to the Queen after the murder of Lord Mountbatten and also watched the Essex cricket team win their first ever trophy when they beat Surrey at Lords in the Gillette Cup final. However, I was not unhappy when it was all over. I wanted to get back to a normal lifestyle and there were pressing political issues I wanted to take up once I was freed from the neutrality all Mayors must observe during their year in office.

Don and Gail and their three children paid a return visit during the summer of 1980. Valerie and I took them to a holiday let in North Devon for a week following which they spent a week in Maldon. Their three children stayed with various friends because we could not accommodate them all and Eddie and Eric developed friendships which last to this day. It was a sad time for them, though. Karen's death was a huge shadow that hung over them.

CHAPTER SEVEN

HAVING MY CAKE IN BANBURY

Growing old is like being increasingly penalised for a crime you haven't committed – unknown

I would never have moved from Essex to Banbury if I had not been messed around by senior management at Northcliffe Newspapers, owners of the *Essex Chronicle Series*. I was content with my lot, but unbeknown to me once you started on the Northcliffe management ladder you were expected to move wherever the company decided to send you. They felt they owned you lock, stock and barrel.

After four years I had earned my Editor's spurs at Romford and was ready to manage a larger paper within the company's Essex empire. I never entertained the thought that I might move out of the editorial department. In those days it was rare for any journalist to think about the commercial side of the business. When, during the summer of 1979, it was decided to launch a new evening paper for Chelmsford and Brentwood in 1980 I was in the frame to be its Editor. It was a bold move by Northcliffe because the national economy under the new Conservative government was in a mess and was about to get much, much worse.

Essex, however, was still thriving and prosperous; so much so that some weeks the *Chronicle* turned away pages of advertising because it could not print enough of them on its small press. I am sure the apparent abundance of advertising and the belief it would continue was one of the main reasons why it was felt an evening paper would succeed. It proved to be the wrong decision at the wrong time for the wrong reasons. I recorded what a disastrous decision it was to launch an evening paper in mid Essex and why in a book I wrote in 1987 titled *Once a Week is Enough*.

My rival for the Editorship was the *Brentwood Gazette's* Editor, Derek Hales, who was older and more experienced. Much to just about everyone's surprise in October I opted instead to become Assistant to the Managing Director of all the group's Chelmsford based newspapers under John Saxton, a move which astonished most of the journalists I knew, but one that paved the way for future advancement beyond anything I could have imagined at the time. With hindsight it was one of those life-defining moments which were to influence many things in future years. I had huge respect for John. He gave me valuable experience in building project management, finance, advertising, marketing and labour relations, to add to my editorial skills, and taught me a lot about managing a business and the pressures when things go wrong, as they did just before the evening paper was launched. We forged a friendship in the midst of some difficult working days which still endures today.

One of the more unusual situations I had to deal with, and one that convinced me the print unions were living on borrowed time, came when the company tried to get the press crew to print a Tuesday paper we had won the contract to produce. Tuesday was an easy day for the men who printed our papers; it was a day they did some cleaning and maintenance before the big printing jobs on Wednesday and Thursday. More often than not they loafed around playing cards, chatting and killing time. A three hour print run was not a difficult task, but they refused to take it on, even though they were being paid to work. It wasn't until I found out the real reason for their refusal that the penny dropped: only half of them ever turned up on any given Tuesday - the rest were amateur photographers taking house pictures for estate agents' advertisements which then appeared in our own papers! They had set up a very lucrative sideline; the money they earned was shared between them. We had to stop it, but it took several meetings to get their agreement.

A few months later the Inland Revenue came down heavily on several newspaper companies because of cash-only pay packets they had been making up and passing on some weeks simply to get their papers printed on time. Names like Mickey Mouse and Donald Duck were on the payroll. It was industrial anarchy, but it was the only way at that time managements felt they could keep industrial peace. Whenever John Saxton tried to tackle similar practices the threat of a strike at Chelmsford with the inevitable warning of a knock-on effect elsewhere in the Northcliffe empire invariably ended with a telephone call from head office telling him to give in. Six years later Eddie Shah and Rupert Murdoch took on all the print unions and changed forever the way newspapers were produced. Tens of thousands of print workers lost their jobs and the unions their power. More than 5,000 print workers employed by Times Newspapers alone were made redundant. Times' management had to negotiate with eight separate unions and 65 'chapels', or shop floor groups.

Soon after I became John's assistant I was nominated by him to take part in a pioneering Northcliffe management training course based in Cheltenham over a six month period. The plan was that eight potential Managing Directors from across the UK would undergo intensive training in all aspects of the business and particularly accounts, advertising and marketing.

The week-long courses every month were held at the palatial Queens Hotel and were to be my passport to greater and better job openings in the not-too-distant future. I was the only journalist among the eight, but I got on well with the rest of the delegates and certainly learned a lot in a short space of time.

Every Wednesday the good and the great from Northcliffe would travel down the A40 from London to Cheltenham to have dinner with us and see how we were getting on. I was careful not to drink too much during such meals because around 10.00pm we were asked some fairly pointed questions about the company and its future. More than one colleague stumbled over his words.

Course organiser was Harry Levy, a likeable cheery chap from head office who took our many jokes and pranks in good humour. Harry's only problem was that he enthusiastically embraced an American management technique all the rage at the time which supposedly bonded people together through outward bound type training. When we learned what he was up to and what he intended for us it did not go down well with those, including me, recently married who wanted to go back home on a Friday night. Harry's plan was for us to be taken to the Brecon beacons in Wales at the end of one week and left up some mountain from where we were expected to find our way back to a nominated hotel 20 miles away. Harry wanted to know our shoe sizes etc so he could kit us out. I rebelled and said I would do the 20 miles in less than an hour because I would find a telephone box, ring for a taxi and see him in the hotel bar. Harry was not amused. I thought it was lateral thinking at its best. It earned me a black mark - but 10 out of 10 in my book for initiative. The following day Harry decided I was not a suitable candidate so I was allowed to go home while the others trooped off in the rain to Wales. Journalists have always made poor subjects for such training!

A few years later an Editor with another newspaper group had no choice but to take part in one such bonding exercise during which the organisers made all the delegates reveal something they were scared of doing. The idea was that your team would help you overcome the said fear. My Editor friend, who I promised will remain nameless, foolishly let slip he could not swim. The team did get him out when he was told to jump in the deep end of a swimming pool, but it didn't make any difference when they were all back at work, except for the fact he felt he had been humiliated.

Despite my rebellious streak I was taken on one side by Northcliffe Chairman Jack Wallwork in March 1980, just as I was coming to the end of my Mayoral year, and told he wanted me to move from Chelmsford once my management training was over. By now the evening paper project was already in big trouble even before its launch and John Saxton was on the verge of a nervous breakdown which nearly destroyed him. I had no objection in principle to a move and neither did Valerie, although it would mean leaving her family set-up in Essex. The job on offer was Deputy Managing Director of Gloucestershire Newspapers based in Cheltenham with the carrot I would become Managing Director two years later when the incumbent retired. It was promotion to a daily newspaper set-up so I waited with some interest for the terms and conditions to be sent to me. Several months passed without me hearing anything.

In the meantime the evening paper was launched on April 14. It was truly awful – a disaster in every sense from day one. Everything that could go wrong did; fatally, the news coverage was nowhere near good enough. The Chelmsford journalists, used to a leisurely pace of working on a weekly newspaper, could not make the transition demanded of a fast moving evening paper operation. One senior departmental manager quit on the first day because of the 'pressure'.

John Saxton's attempts to find out when he would be losing me hit a brick wall. I didn't like to pressurise him because he was busy trying to salvage the evening newspaper (it closed two years later after losing nearly £3 million). The longer I stayed the longer he had somebody he could delegate some of the responsibility to when he was under the worst pressure. I arranged portakabins for new staff, supervised building work and kept an eye on most departments for him. The other journalists thought I had lost my marbles, but I enjoyed the work in the following two months. It was better than working in the news room where the atmosphere was dire and morale at rock bottom.

Out of the blue on the first Thursday in July John took a telephone call from Jack Wallwork during which he was told to inform me that I had to report to the Cheltenham office the following Monday morning. I assumed I was too junior for him to personally ask me! There was no mention of what I would be paid extra (if anything), a car or accommodation. When Northcliffe said 'jump' you were expected to jump and not ask too many questions.

I went home feeling very unhappy and after discussing it with Valerie decided I would not go. John had the difficult job of telling London head office I had turned down the move. The following week he had the even more unhappy task of telling me that if I did not go he had been told he might have to sack me. Apparently, I was the first senior employee within Northcliffe's vast regional newspaper empire ever to refuse a move. They were not prepared to let me set a precedent and get away with it.

Nobody likes to be bullied. It has always brought out the worst - or best depending on your view – out of me when put in such situations. I did what all journalists did at that time and quickly got hold of several weeks' copies of *UK Press Gazette* where most newspaper jobs were advertised. One caught my eye - **Editor wanted for large, broadsheet weekly paper in Oxfordshire**. I quickly sent off a letter and cv.

John frantically tried on my behalf to find out from Northcliffe HQ in London what really was going on, and when he might be expected to hand me my notice and lose me. For several weeks the silence was deafening. In the meantime I was invited for an interview at the *Banbury Guardian*. Then came a fateful week. Jack Wallwork came to Chelmsford in his chauffeur driven car for a board meeting after which he tried to convince me why I should go to Cheltenham. He promised me a bit more money and a better company car sometime in the near future. The company would also pay all removal and accommodation expenses.

I asked for a few days to think it over and went home to consult with Valerie. I was all for telephoning Banbury to say I would not be attending their interview after all. Valerie urged me to delay any decision and go and see what was on offer in Oxfordshire. It was wise advice.

I went by train, which gave me plenty of time to do some thinking, and was interviewed by *Heart of England Newspapers* Editor-in-Chief John Algar. He and I got on well from the outset. Some people described him as 'old school', but to me he was someone who knew a good newspaper from a bad one and had high standards. The more John and I talked, the more I warmed to him. I liked what I heard about the challenge the *Banbury Guardian* would pose because it was in a slump and I felt comfortable about how I could arrest it. By the time I got back to Heybridge five hours later John was already on the telephone offering me the job. It even paid more than the Cheltenham job and I got a better car. I accepted there and then. It felt right, while Cheltenham didn't.

The following Monday John Saxton had the difficult job of telling Jack Wallwork that despite personally seeing me - something that didn't happen too often where job appointments were concerned - he had failed to get me to move to Cheltenham. I understand the telephone line was hot when John revealed I had already fixed myself up with another job and had handed in my notice. They couldn't even sack me! A few days later I received a terse two paragraph letter from Mr Wallwork's office which said I had made a big mistake. I knew I had burned a lot of bridges behind me as long as he was Northcliffe's Chairman. Fortunately he retired before I needed Northcliffe again.

Soon after I left the *Essex Chronicle* I was relieved I did not have to deal with one problem the company encountered. A Deputy Editor decided, without any warning, to become Caroline instead of Alan. No matter how much training managers get there is no way they can be expected to know how to handle such a problem. To make matters that bit more difficult for the company the print unions made it clear that if Caroline strayed into the production area there would be trouble. They said an immediate mandatory chapel meeting would be called which would disrupt production of that week's papers and there was every possibility they would go on strike. They were not prepared to let a man dressed as a woman enter their very masculine domain.

John Saxton could have well done without the problem - he had enough to deal with because of the failing evening paper - but he handled the matter tactfully. The company's lawyers advised him Caroline could take legal action, which she would probably win, if she was sacked. They also warned the subsequent publicity would not be pleasant. She was allowed to remain as a sub-editor until she moved to another company two years later, but she was not allowed anywhere near the room where her pages were put together by the union dominated production team. I am glad it was not my problem to resolve.

The move to Banbury meant I had to resign my council seat. I was sorry to leave Maldon Council but the work I had put in had made a difference to the people of Heybridge in particular. In the resulting by-election the Liberals had a good candidate in Jim Goldring who won easily. It meant the party retained all three seats for the two Heybridge wards. Jim was in his sixties but like many others he had been attracted to the local party because of our campaigning work in the community. Andrew Good took over as leader of the Liberal group and did an excellent job for several years before he moved to Colchester as a chief officer on that town's council. At the next set of Maldon Council elections the Liberals won five more seats.

Valerie was already several months pregnant by now. The move was not easy for her as it meant finding and setting up a new home in addition to coping with me living in 'digs' for several months. There was no easy route between Heybridge and Banbury – it was a minimum three and a half hour car journey cross country through small towns each of which seemed to have horrendous traffic problems of their own.

I was found accommodation with one of my new company's printers, Dermot Gallagher, who went on to become a top football referee in the Premier League. Unfortunately Dermot's shift work meant I got little sleep because when he came home around 2am he always woke me up while making a meal and watching television. I rarely managed any solid sleep. The company eventually agreed to pay for me to stay at a local hotel for the last few weeks before our move.

I didn't get off to the best of starts. A month into my new job I caught a nasty virus which laid me low for nearly three weeks just when I was putting into place my plans to rejuvenate the *Banbury Guardian's* news coverage. At first I struggled into work each day feeling dreadful but determined to get on with the job. It soon became obvious I was not well. I was not registered with a Banbury doctor and as a result did not seek medical help right away. I thought I could shrug it off in a few days, but I was eventually consigned to bed with a high temperature, headache and general sickness. Valerie had to come and collect me – I was too ill to drive back to Heybridge. A 21 day course of antibiotics restored my health.

Fortunately the *Guardian* had a very capable Deputy Editor, Beverley Rigby, and a hard working sports editor in Andy Martin. Beverley was a first class journalist, popular with the staff but also someone who would not stand any nonsense. In the following years she and I forged a strong team. She edited the paper for several weeks in my absence and then enthusiastically backed the wholesale changes I wanted to make.

When I returned to work I was ready to introduce new ideas into the news room. These involved changing a culture which had been allowed to develop whereby the paper was filled each week with too many stories about Cherwell District Council. Chief reporter Keith Wood, a thoroughly decent man, loved local government and if all I had wanted every day was enough copy to fill the paper, he would have provided it. Cherwell's councillors and senior officers loved our coverage. Unfortunately, the readers did not share Keith's enthusiasm and sales were in freefall.

My job was to arrest the decline and motivate the rest of the staff into providing a greater variety of stories. They had got so used to Keith filling the page lead slots with his own material they had almost given up trying. I encouraged them to bring in their own stories; gradually Keith gave them the chance to tackle the big fires, accidents, crimes etc. It was hard going because I knew Keith did not like the work practices I was imposing on him. He and I had some strong exchanges of opinion. He also had the difficult job of telling some councillors why their names did not appear in the paper as regularly as they had before, but to his credit he carried out my instructions. He had no choice!

Inevitably, this meant we put Cherwell Council under greater scrutiny and carried some stories that were critical of them. I took one call from the Chief Executive who made it quite clear he did not agree with the direction the *Banbury Guardian* was taking. When he didn't get the response he was looking for, my invitations to some social events dried up. Big deal!

I had one other member of the news room awkward squad to tackle. This was Ted, the 'entertainments' reporter. Ted spent most of his week doing the television listings, which already came in typed, an entertainments round up page and little else. It was hardly a full week's work and a luxury no weekly paper could afford. However, he had been allowed to do his own thing for some time so custom and practice had set in. I knew a day of reckoning would have to come but first of all I had to sort out the news coverage and Keith.

Events then took a hand. One Monday morning every reporter but Ted was out of the office on various stories when all the telephones started ringing. Ted did not answer any of them. Beverley and I dashed into the reporters' room and took a spate of messages before the phones quietened down. I was furious that Ted did not offer to help and asked him why he was not prepared to take messages for his younger colleagues? His grumpy reply was: *'Not my job'*.

I knew this was a challenge I could not ignore. I sat down that afternoon and wrote out a new job spec which allowed him two days a week to do his entertainments and television reports, but required him to do three days of general reporting. Because he rarely left his desk and did not drive, I said he could claim on his expenses for the taxis he would need to book to get him to any council meetings he was asked to report on. To my amazement I discovered he had rarely been asked to report on a parish council meeting, never mind the other evening jobs all the reporters were doing every week.

Ted gave me a thunderous look, but wisely decided not to argue with me in front of the others. The next day he came into my office, produced a battered sheet of paper from his pocket, signed it in front of me and said it was his month's notice. I told him not to be silly and gave him a day to think things over. Beverley told me he had threatened to resign on several other occasions following which he had always got his way. This time he picked the wrong man to challenge!

Wednesday was press day when I had to meet a noon deadline and then go to Leamington Spa to see the paper to bed. Ted said he still wanted to resign. I didn't have the time or the inclination to debate the matter further. I had already told John Algar what had transpired and had his full backing to deal with it any way I wished. To Ted's astonishment I said he didn't need to work all his notice – he could leave that Friday. Most of the staff thought there would be some sort of reconciliation once I had got that week's paper out of the way. They didn't know me very well. The only way Ted was now going to be part of my team was if he accepted the new working conditions I had given him. There was no way he was going to be allowed to continue doing just what suited him. Apart from other considerations, it would have been unfair to the other reporters.

By Friday lunch-time it was obvious I was not going to change my mind, despite a telephone call from a bossy woman from a local dramatic society who said we could not let a *'legend in Banbury'* leave. In case anyone had any doubts about my determination not to back down, I took the afternoon off. The rest of the staff had a hasty collection while Ted cleared his desk, packed up his typewriter and walked out of the office never to return. I advertised for a new junior reporter. After that little episode I never had any trouble with Keith or the rest of the team.

Ted did not get another job for several years. By one of life's quirks of fate I met him again many years later when he was by now doing general reporting for Banbury's free paper called *Focus*. I was asked to return to the town to do some consultancy work by my old employers and discovered Ted was one of the staff. He was gracious enough to tell me I had been right to accept his notice, that he was wrong to challenge my authority, but how for many years he had hated me for doing it. We got on well after that.

The *Banbury Guardian's* smart, well maintained office in those days was in a renovated old building 30 yards up the road from Banbury Cross of fairy story fame. Traffic used to queue for 10 miles out of town on the main Oxford road most days before the M40 was built. We had a car park at the back of the building large enough to accommodate everybody's car, a luxury few journalists enjoy nowadays.

Part of my plans to change the office culture involved a meeting of department heads every Thursday morning to look at that week's paper and plan ahead. I was surprised such meetings had not taken place before I arrived, but they hadn't and what I regarded as normal practice was regarded with suspicion by both Keith and my chief photographer, Ian. We started off by reviewing the paper page by page, analysing the good and the bad and noting any follow ups. We would then move on to discuss the week ahead and how to use the reporting team. I wanted to involve everyone in the decision making process, something which had been left to Keith until then. These meetings also allowed me to defuse any news room tensions between reporters and photographers and I even allowed myself to be persuaded to change my mind and bow to local knowledge when appropriate.

When it comes to any sort of change in their routine journalists like to think of themselves as liberal-minded people, but my experience is that most of them are conservative with a small 'c'. After a few months I brought in another innovation – every first Thursday in the month I held a staff meeting which allowed even the most junior reporter to have a say. It took three months before the journalists realised it wasn't some sort of management trap!

Soon after moving to Banbury I was invited to become a Rotarian. My predecessor had been a member and I was expected to follow suit. Fortunately, I didn't make a snap decision because within a few days I was also asked if I would join Round Table and the Lions. All three organisations do good work in the community. I delayed any decision on the grounds I was too busy changing the newspaper; I was glad I did because I discovered that both Round Table and the Lions believed the local Rotary club gained more than its fair share of coverage at their expense. Whether this was true or not I had no way of knowing, so I didn't join any of them. Instead, I wrote to all three chairmen and said I would be delighted to come to the occasional meeting and offered my services as a speaker. All three took me up on the offer and I ensured everyone got a fair deal on our news pages for their charity work.

One invitation I felt safe in accepting was to become a director of Banbury United. The club are still the main football team in that part of Oxfordshire, although they struggle to survive in the Southern League. Before my arrival in town they had had a few moderate to successful seasons. They had remained solvent after selling two players to Derby County for reasonable transfer fees, but by the 1980s they were in decline and the money had run out. Their ground was not easy to find down a narrow lane running alongside the railway line. If they had a couple of wins it was nearly cause for a civic reception - the old joke that they did a lap of honour when they won a corner was not far off the mark. As Editor of the local paper I was invited onto their board of directors. My predecessor was a tennis fanatic who declined the 'honour'. For two years I enjoyed the experience, but I cannot say I improved the team's fortunes. I was amazed even in those days how much players at that level wanted paying. It was a far cry from watching Burnley.

I never minded a bit of humour creeping into any paper I edited as long as the story justified the effort. April 1 is an obvious day for journalists to have some fun and see how many readers fall for whatever surprise you spring on them. The only year we came up with a good idea while I edited the *Banbury Guardian* was when I approached Lord Saye and Sele, owner of one of the area's major tourist attractions, Broughton Castle. He happily played along when I suggested we run a front page story and picture launching an appeal for £50,000 to move the castle four feet to the right because it was in danger of falling into the moat. We carried comments from 'expert castle movers' and his Lordship. Despite directing readers to page seven where they were reminded of the date, we received several cheques from generous donors which I returned with a covering letter.

At the *Essex Chronicle* they ran an advert for an open day on the Sunday after April Fool's Day at Great Totham Treacle Mines. Totham is a small Essex village – its roads were gridlocked with people trying to find the mines! The best prank award, however, goes to the *Leicester Mercury* which carried a story about a new town planned between Shepshed and Coalville to be called Coalshed.

Such harmless fun was fine and provided some welcome relief from the everyday diet of crime, court and council stories. There were other times when it was sensible to let office humour flow within reasonable bounds. Bad language, however, was banned in all my news rooms.

Poor Keith Wood found himself the victim of an office prank which he took in good heart. He did a story about a local member of the House of Lords which he got wrong. His Lordship telephoned to complain, but Keith was out of the office. He said he would ring back later. Keith was apoplectic when he heard. He was apt to doff his cap at nobility! A reporter who was a good mimic could not resist going to another office to pretend he was the complaining Lord. We all kept our heads down when Keith answered the phone, but tears rolled down our cheeks when we heard him mutter: '*Yes, I am a silly arse your Lordship.*' At that point Keith realised he had been well and truly had.

Editors have to have a thick skin at times when dealing with the public and the things they complain about. I always had a policy of correcting anything we got wrong as soon as possible and holding up my hand and apologising unless the lawyers were likely to be involved.

I had more silly complaints while in Banbury than at any other time of my career. The eagerness of townsfolk to whinge and moan about the most trivial item was something I never understood. One irate reader bent my ear about a front page colour picture of a girl surrounded by multi-coloured teddy bears. The *Banbury Guardian* was one of the first weekly papers to use colour and was proud of the quality. When I got a word in and asked what he was really complaining about, he said it was obvious to anyone with half a brain that the teddy bears had been made in Korea and not the UK. '*You should be ashamed*', he told me.

Another complainant who got a small correction in the next edition ended his tirade with the comment: '*And this is not the first time I have had cause to complain about your paper.*' I had no idea who he was so I asked when was the last time he had complained. '*Twenty seven years ago,*' he replied. I told him we had not done too badly if we had made only two mistakes in 27 years.

It was while living in Banbury that our first child, Georgina, was born on January 31 1981 at Horton Hospital. We managed to move into our new home just in time; workmen were ripping out an old kitchen on the day Valerie's waters broke while she was in the local bank. We were now proud parents.

Neither Valerie nor I really settled in Banbury, possibly because any move from Essex was never going to be easy. I enjoyed being Editor of the *Guardian* and working in the revamped news room with some good, young and now motivated reporters. But the town was not overly friendly and had a big chip on its shoulder about Oxford. I did improve the paper's circulation and also recruited more than 50 village correspondents across Oxfordshire, Warwickshire and parts of Northamptonshire. Once a year I got them in to thank them, give them a glass of wine and some cheese and chat about how they could do even better.

My position meant I had to be very careful about engaging in too much political activity. Nationally the Labour Party under Michael Foot was in turmoil and near to civil war. The Conservatives under Margaret Thatcher were also unpopular as unemployment and inflation soared. Into what was a very fluid political situation stepped four leading Labour MPs who set up a new centre right party called the Social Democrats. The Gang of Four, as they became known, formed an alliance with the Liberal Party and for a brief 12 month period topped every opinion poll. Banbury, one of the safest

Conservative seats in the country, was designated as an SDP sphere of influence. I helped to run one branch and delivered some leaflets, but I had to ensure I kept well out of the public eye.

Like most local papers – despite what politicians from every party will tell you - the *Banbury Guardian* was politically neutral which disappointed the SDP's naive and politically immature officers who thought having me on board would ensure they got preferential treatment. They didn't. Ironically, I got on much better with the new local Tory MP, Tony Baldry, now Sir Tony, than I did with most members of the SDP – signs of a future change of political direction.

One benefit of being the *Banbury Guardian's* Editor was private medical insurance which included a free non-compulsory annual check-up with a Leamington Spa doctor. Some of my fellow Editors refused to take part, claiming they did not want the company to know too many of their personal details. I had no qualms. My first visit produced a shock, though, when the doctor expressed alarm at a growth in my thyroid. There and then he made immediate arrangements for me to undergo tests which a few weeks later resulted in an operation at the Nuffield Hospital in Oxford when part of my thyroid was removed. I took several weeks to get over the operation and once again Beverley Rigby did a good job of editing the paper. It was a shame she never got the Editor's job when I left. There were very few female Editors in those days; thank goodness that is no longer the case.

I had been in Banbury for two and a half years when John Algar took me on one side and told me he had quietly spoken about me to the Editorial Director of a large newspaper group based in Worcester. *'Would I like to meet him for a chat?'* During our weekly private chats while I was in Leamington putting the final touches to the paper John made no secret of the fact that he felt I could go on to greater things in the newspaper industry.

I wasn't unhappy at the *Banbury Guardian* and wasn't actively looking for a new job. Valerie and I had started, at last, to settle in Oxfordshire and make friends. But I also knew that after all the changes I had made in the news room and to the office culture it was time to let things settle down and bed in. Some people would have been satisfied with an easy life, a 9-5 job with a few perks, but not me. So when I received a telephone call inviting me to travel to Worcester to meet a Mr John Hardeman I knew I had nothing to lose by going to see him.

What followed was the strangest interview of my life. John was Editorial Director of the Berrows newspaper group which consisted of two evening papers (Worcester and Hereford) and a string of weeklies throughout Worcestershire and the West Midlands recently bought by Reed International, then owners of the *Daily Mirror*. John needed a right-hand man to help him manage the weekly editors, some of whom he wanted to replace. The papers were a mixed bunch, ranging from the top selling *Hereford Times* to the struggling *Redditch Indicator*. They were a mix of free and paid-fors.

When John interviewed me I soon got the impression he had already made up his mind to offer me a job; he went out of his way to sell the company. About 90 minutes into our meeting he took me for a walk round head office and I discovered I would become the group's Managing Editor if I accepted his offer. At this point I had not said more than a few dozen words, but I knew it was a massive career opportunity. There was a sizeable salary increase, a better car and the chance to join a big newspaper company. I drove back to Banbury and submitted my resignation to John Algar along with a personal letter of thanks. It meant another house move, but this one proved much easier. We sold our Banbury home quite quickly and bought a lovely property overlooking the Malvern Hills on the edge of Worcester.

I joined Berrows in March 1983 and immediately began to work on editorial strategies and training for the 18 weekly titles. Valerie was pregnant again and Timothy was duly born at Worcester Hospital that September. I had hardly got going in my new role when on May Day the Managing Director of the Stourbridge end of the company had a massive heart attack in his garden and died instantly.

Sad as it was, it was another of those breaks which have been a feature of my life. Berrows had nobody with senior management experience available, but they knew I had from my time at Chelmsford and the Northcliffe management training courses. After a quick interview with group Managing Director Roger Rix I was on my way to a large office in Stourbridge where I took control of the paid-for *Kidderminster Times*, the *Stourbridge County Express* and free papers in Dudley, Stourbridge, Halesowen and Ludlow.

I inherited three big problems to go with the large office: the print unions were militant and looking to make trouble; the senior staff had got used to perks few others had; and on top of that I was told talks were talking place to merge all the papers now under my control with those of the rival free newspaper company, Bullman Newspapers, run by entrepreneurs Chris and Pat Bullivant, Jan Wilde and Geoff Hickman. All I had to do was keep a lid on things for six months. Talk about a poisoned chalice

Within 48 hours the main print union, the NGA, were demanding talks even though my predecessor was not yet in his grave. I told them I had to be given time to find my feet, analyse the local situation and get to know people first. That bought me about five weeks. I knew how to stall from handling the unions in Chelmsford.

The perks enjoyed by a few senior managers were speedily dealt with: I stopped all car valeting and sold the stocks of expensive wines held for the company by two local hotels. When I received the final bills I was amazed how much was spent every week on wining and dining at the very best local establishments. When I checked I discovered quite a bit of it was done on Sundays when family members were invited. One advertising manager came to see me to complain about the termination of the valeting contract. He said he needed his car valeting because he had spilt a bottle of milk and it stank. I told him to get a bucket, fill it with some soap and water and do it himself. Problem solved!

Meanwhile talks continued with the Bullman executives while I had the job of getting the papers out on time. Eventually, I could not put off the NGA talks any longer and a day was set for the first showdown. I knew from my Essex days what their tactics would be: outrageous demands coupled with smiling threats. I also knew I could expect a long day(s) of negotiations followed by a letter setting out their 'totally reasonable' requests for pay rises somewhere in the region of 10-15% above inflation. They did not know it, but their jobs wouldn't be there in a few months' time, never mind a pay rise.

The morning of the meeting I was highly strung at home and when I could not find one of the socks I had placed on a chair the night before I ranted and raved, blaming everyone in earshot before doing what I should have done at the beginning and simply gone to a drawer for another pair of socks. Georgina and Valerie had the good sense to keep out of my way.

My Stourbridge office had windows all down one side - when the sun was shining it became something of a glasshouse. Two hours into the meeting I went to my pocket, pulled out a 'hankie' and saw the look of amazement on the faces of several hard-bitten print union officers as they watched me wipe my face with a sock and put it back in my pocket. They must have thought they were dealing with an eccentric madman. They duly put their demands in writing and I duly took time to deliberate over them.

Fortunately, just as we reached the point where they were about to go on strike, work to rule or carry out some other industrial (in)action and stop producing the papers, a deal was announced between Reed International and Bullman Newspapers whereby each would have 50% of a new company and all production would be transferred to Bullman's non-union set-up situated between Redditch and Alcester. The paid-for *County Express* was closed leaving Bullman's free *Stourbridge News* with a money-making monopoly. Other titles in Bromsgrove, Redditch and Kidderminster were shut or amalgamated. It was sensible rationalisation which produced a good newspaper for each town. The entire production staff at Stourbridge was made redundant.

I expected to go back to my original job with John Hardeman as Managing Editor at Worcester, but Chris Bullivant had other ideas, which he probably came to regret in later years. He asked me to stay on as joint Deputy Managing Director of the new company. I liked Chris and his entrepreneurial free-thinking ways, but from the outset I had a problem with his wife, Pat, who was boss of each paper's advertising departments. From day one she and I simply didn't like each other. Later it was to cause much trouble and lead to a rift which has never been healed. Chris and I made a good team. He had one good idea in 10, but it was often a corker. I had the job of dealing with the other nine and ensuring the smooth running of what was by now a very large newspaper group covering the West Midlands.

CHAPTER EIGHT

BRITAIN'S FIRST FREE MORNING PAPER

Consensus is the process of abandoning all beliefs, principles, values and policies in search of something nobody believes, but to which no one objects – Margaret Thatcher

I enjoyed my first few months working with Chris Bullivant. He came into work each morning full of new ideas, while I brought to the company regional newspaper experience and a better understanding of the editorial side of the business. The Editors welcomed me as an ally. There was a lot to sort out as several long established papers were closed or amalgamated with newcomers. Some egos had to be smoothed and several people made redundant. It was the first time I had worked alongside the new wave of entrepreneurs who shook up the regional press when they launched free newspapers as opposed to freesheets. The *Solihull Times*, for instance, had more than 70 pages of editorial each week in a 120 page paper. The conventional press had no answer except a few years later to pay millions of pounds to buy out these 'interlopers' who had invaded their traditional territory.

Decision making was much quicker and often on the hoof, which I enjoyed. I had to learn one important new skill - how to handle groups of estate agents in all the towns where we had titles. They had seats on our main board as part of the price we paid for getting most of their advertising. They also shared in the annual profits, but, thankfully, rarely tried to influence editorial content. Once every six months we got them together over a glass of wine and some food to discuss trading conditions and any price hike we were about to impose. Chris handled them brilliantly. Once we got the majority of estate agents to advertise with us, other advertisers followed them into our papers. It was a clever tactic and one our opposition could not match; some of them felt it was beneath them to even try.

One afternoon in October 1983 Chris and I were pondering an attack on our strong Redditch weekly paper by the largest newspaper group in the Midlands, the powerful *Birmingham Post and Evening Mail* organisation. They had their own much smaller weekly paper circulating in Redditch which they used to start under-cutting our advertising rates to the point where they might as well have given the space away. We considered Redditch to be vital territory for our financial sustainability and did not want to lower what we charged advertisers there because of the inevitable knock-on effect elsewhere in our empire once word got out. We knew that if the *Post and Mail's* management really declared war on us they were strong enough to sustain any financial losses they might suffer. Fortunately for us they didn't resource their attack properly and never matched the editorial quality of our own paper. When we refused to cut our advertising rates, and they didn't attract enough new business quickly, they lost interest and terminated their attack.

Long established newspaper groups like the *Post and Mail* thrived where they enjoyed a monopoly, but had no real idea how to fight back when the weekly newspaper entrepreneurs invaded their patch. Within six years the *Mail's* paid-for Walsall weekly paper lost 80% of its circulation to a free newspaper interloper. It was the same story in Solihull and Sutton Coldfield. It was an unequal battle: their stiff-necked, smart suited male advertising reps were no match for our well paid and incentivised dolly birds trained by the impressive Jan Wilde. One car dealer told me that it was worth the cost of his regular half page advertisement just to have our 'girl' walk onto his forecourt for a 10 minute chat with his staff.

In a throwaway remark Chris said it was about time the *Post and Mail* had some real competition in its own heartland to keep it occupied; he outlined to me how he had been wondering for some time whether a free daily paper – morning or evening - might work. As yet nobody had ever tried this in the UK, although the *Metros* were to do so with great success 20 years later. Ever an optimist at that time, I said I saw no reason why it could not work given the right financial backing. It was the start of the most adventurous and exciting phase of my newspaper career.

Encouraged by my enthusiasm, Chris went off to talk to his business partners at Reed International who gave it a cautious welcome. At this stage they were neither in nor out. Chris asked me to put some meat on his idea and prepare a report for consideration at the Bullman board's next meeting under the cover of my work at Stourbridge. Secrecy was paramount, although I doubt whether the *Post and Mail's* senior management could have got their minds round what we were planning, even if they had known about it. I had only the flimsiest of evidence to work on, although research at Companies House and elsewhere did give me an insight into how the *Post and Mail* operated and the numbers of staff involved. It soon became obvious that while we would be up against a well established company with a good reputation in Birmingham, its management was top heavy and the company was vastly over-staffed. We were encouraged by its failure in Birmingham's satellite towns to defeat our weekly opposition and its nightly losing battle with the *Wolverhampton Express and Star* in the Black Country.

Finance was always going to be the key. Chris had some money from the weekly papers deal with Reed International and was prepared to use it. However, he needed much more than he could raise on his own if we were to have any chance of success. Reed showed some interest, but would not commit financially. They wanted the printing contract for their Worcester press and production set-up and were prepared to give us expert help when it came to setting up delivery teams. It was an exciting few months full of daily twists and turns. Both Reed and Chris came close to pulling the plug on more than one occasion. Somehow we managed to keep it secret from all but a few people - the *Post and Mail* never got a sniff of what was going on under its nose until we were ready to tell it and the rest of the world the following August.

By the spring of 1984 Chris was determined to go ahead. He and his financial advisor Stan Biddle, a retired bank manager, found excellent new offices just off the Hagley Road in Edgbaston. Stan did a superb job in quickly furnishing them with all the desks, chairs and other equipment needed.

I had the job of building an editorial team from scratch - a difficult job because I was unable to tell them what we were really planning to do. Amazingly, more than a dozen journalists soon left their comfortable jobs to join the venture. Today most of them say it was the most enjoyable time of their working lives. I brought Malcolm Ward back from the Middle East to be Deputy Editor, persuaded a Deputy News Editor, Richard Creasy, to defect from the *Express and Star* and recruited some people from my old paper in Banbury. Others came from the weeklies round Birmingham I was theoretically still in charge of including Mark Higgitt, who became Chief Sub-Editor. I quietly interviewed and employed the best reporters, sports staff and subs and told them this was their chance to make a name for themselves in the industry.

Pat Bullivant headed up the advertising side, but we rarely talked. That was Chris's job. I didn't envy him. Instead, if I wanted to know anything about the advertising department, I went to her number two, Jan Wilde, the best advertising manager I ever worked with. She and I got on well and shared the same, often daft, sense of humour. She was good at handling people and getting the best out of them.

We had one big stroke of luck when Reed International gave us the top two men in the newspaper industry to organise the delivery rounds - Roger Sparrow and Mervyn Donnelly were seconded from the *Evening Gazette* at Colchester. The hard work they put in and the teams they organised in a city they did not know earned my admiration. Happily, I knew both of them well from my Maldon days so we had an instant, excellent working relationship. They had the hardest job of all when at the June board meeting we decided to launch a morning rather than an evening paper which we wanted delivered free into 300,000 homes four mornings a week from October. In hindsight we should have gone for the jugular and done a free evening paper, but at the time it was one step too many.

The sheer size of the print run meant no printing press in the area could deliver what we wanted in the timescale during a normal working day and do their other day-time jobs. Printing from midnight to 5am at Worcester just down the M5 was much easier. Roger and Mervyn recruited and trained 100 area agents each of whom controlled 3,000 boys and girls who delivered on average 100 papers each. I cannot praise enough their achievement in setting up such an extensive network of part-time staff because we had very few complaints about non-delivery once the *Daily News* launched.

We did have some print union problems to overcome. The NGA (National Graphical Association) had one of their strongest branches in the country in Birmingham and the West Midlands and they were determined to extract maximum wages for anybody who worked for us. We had several unproductive meetings with them. They only moderated their expensive demands when we threatened to print at the non-union *Nottingham Post*. After that we got on well with the union's officers who realised our working terms and conditions were better than most of those available elsewhere in the area. I recruited John Clegg from our weeklies to run the pre-press operation. It was another inspired appointment.

Chris told me that in addition to seeing if a free morning paper would work he had the secondary aim of crippling the *Birmingham Mail* to such an extent its owners would consider selling all their newspapers in the Midlands to him or Reed. In October 1984 the *Birmingham Evening Mail* sold 304,000 copies a night. Just over a year later the *Mail* had lost a third of its circulation - 100,000 copies a night. We did not see ourselves in competition with the *Mail's* sister paper, the *Birmingham Post*, a regional business paper that was losing money.

Most people within the newspaper industry said what we were attempting couldn't be done and that we would not last very long. The Newspaper Society, controlled by the big players, poured scorn on us at every opportunity. Change was not a word they embraced. New ideas were not welcome. Even so there was great interest in the idea, especially when Reed took the decision to be financially involved a few months after our launch.

One of my key jobs was to publically refute whatever criticisms were directed our way and talk up what we were doing both in Birmingham and elsewhere. Once news broke there was a rush of people from around the world who wanted to know more. Visitors came from South Africa, Australia, France and the United States. The big regional newspaper owners in the UK continued to rubbish us at every opportunity, but that motivated *Daily News* staff even more. We were underdogs, but we soon showed we had bite. I was asked to speak at conferences nationwide and appeared on BBC's *Newsnight* and other television programmes. I was also in demand as the public face of the *Daily* News in Birmingham.

It meant long working hours but there were perks: as Managing Director and launch Editor of a daily paper I had a regular seat in the directors' box at Aston Villa where the then Chairman Doug Ellis always invited me to stay on after a match and have a drink in his private lounge. He introduced me to interesting people like the violinist Nigel Kennedy, an avid Aston Villa fan. I befriended Pat Roach, a television star in Auf Wiedersehen Pet, and mixed in the company of among others Jasper Carrott, Don MacLean and Villa manager Graham Taylor. At one event at Birmingham's NEC I sat two rows behind Prince Charles and Diana Princess of Wales.

I was privileged to manage a hard working editorial team, many of whom used their experience on *the Daily News* to get good jobs on national papers in the years ahead. I tried to make the work as enjoyable as possible and inject fun into our attempts to scoop the *Mail*. There was no way we could compete with the large number of reporters they employed across the whole of the West Midlands, or their bumper pagination some days and extensive coverage of local councils and courts, but we did go all out to get our own stories and offer a different read four mornings a week. When I meet ex *Daily News* reporters nowadays they tell me the paper gave them some of their most enjoyable working experiences.

There were occasions when I needed the judgement of Solomon to sort out problems. A year after we launched we had more than 200 full-time staff on top of the part-timers delivering the papers each day. Birmingham City Council required us to employ a percentage of staff from ethnic minorities if we were to get any of their advertising budget. It proved impossible to recruit Asian and black reporters – there weren't any available. We had to discriminate against the white candidates we really wanted to employ when it came to recruiting advertising, accounts and reception staff to achieve our quota. One black girl, who had an appalling attendance record, made it clear she did not want to do much work when she did bother to turn up, but we felt we couldn't sack her because of the council quota.

An Asian receptionist stole several hundred pounds from money taken over the counter for classified advertising. When we sacked her she appealed and brought her husband along to defend her; his main argument was that it was not his wife's fault if we put temptation in her way. One very attractive black girl was an excellent advertising representative. I was disappointed when she handed in her notice so I asked to see her to find out if there was any way we could persuade her to stay. Her honest answer was that she could earn a lot more money as a prostitute and intended to make that her career. There was no way I could compete.

One Saturday evening I called into the office on my way home from Villa Park. Nobody worked at the weekend so I was surprised to hear noises coming from the boardroom which contained filing cabinets full of confidential papers. Somebody had forgotten to lock the door. Spread out naked on the boardroom table were two of my reporters. I don't know who was more embarrassed. They quickly scrambled to get some items of clothes on while the male muttered: '*We only came in to do our weekly expenses.*' The question was what should I do? The boardroom was strictly out of bounds, yet both were good reporters and single. They assured me they had not touched the filing cabinets. Did I discipline them? No, I didn't, but a few weeks later I decided the table had to go.

I was always keen to ensure line managers did regular staff appraisals. Not only did I regard them as a valuable way of finding out how people felt about their work, but it also gave both sides the chance to discuss career opportunities. The danger of such a policy is that it can become a moaner's charter. One solution I found that really worked was to invite the 'chronic complainers' to sit on the company's health and safety committee where they would meet fellow whingers for a couple of hours a month. I insisted that proper minutes were taken and sent to me for perusal, following which I would have a meeting with the chairman to decide any necessary action. It enabled me to quickly deal with people who wanted to tell me about ice in the car park or the poor taste of coffee from a machine. It also meant I dealt with only one chronic complainer within the entire company, because any attempt to engage me between meetings was referred to the said committee. I insisted they meet at 3pm on a Friday which meant that if they wanted to ramble on and on they did so in their own time, not the company's.

Two appraisals revealed a very personal problem: a smelly manager. Both women wanted something done about their boss who did not use deodorant. They claimed it affected their work, particularly on hot summer days. It was my job to call in the manager and tell him to improve his personal hygiene. A few months later an industrial tribunal in Birmingham ruled in favour of a company which sacked an employee for 'smelling' and wearing clothes with food stains. I am glad I didn't have to do that.

The job move into Birmingham also meant moving house from Worcester to be nearer my new work base. The M5 was being extended from two to three lanes at that time and often it would take me two hours each way to get into the city from Worcester. In 1985 Valerie and I decided to move to Barnt Green in the Lickey Hills south of Birmingham near to where the Bullivants lived, but made the disastrous mistake of buying a small modern house neither Valerie nor I liked from day one.

Only a few months before the move Valerie's mother, Ann, collapsed and died - a shock to everyone in the family and one Valerie still feels to this day. It was so unfair. She was the lynchpin of the family and someone I had grown to love. She adored Georgina and our second child, Timothy, born at Worcester Hospital in September 1983. Ann was a regular visitor to our home in Worcester and the perfect grandmother. Her life was ended far too soon. She collapsed with a brain haemorrage during a lunch break at Braintree College from where she was rushed to Chelmsford Hospital. She died two days later without recovering consciousness. I was in Jersey addressing the Guild of Editors conference when I got the news and flew straight home. I sobbed when she died - it still brings a tear to my eyes today. After Ann's death we decided to have a third child and Robin duly came along in 1986 on the same day as our wedding anniversary, June 3. He was born at Bromsgrove Hospital.

We were still in shock when we moved to Barnt Green, but we had the good sense after a few months to do something about a house neither of us liked. We sold again and moved to nearby Cofton

Hackett into a much larger house with a big garden. We stayed there nearly two years before moving back into the heart of Barnt Green village. Valerie was happy to be near the shops, the local school and her friends who often popped in for a coffee after doing their shopping. We made many friends during this time, but I was too pre-occupied at the expense of anything else with making a success of the *Daily News*. I was not easy to live with. I had far too many migraines - weekends were often spent in bed recovering. As a result I missed out on the children's early lives and regret it now. Fortunately, Valerie more than made up for my lapses.

Despite the prophets of doom the *Daily News* survived a traumatic, hard working first 12 months after which Reed International bought out Chris Bullivant and took full control. This meant saying farewell to Pat Bullivant – as far as I was concerned it wasn't a day too soon. My friendship with Jan Wilde and her husband, Paul, though, continues to this day.

Reed appointed Phil Harris as chairman of the company to keep an eye on what was by now a considerable investment. He and I worked on improving advertising revenues which steadily grew throughout 1986. Phil was an extravagant spender compared with what I had been used to. He had a big company mentality, believing the only way to succeed in Britain's second city was to spend lots of money in a dash for growth; profitability would follow. He gave all the staff annual above inflation pay rises and eye-watering bonuses, including me. Our costs rose quite dramatically.

Every time we hit our monthly sales target I would discover our cost base had risen because of Phil's spending. There were times when I felt uneasy, but he was Reed's man, spending their money so I felt I could not complain too much. There were no warnings at the monthly board meetings that anyone else was unduly concerned. The five London based Reed directors asked questions about revenues, but didn't seem too worried about soaring costs.

Phil brought in human resources staff we did not need, a bonus system which he said helped us keep key staff and organised training sessions at expensive hotels which were fun but I doubt brought in any extra advertising revenue. We wined and dined the good - and some of the bad - in Birmingham and bought a racehorse we called

Birmingham Pride. Phil loved horse racing so this was a way for him to indulge his hobby at the company's expense. The horse failed miserably and was still running well after every other horse in the field had finished. I never saw it run because I had better things to do than spend my days at a race course. Phil invited key advertisers to join him for a fun day out while I ran the business. I did not know it at the time but the cost of buying and maintaining Birmingham Pride changed Reed's mind about Phil. They began to take a closer look at what we were spending their money on.

The original intention was for me to be launch Editor for three months, combining it with my role as Managing Director. It meant that some weekdays I left home at 8am and did not get back until midnight. I also still had the weekly *Solihull Times* to manage. Three months became six and six became 12. I would perform the Managing Director's role until early afternoon, edit the paper until around 7pm and either take part in some company entertaining or deal with the Worcester production managers until 11 o'clock. At every board meeting I would try and get agreement to promote my deputy, Malcolm Ward, but there was a general reluctance by other board members to let me relinquish the Editorship as by now I had become the public face of the venture.

After two years events conspired to force the board's hand when I collapsed from stress one evening. I was at a reception and film premiere with Phil and some advertisers when I suddenly felt poorly. As the evening progressed I felt overwhelmed and told Phil I had to go home. He could see something was wrong and told me he could handle the rest of the evening as by now the film was well underway. I started crying on the drive home. I couldn't stop. I didn't know what I was crying about. I just wanted to cry. It had never happened before (and has never happened since). When I got to Barnt Green Valerie immediately called a doctor friend who told me I had to ease back, or else! In addition to showing all the warning symptoms of acute stress a few days later I discovered I had a stomach ulcer brought on by my lifestyle and taking too many pain killers to ease my migraine attacks. I was permanently tired, short tempered and not much fun to be around at home. My own GP bluntly told me what I was doing to my body. I had the good sense to listen.

This forced Reed's hand. They were very good to me. Malcolm was appointed Editor on the understanding I kept an eye on the editorial direction of the paper and also maintain staff morale. The latter was not one of Malcolm's strengths. He was a good newspaper technician and a better page designer than I ever was, but he did not excel when it came to handling people. Reed knew I had played the leading role ever since that first conversation with Chris Bullivant and recognised my efforts by making me Chief Executive.

I was happy to hand over the editorial reins to Malcolm who did an excellent job of re-designing the paper and together we sharpened up the news coverage. He was less successful in keeping a happy team. There were times when he allowed his personal problems to cloud his judgement. His senior team always knew when his love life was in disarray and learned to keep their heads down if he came into the office in a bad mood.

Unfortunately, soon after I became Chief Executive, I had to sack a senior advertising manager who I caught fiddling his expenses. There was no way I could check everyone's expenses every week, but I used what I called 'dip-stick' management to select a few from each department for detailed scrutiny and occasionally query them. Senior managers had a company credit card they could use for petrol and entertaining which required me to trust them to use it only for proper company expenditure. I became suspicious of one manager whose petrol bill seemed to be much higher than I thought was realistic. An investigation revealed he was filling up his wife's car as well as his company one. I called him in and fired him on the spot. He said he would take the company to an industrial tribunal, but he never did. He was lucky I didn't call in the police because I am sure we would have found more fiddles if we had conducted a detailed investigation. If someone is fiddling it is a fair bet companies never find out the full extent.

Throughout 1987 advertising revenues continued to grow but we kept falling just short of actual profit. By now others were considering emulating what we had achieved, while the *Birmingham Post and Mail* was experiencing financial troubles of its own. Secret talks began between Reed International and the *Post and Mail's* management, thus achieving one of the two original objectives. The talks ran into trouble over who would pay the redundancy money to the 300 people both sides agreed needed to be culled because of over-manning. Reed could have bought the *Birmingham Post and Mail*, its other newspapers and printing operation for £8.5 million, but at the last minute rejected the deal. A few months later the *Mail* sold out to an American company for nearly ten times that amount.

It was a poor decision by Reed's top brass. I was not surprised when a few years later they pulled out of newspaper publishing altogether. It started me thinking about my own future, but first I had to travel round the world after accepting an invitation to address the Pacific Area Newspaper Publishers Association conference in Adelaide and also speak at Melbourne University about the *Daily News*. The conference organisers gave me a round-the-world first class air ticket for my troubles. After I gave my 35 minute talk - which I felt very nervous about beforehand - I enjoyed myself in Adelaide for four days with other Australian and New Zealand newspaper executives. I travelled on to Hawaii where I toured Pearl Harbour and then, despite an airline strike which nearly stranded me, moved on via Los Angeles to Boston where I met up with Valerie, the children and Don and Gail Macuish.

I returned from Australia in late September 1987 and began to seriously think about setting up my own company. I was approaching 40 and felt if I didn't do it soon I would never do it. I had a comfortable and manageable role with the *Daily News* - perhaps too comfortable - with people to run round me and do whatever I needed done. I was a regular speaker at major conferences in the UK and judged beauty contests galore in Birmingham's clubland (it's tough at the top!) I also knew there were still plenty of local newspaper monopolies open to attack and opportunities for new start ups. Towns like Leamington Spa and Stratford upon Avon had only one newspaper and were vulnerable to any newcomer.

Events once again conspired to force my hand. In the first week of January 1988 Phil Harris submitted a plan to me and the other four local members of the *Daily News's* board of directors (Editor, Production Director, Advertising Director and Chief Accountant) that I did not like one bit. It involved changing the paper we had fought so hard to get off the ground against all the odds into a number of small weekly papers based on Birmingham's different districts. I thought it was suicidal just at the time when the *Daily News* was breaking even some months and possibly on the verge of turning in a profit if we seriously attacked our bloated cost base. I could not see how small local papers in the different Birmingham districts would attract more than cheap very local advertising. Unfortunately, he persuaded the other four it was the way forward which left me, their Managing Director, out on a limb. At this stage the five London-based Reed International directors were not involved but I presumed - wrongly as it turned out - they had already given some sort of approval; after all Phil was their man protecting their interests and considerable investment. The necessary new funding would have to come from Reed.

I voiced my strong disagreement and said I hoped that after reflection the plan would be dropped. To my mind it made no sense and when it was not raised again at any meeting I attended I didn't give it another thought. I was too busy dealing with other matters. Undeterred by my opposition, Phil proceeded to plot behind my back. For two months he held secret meetings with the other directors and worked out a plan he hoped would get approval at the April board meeting. I found out by pure chance what was going on when I wandered into one of their secret meetings. I was furious, called them traitors to their faces and then left them to it. Once he knew he had been rumbled, Phil put me under intense pressure to 'fall into line'. He made it clear that if the plan was approved by the full board and I voted against it my position would be untenable.

It wasn't a happy situation to be in with a big mortgage and three young children. The other directors also went to work on me, encouraged by Phil. They patronised me, said I had put up a good fight and urged me not to sacrifice my career. I gave each of them an icy stare while outwardly remaining calm. Inside I felt the strain. My mind raced as to what I would do if I found myself out of a job in the near future. Out of the blue I was invited to join a four day press trip at the end of March to Toronto and Niagara Falls. This gave me the chance to get away from the office and do some serious thinking. For several hours I stood at the Falls thinking about what to do and even had a surreal moment when a couple tapped me on the shoulder and asked if I *'was David Scott?'* They were from Maldon and on a round-the-world trip. Phil, desperate to convert me at the last minute, even rang me at my Toronto hotel to try and get me to change my mind, but I came home more determined than ever to stick by my guns, vote against the plan and, if that meant I lost my job, then so be it.

The next board meeting was due a few days after my return: I knew it was my last chance to make my case and stop the demise of the *Daily News*. The night before that fateful Friday I hardly slept as I turned over in my mind what I was going to say and the personal implications for me. Would they pay me off right away? Would I be asked to clear my desk after the meeting? Where should I look for a new job? How many bridges was I burning? What would I say to the people I had encouraged to come to Birmingham who had left more secure jobs? I was certain I would be outvoted 10-1.

Phil's plan was item number four on the agenda. The first three items did not register on my radar and were quickly dealt with. When the time came Phil spent 20 minutes confidently explaining why he felt his proposal was the way forward. I listened to what I thought was the death knell for the *Daily News*. The other four local directors nodded at the right times, but the five London directors' faces were set as if they were playing a game of poker. It looked like minds were already made up and I was going to be presented with a fait accompli.

When Phil finished speaking he invited comment from others and looked straight at me to signal it was my turn. Before I could speak Roger Rix, my former boss at Worcester and a Reed man, butted in. The next 10 minutes were savage. He slammed the plan as *'ill conceived',* *'unlikely to succeed, ' not something Reed would like to get involved in'* etc etc. In other words the London men were shafting Phil. I could hardly believe my ears. The other four local directors were horrified. One found it hard to shut his gaping, open mouth. They had assumed Phil had got the London directors on board before submitting his plan to a formal vote? He had assured them the meeting would be nothing more than a rubber stamping exercise.

I quickly realised this was board room politics at the highest level and other factors were in play. While the rest of the local directors dithered and one looked visibly shaken, I took the high ground and said that everyone knew I was against this plan, but that in fairness as Chief Executive I would outline why my team believed in it before giving a personal opinion on why I thought it was badly flawed. Then I extracted my revenge. I asked the other four local directors in turn to explain why they supported it and why they had wasted so much valuable time on the scheme despite my opposition. I questioned how much it had cost us and asked whether as a result of all the work that had gone into Phil's plan we had taken our eye off the primary task of bringing the *Daily News* into profit. Two were nearly speechless and spluttered their way through a few painful sentences, while one looked as though he was going to be sick. I wasn't in the mood to let them off the hook. I had suffered several months of anger and stress; their few minutes of anguish were nothing compared to what I had gone through. Whoever said *'revenge is a dish best served cold'* must have had me in mind.

Phil was as red in the face on the outside as he must have felt inside because he knew I had the deciding vote; he and the other four local directors were lined up in support of his plan and the five Reed men were apparently against it, although I knew that without financial backing the plan was going nowhere anyway. When put to the vote I sided with the Reed directors and the scheme was defeated 6-5. They had gambled I would stick to my guns no matter what the personal cost could have been - they had been right. We had a recess for coffee at that point and I went to the toilet. One London director followed me and said: *'Well done. We trusted you would not back down.'* I only wish he had warned me in advance.

The board's refusal to back their own chairman's plans for the future left Phil exposed. I did some quick thinking and realised that behind the scenes Reed wanted rid of him and his high spending management style there and then, but I saw an opportunity open up and took it. Before Phil could be summoned to London to face the chop, I spoke to him the following Monday and said that rather than him being forced out - as I was sure would happen later in the week - I was willing to leave on my own terms if he cut me a good deal.

There was no way the company could afford to lose both of us at the same time. Reed were always watchful of any tremors that would affect their share price. Phil knew I had saved his job for a while: in return he was very good to me. Between us we negotiated my departure for early August 1988. I got a lump sum in lieu of notice, my company car for six months and a lot of goodwill all round.

Between April and August I did very little work of consequence at the *Daily News* while I plotted my next role. I had a free hand. So did Phil. After I left he secretly took the plan Reed and I had rejected to the *Birmingham Post and Mail's* new American owners who gave him the go ahead. It proved to be a very costly flop. He spent a lot of their money in a very short space of time to no avail and was fired along with those *Daily News* staff who followed him. Phil never had another job in the regional press.

There was no way I was going to tell any of the *Daily News's* senior managers what I intended to do when I left. I had learned not to trust any of them. All I did do was give Phil an undertaking I would not poach any of the senior staff. They gave me a big send-off at a lunch held at the Plough and Harrow Hotel and an expensive clock made in Birmingham's jewellery quarter.

The *Daily News* did eventually make a small profit but the recession of the early 1990s crippled it and in June 1991 it was turned into a large weekly paper on a reduced circulation. It was a brave experiment which paved the way for others with the money and the ambition to make free daily newspapers succeed.

I set my sights on launching weekly papers in Leamington and Stratford. I had the plan but not the necessary finance. It was then that I made a big mistake because I approached Chris Bullivant who was also looking for a new venture. I should have known better and blame only myself for what followed. He agreed to put up the money; in return I agreed to give him my services free for a couple of months while we found offices and recruited staff. The only condition I placed was that his wife would not be involved. I was adamant I never wanted to work with her again. Chris knew my feelings and assured me she was too busy with the new weekly papers they had launched in Bromsgrove and Redditch to be involved anywhere else. I left it to him to explain to her our agreement. Over the next few weeks there was never any hint within my hearing that she had any interest in what we were doing.

We found new offices in the centre of Leamington and approached and succeeded in persuading a number of people to take on key positions including Advertising Manager and Editor. Beverley Rigby was offered and accepted the latter position. She had left the *Banbury Guardian* before I did to join the BBC because she knew there was no way she would be promoted when I moved on. It was the *Banbury Guardian's* loss. I am sure *Heart of England Newspapers'* decision not to make her an Editor was based on her sex rather than her abilities. I knew John Algar rated her highly so it had to be a decision further up the management chain. I was glad I was able to offer her an Editorship, even though our working partnership did not last very long. Fortunately, our friendship has.

Chris worked his magic with the estate agents to ensure we got some of their advertising from week one and somehow we kept our plans under wraps. The existing newspapers had, as I suspected, abused their monopolies so we found a receptive market for an alternative.

I put in a lot of unpaid work to get the whole scheme up and running and all went well until the Sunday night before we were due to launch our first edition the following Thursday. I was in bed when Chris telephoned to say that next day his wife would be in the office to take over the running of the advertising department. He said he was unhappy with the way it had been set up and the manager should be fired. There was no consultation, no prior warning. So much for a 50/50 partnership! He gambled that I was too far committed to do anything about it. He was wrong! I told him that if she came in, I would be out. He didn't believe me. He was wrong again!

The next morning I was first in the office. I sat at my desk waiting for the two Bullivants to arrive. Chris came in to explain that, in his opinion, we needed his wife's expertise. I accused him of breaking his word, cleared my desk, packed my private belongings and left after telling him I should have known better than get involved with him again. I was out of work with a family to support.

My first call was to my financial advisor Brian Foster in Sutton Coldfield who I had first met in 1984 when he volunteered to write a weekly financial column for the *Daily News*. Since then he had become a good friend. I regularly enjoyed his marvellous hospitality, along with my son Timothy, in his private box at West Bromwich Albion's games. He calmed me down and then put me in touch with an excellent solicitor in Birmingham. There was the small matter of my 50% holding in the Scott/Bullivant company to sort out. Solicitors don't come cheap but the lady Brian found for me was worth every penny. While the legal wrangle was being sorted out the new paper was launched in Leamington.

Over the next two weeks I hardly slept while I tried to decide what to do. Most nights I got up around 2am and did a lot of thinking. Some of it was emotional. Most of it was telling myself what a fool I had been. Finally, after giving myself yet another good talking to, I opted to see what I could do on my own with no interference from any partner. It was one of the best decisions of my life and one that was to give me 25 years of fun, travel and a good lifestyle. However, it didn't feel like that at the start.

I knew it was going to be a big personal test. First of all, I had to stop feeling sorry for myself. I burned with anger, but I knew that was destructive. I had to adopt a far more positive attitude, put the past behind me and work out how I was going to make my future living. What I didn't know then was that between them Chris and Pat Bullivant had just done me the biggest favour of my life. They had forced me to go out and make something from nothing.

After a few weeks of legal wrangles over my 50% holding Jan Wilde telephoned with a proposal. She said the only winners in the end might be the respective lawyers so she offered to buy my 50% holding. She had set up Bullman Newspapers in partnership with the Bullivants and felt she could work with them again for a short time. I agreed to sell my shares to her, thus severing any links with a plan I had carefully constructed only a few months previously. I never saw the Bullivants again. Jan sold her shares to them a while later.

I had many contacts in the newspaper world. What I didn't know was whether they would give me any work. I decided to test the water by setting up a media consultancy. I prepared a brochure, mailed it out and then waited to see if I would be offered any work. I didn't have to wait long.

My first job was to sort out for the teachers union the NASUWT their monthly newspaper; work offered me by a Barnt Green church friend Paul MacCloughlan who was the union's treasurer.

Soon after Northcliffe newspapers Managing Director Ian Park invited me to lunch in London to discuss working for them. He had replaced Jack Wallwork, he of my Chelmsford days. I had a clean slate as far as Ian was concerned. We got on well and a few days later I was asked if I would spend some time looking at the *Derby Evening Telegraph* set up. A new Managing Director had been appointed in Derby and he needed somebody with an editorial and free newspaper background to work alongside him. That new MD was Steve Anderson-Dixon who in later years was promoted into top management jobs within both the Northcliffe and the Trinity Mirror newspaper empires. I was up and running. I spent 20 months working a couple of days a week with Steve and enjoyed every minute of it.

CHAPTER NINE

OH, I DO LIKE TO BE BESIDE THE SEASIDE

You don't get older, you get better – Shirley Bassey

With the benefit of hindsight going it alone was a tremendous gamble. It could have gone awfully wrong. For the first two years I was kept busy with consultancy work all over the country, which meant I had to get used to hotel life. I have never been one for hanging round a hotel bar so most evenings it meant having a meal, reading plenty of history books and watching television.

I found the long car trips to Carlisle, Hull, Grimsby, Liverpool, Derby, King's Lynn, Canterbury, Banbury, Exeter, Tunbridge Wells, Southampton, Leicester, Haverfordwest, Aberystwyth, Carmarthen Swansea and many other places round the UK quite exhausting. Quite often I would do a day's work and then have a six or seven hour drive home through all sorts of weather. I found coping with freezing fog the hardest; after a few hours I would openly talk to myself while driving to keep up my concentration. A couple of particularly bad Friday night journeys home made me realise it was better to find a hotel en route and get a good night's sleep before carrying on the next morning.

I took all the work offered which got my name known within several large newspaper groups. Gradually the consultancy work evolved into doing some training as well. I would identify a company's problems and then be asked to help resolve them. This often meant training the relevant staff. I started off with two courses - sub-editing and management. Fortunately, I had kept a lot of notes and examples from my time as training officer at the *Essex Chronicle* plus my various editorships. In the next 12 years I built up my portfolio of 24 courses covering just about every journalism subject but feature writing. I also started running refresher courses and mock exams for trainee journalists taking their national exams. Today I have a file full of 'thank you' letters and emails from successful candidates. Each course required a lot of research, but I enjoyed it. I didn't want to teach just from a text book; anyone with half a brain can do that.

I soon discovered too many lecturers running media degree courses were academics who had never been anywhere near a news room. One university journalism course manager said she did have news room experience because she had been a village correspondent for her local paper. How can someone lecture on journalism who has never actually worked for a newspaper?

From the outset I wanted people attending my training courses to not only understand the theory, but to be able to apply it in the workplace. This meant giving them real examples to study, not made up ones. I had another advantage which newspapers soon recognised - I could empathise with everyone I trained from the most junior reporter to the most senior Editor because at some stage of my career I had done their job. I also adopted a company slogan which raised a few smiles – *if you think training is expensive, try ignorance*!

In time different law refreshers became the most popular and sought after courses which meant I had to do a lot of reading to keep up to date. I found it a fascinating subject. Ironically, the people who needed a law refresher course the most – Editors and their senior staffs – were often the people who did not attend one until after they had run into legal trouble. Sometimes I was called in after a newspaper had already paid a large sum settling a libel action or been given a rollocking by a judge for committing a contempt.

I ran a one day law refresher at the *Reading Post* during which the room went very quiet. *'Would you mind looking at page seven of today's paper?'* said one delegate. When I did I knew straight away they had identified a victim of rape contrary to the Sexual Offences Amendment Act. They sweated on that one for several weeks, but got away with it. They were lucky.

Before I reached the stage where I could offer a full package of training courses to companies the UK economy went into recession.

The inflationary pressures created by Chancellor Nigel Lawson's policies and in particular his 1987 budget were one of the reasons given for the UK's entry into the European Exchange Rate Mechanism in October 1990. This was supposed to help restrain inflation which had been approaching 10% in the UK. However, the economy fell into its third recession in less than 20 years, with unemployment coming close to three million by the end of 1992. During this period the Tories ousted Prime Minister Margaret Thatcher, but to everyone's surprise managed to win the 1992 General Election under John Major's leadership after late slip-ups by a Labour Party led by Neil Kinnock. Their honeymoon didn't last long.

Black Wednesday is the name given to 16th September 1992 when the British pound and Italian lira were forced by currency speculators to leave the European Exchange Rate Mechanism (ERM). The ERM was started in 1979 as an agreement between governments to peg their currencies to each other. Each currency was allowed a 2.5% band either side of their fixed peg rate, outside of which the currency was not supposed to move. John Major was a strong advocate of the system until days before the pound's unceremonious exit. Some economists argue that the pound was doomed from the start, entering the system, as it did, while the UK was in recession.

Nevertheless, the final seeds of doom were sowed in August 1992. That month the newly reunified Germany defended the deutschmark from a steady decline brought about by the uncertainty over its economic strength and raised interest rates to 9.5%. This started to threaten the fragile pound, which moved ever closer to the edge of its band. John Major tried to 'talk up' the currency, and took every opportunity to promise that it would never be devalued. The money markets and the financial world in general smelled blood.

On 16 September the British government announced a rise in the base interest rate from an already high 10 to 12 percent in order to tempt speculators to buy pounds. Despite this, and a promise later the same day to raise base rates again to 15 percent, dealers kept selling pounds, convinced that the government would not stick with its promise. At 7pm Chancellor Norman Lamont announced Britain would leave the ERM and interest rates would remain at the new level of 12 percent - the next day they were back at 10%. A large number of businesses failed and the housing market crashed. It was many years before the Tories recovered their reputation for economic competence.

I had seen the warning signs two years' earlier when Nigel Lawson's economic boom evaporated. There were worrying pointers about the state of the UK economy well before September 16 1992. Newspapers are always among the first to feel any economic chill. I began to hear that advertising was starting to dry up in key areas like jobs and motors and the big supermarkets and large national companies were no longer using the regional press to the same extent. In response newspapers started to cut back their spending on both consultancy and training in anticipation of continued reduced revenue. They didn't believe it was going to be a short term problem; they were right. I could see trouble ahead for the work I was trying to get.

In January 1990 I made my first visit to Torquay to advise Ian Park about what to do with a free paper Northcliffe had bought called the *Weekender*. Having paid a lot of money to an entrepreneur for the title, they then had no idea how to manage it effectively and maximise its potential. Some of Ian's senior colleagues in London intensely disliked free papers and treated them with the same disdain they would for something they picked up off the bottom of their shoes. All they wanted to do was protect their existing paid-for evening papers, in this case the *Torquay Herald Express*, from any rivals. They never did learn from the entrepreneurs.

I spent two weeks at the Grand Hotel on the seafront, visited the *Weekender*'s office in Paignton on numerous occasions, met the staff, asked lots of questions and then did a report. I discussed it with the Managing Director, Pat Aldridge, and her team and returned to Barnt Green to carry out work for other newspapers. Three months later I had a telephone call from Ian. He asked me to return to Torquay because the changes I had recommended and he had agreed had not been pushed through. He was not happy and when Ian was not happy it was time to move quickly – or else! The *Weekender's* editorial staff foolishly ignored the recommendations in my report in the hope everyone would forget about them. Ian was furious and threatened to sack the entire editorial team. He was not a man to cross and definitely not someone you could afford to ignore if you wanted to keep your job. The Editor duly got his marching orders. I persuaded Ian that the deputy, Nick Pannell, and photographer, Steve Pope, were worth keeping. They vindicated my decision but never fully understood how close they came to following their Editor out of the door.

To this day I have no idea what made me offer to become the new Editor and make the changes Ian was looking for as long as Northcliffe allowed me to develop my training courses and be away some days each month. It was just a gut feel I had that it was something I had to do. Ian and Pat jumped at the chance to get me on board. I was never on the payroll – I invoiced them every month for my work based on the previous Editor's salary. It saved them National Insurance and pension payments. It was another of those strange moves in my life that proved to be the right one, although there was no way of knowing it at the time. I started work in August and the recession bit soon after. Much of my consultancy and training work dried up for a while so the money I earned from editing the *Weekender* helped pay the bills at a key time.

I got on well with Pat Aldridge and *Herald Express* Editor Jim Mitchell. Together we put some of the best features of the *Weekender* into the paid-for title, re-positioned the free so it did not damage the evening paper and moved everyone into head office in Torquay, which enabled the company to get rid of the *Weekender*'s office on an industrial estate in Paignton.

At first it wasn't easy because there was bad feeling between the two editorial teams, most of it caused by inflated egos and personality clashes. Much of it was silly nonsense, but Jim and I teamed up to deal with each problem as it arose. He was my sort of Editor – tough but fair. He was a commanding figure in his news room and every day rolled up his sleeves to pitch in with advice to his team on the big stories of the day. He did not tolerate fools gladly and stamped his mark on every edition. He would have hated the role played by many Editors today who have to attend time-consuming meetings rather than working alongside their reporting teams.

Pat was the best people-orientated Managing Director I ever worked with. She really did care about the people she employed, took a personal interest in their careers and, when required, their personal lives. It was a loss to the newspaper industry when illness forced her to retire early in 1995. She and I still meet up regularly.

It took me two years to come to terms with the slow pace of working life in South Devon after what I had been used to in the West Midlands, Birmingham and Essex. Most people had one gear – slow. Things got done - eventually. But they saw nothing wrong in not always doing what they were asked to do, and there was a distinct lack of enthusiasm for any role that might involve leadership or extra effort. Later I discovered this lack of drive was the norm right across the board in Torbay and not confined to the local newspapers. It was baffling and sometimes frustrating. And not at all what I was used to. I didn't come to terms with it until I visited Torquay Library and started reading a book about the Home Guard in Devon. In 1940 many men volunteered for Torquay's 'Dad's Army' but officers had to be brought in from Plymouth and Exeter. I realised I was fighting history and gave up trying.

I started to write a regular column under the name of 'Ken Weeder', an anagram of *Weekender*. Most of the readers never worked it out. In 1995 I won the Columnist of the Year award in the South West Press Awards just a month before I left the paper.

There were other highlights including helping to raise tens of thousands of pounds for a children's hospice, but the company's heart wasn't really into free papers and I had an increasingly tough job maintaining staff morale. I also came under attack from a Liberal Democrat Mayor who accused me of not carrying enough pictures of him during his year in office. The bloody cheek! He got short shrift from me and the company.

The move to Torquay was tough on Valerie. She loved our home in Barnt Green in the centre of the village, was happy at the local Baptist church and had many friends. In hindsight relocation saved us from a lot of anguish which was yet to come at the church, but at the time she did not want to move to Devon. I fully understood why. However, my work had to have priority. There is no doubt that if we had not moved I would probably have had to seek a job somewhere in the country and not been able to develop and keep my own company going the way I did.

For three months I lived in a flat the company provided which was owned by one of its secretarial staff, Virginia Griem. I cooked - not very well - and travelled back home on Fridays. Valerie and I immediately started searching for a new home; first in the South Hams and Totnes and then in Torquay and Paignton. It wasn't easy. For a variety of reasons we didn't see anything that compared with our lovely home in Barnt Green, which sold very quickly. After several futile 400 mile round trips between the Midlands and Torbay we eventually found what proved to be a lovely family home in one of the nicer districts, Wellswood, near to shops and in the catchment area for an excellent junior school for Georgina, Timothy and Robin. We christened it Ferndene and moved in the weekend before Christmas 1990. The previous owners had lived downstairs and rented out the five bedrooms upstairs to students, but we ripped the house apart and turned it back to something like its original state. It took several years and more than £60,000 to do all the work, mainly carried out by someone we were to get to know well over the years, Ian Plumridge. Ferndene had a large garden and eventually a sweeping drive when we took away the steep steps and replaced them with tarmac. It was to be our home for the next 15 years.

The children settled very quickly and enjoyed Warberry School where headmaster Peter Vear cared passionately for all his children. He also managed the school football teams and was glad to have first Timothy and then Robin available to score the goals that for several years made the school football teams the best in Torbay. I enjoyed watching many of their games. I was a very proud father when Tim scored in a South Devon schools cup final win on Torquay United's ground. Robin also excelled at chess after being encouraged by another teacher, Mr Tim Onions. He showed at an early age he was a quick learner and had a concise, clear mind. He and two other Warberry pupils represented Devon in tournaments all over the UK for two years until Robin began to miss home so much he did not want to go any more. Georgina, Tim and Robin passed their 11 plus exams and went to the local grammar schools.

We rented a site at Preston near Paignton and had our own beach hut made for us by Ian. Valerie took the children there summer weekday evenings after school where they played on the beach, learned to surf and had tea. I joined them after work when I was home. We enjoyed some glorious family evenings at Preston and the children had idyllic summers for ten years. I went to the beach hut and chilled out on Saturday mornings with a batch of newspapers. It was the quietest day of the week because holidaymakers were either travelling down the M5 to Devon or on their way home in the other direction. There were several church families nearby at other huts so we got to know quite a few people, but it was hard work at first making friends for both Valerie and I - South Devon was nothing like as friendly as Worcester or Barnt Green.

Valerie's health suffered for a while and she felt very lonely. She played the major part in bringing up the children during this time, planned and master minded all the work on Ferndene and kept an eye on things while I was away. She tackled it all with gusto, giving the children lots of encouragement, time and love. She devoted all of her considerable energies to running a good home and bringing up three children while I built the business. I could not have done it without her.

One good friend I did soon make was the Reverend Andrew Green at a time when he needed all the friends he could get as he dealt with a succession of problems at Upton Vale Baptist Church, which we started to attend as soon as we moved to Torquay. He and I spent two weeks in 1992 in Virginia and Pennsylvania touring Civil War battlefields together and had a great time. We flew to Washington, picked up a car and then booked into hotels wherever we ended up in an evening. We visited Gettysburg, Bull Run, Harper's Ferry, of John Brown fame, the old colonial town of Williamsburg, Appomatox where Confederate General Lee surrendered to Yankee General Grant, the Shenandoah Valley and had three nights in Washington where I sat in a space shuttle on display in the Smithsonian Museum. Gettysburg was particularly moving. The three day battle was well explained at the on-site visitor centre. Three years later Andrew asked if I would like to accompany him to Brazil when he was the main speaker at a conference for South American Baptist missionaries. It was another memorable trip.

By 1994 the recession was over and demand for my training courses returned. Newspapers were spending on training again. Most of my work involved sharpening up journalists – from junior reporters to Editors - on short intensive two or three day courses. Law refreshers, in particular, were very much in demand. The effort I had put in doing the preparation work at last paid off.

Many of my courses were held within companies and this involved yet again more travel. For my 'open' courses I used the beautiful Regency Hotel at Solihull next to the M42 until a large concern bought it and standards dropped alarmingly. After one particular bad day in 1996, when the room was not set up prior to my arrival, the food was dry and tasteless and nobody in management appeared to care, I decided to move to the Prince of Wales Hotel at Berkeley between Gloucester and Bristol which I had found by accident when doing some in-house training at nearby Dursley. It was a good move because it was not only an hour and a half each way less travelling for me but it was privately owned and as such much more comfortable. The food was first class too. Over the years I have been well looked after by the hotel's staff and management.

I left the *Weekender* in September 1995. They didn't need me any more and I needed the early part of the week to prepare for my training courses, do basic admin and accounts etc. Most weeks I left home on a Tuesday afternoon or Wednesday morning, not returning until late Friday night or the occasional Saturday night. In addition to the training there were still some short-term consultancy jobs.

My former boss John Saxton was by now Managing Director of the *Kent and Sussex Courier* and *Sevenoaks Chronicle* based in Tunbridge Wells. He employed me to motivate several Editors and sharpen up the two papers' editorial content. I enjoyed all my visits to Kent, but not the drives home round the M25 and down the M3/A303 some Friday nights. After a while I started to go by train. It wasn't an easy journey through London, but it was far less stressful. John always ensured I stayed at a good hotel in nearby Pembury. When he retired I continued to train all their junior reporters and some seniors for many years. I was delighted when some of them became Editors.

I worked hard and earned very good money for the next 16 years. On more than one occasion I gave thanks to the Bullivants. I was happier, fulfilled and made lots of new friends working on newspapers across the UK.

I could have looked for work abroad, but never fancied it. I would have had to commit to being away from home for several months at a time. The only job I accepted outside the UK came about by chance. Steve Hall, the then Editor of the *Exeter Express and Echo*, was contacted by a Crediton businessman who had been asked to try and find someone who could train staff on the Falkland Islands newspaper, the wonderfully named *Penguin News*, and radio station. Steve passed on my name and it resulted in me visiting the Falklands on three occasions over a six year period.

The first time I was meant to fly out I never got off the ground. I was booked on an RAF flight from Brize Norton and duly turned up early one Monday morning only to be told the plane had 'problems'. I did not like the sound of that. Along with other passengers I was kept in a room for eight hours with no food or drink waiting to board only to be told at the end of the day that the flight was delayed for at least another 24 hours. When I asked for some water because I had a migraine I was told by a very rude RAF officer to see what was available in the toilets. When I asked the same officer just when he hoped we would fly out he told me it was not my business to challenge an 'order' and threatened to put me on a charge – he thought I was in the Army. His attitude changed a little when he discovered I was a civilian.

The RAF offered to put me up at their on-site hotel for £45 a night if I would share with a squaddie. At that point I had had enough, collected my bags and drove back home. That flight did not take off for two further days and then got held up another two days at Ascension Island because of more mechanical problems. The Falkland Islands government had paid for the trip so I let them sort it out, while I wrote an angry letter to my MP which he passed on to the Defence Secretary. I got a long reply which said the matter would be looked into and appropriate steps taken. I doubt if they were.

Two months later I tried again and this time I flew out on time, although I wondered whether somewhere over the Atlantic they might press a button and eject me. When I showed my passport to an officer at Brize Norton I got a knowing look. It was the quietest flight I have ever undertaken because most of the people on board had just left their families for six months and didn't want to be going to the Falklands. There was no banter. On board were eight soldiers in battle dress on their way to the Congo to help Brits leave. They were big guys. When we descended to Ascension Island to re-fuel one of them got up to take something from a locker. A pint-sized female RAF officer can storming down the aisle and shouted: '*You are on a charge for disobeying the seat belt sign*'. He sat down very quickly. I didn't move until the others did.

It took 18 hours to get to Port Stanley, but it was well worth it. An hour out two RAF jets came up to greet us; I looked out of the window and there was a pilot waving at me. It was quite surreal. When we landed I had to listen to a 30 minute lecture from a sergeant major about the dangers of picking up objects in fields which just might be bombs or mines. The Argentinians had not kept any record of where they had placed them and our army had given up trying to find them because too many men were being injured. After the lecture I was driven the 40 miles to Stanley across some of the most barren ground I have ever seen.

I was given two pieces of good advice before I left: never criticise former Prime Minister Margaret Thatcher; and don't call the locals Bennies after a famous television soap star actor of the 1980s.

Penguin News editor Lisa Riddell and her small team were very friendly and easy to train because they were keen to learn. In return they educated me about the 1982 war with Argentina. I got the chance to speak to some of the civilian leaders who thought they were going to be shot and was taken to San Carlos Bay, where the troops landed, and on to Goose Green, Darwin and Mount Tumbledown - all scenes of fierce battles. I stayed at the comfortable Malvina House Hotel owned by a former Royal Marine who had fought in the war and enjoyed the whole stay.

While the weather was cold, it wasn't as bad as I had been led to believe. It was, however, very windy. Stanley at that time was how I envisaged life in British villages was soon after the Second World War. There were red telephone boxes, many poles displaying the union flag, an old fashioned post office and a community spirit forged by long established families. People didn't lock their cars; why would anyone steal one? There were a couple of good restaurants and pubs, an excellent hospital and a good school. Food was more expensive, but petrol was cheaper. Tax rates were lower than in the UK.

I made a second trip two years later to do more journalism and law training. On the way I had to spend a night at Ascension Island which was not pleasant. I was bitten all down one arm while I slept in a room full of bugs. I was glad to fly out the next morning. On a rare day off I was taken on a 10 hour trip to see a colony of King Penguins and sea lions. It was one of life's great moments to stand in the middle of hundreds of chattering colourful penguins.

My third and final trip came in 2004 and this time I chose to ditch the RAF and fly by scheduled flights via Madrid, Santiago in Chile and Punta Arenas at the tip of South America. It took three days each way and while I had a lovely 24-hour stay in a smashing hotel in Santiago on the way back, it was not something I would want to do too often. This time I stayed with Pete and Fran Biggs rather than in a hotel. Pete is head of the Falklands own territorial army force, while Fran sells advertising for the *Penguin News*. She is a hard worker who over the years has played a big part in the success of the newspaper. Pete and Fran drove me round the main island in my free time pointing out places of historical and geographical interest. They made my stay a memorable one.

It was a visit with more than one objective. In addition to some further law and journalism training for the newspaper's small staff, I was brought in to train several islanders on how to manage the newspaper and radio station, both subsidised by the Falklands own government. The Argentinians were claiming at the United Nations that because of this subsidy the government had direct control over the media. To counter this, a Media Trust, independent of government, was set up - in effect its board of directors. After training five islanders over several days on how a newspaper operates and the role of an Editor, I addressed the Islands' governing council and explained it all to them. I had meetings with the Governor and the Attorney General and addressed a public meeting following which there was a question and answer session. I also went on two radio programmes to explain what I was doing. Before I left I had one superb dinner at Government House where I was sat next to round-the-world sailor Ellen MacArthur.

The only other foreign trip connected with my work was in 1994 to advise Don and Gail Maccuish in the United States. Don was offered the chance to buy the ailing *Malden News,* the daily paper which had extensively reported on my Mayoral trip in 1979 and which I might have joined soon after if Publisher David Brickman had offered me an attractive job. Thank goodness he didn't. He died in 1992 three years after selling the paper for a million dollars to another Malden businessman, Warren Jackson. I had already met Warren several times and thought him the worst type of loud-mouthed Yankee anyone could ever hope to meet. On the first occasion during the Mayoral trip he was put in his place by, of all people, my wife, Valerie. We were having breakfast with a group of Malden businessmen and he could not resist showing off. He eventually got round to boasting he was on his third or fourth wife. Valerie asked if the others died of boredom. It was the perfect put down and brought hoots of laughter from the rest of the table. Warren had to laugh as well, but the look he gave Valerie was one of venom.

He wanted rid of the paper and its sister titles in nearby Medford and Melrose. Like many other people I have met over the years he thought running a newspaper company would be easy and would give him some prestige. He had bought into a business he knew nothing about because owning a couple of newspapers appealed to his vanity and ego. He thought they gave him some sort of power, a delusion he shared with others I have met in the UK. By the time he realised the newspaper business was not what he thought it was, he had alienated the unions and was in the middle of trying to resolve a strike which had stopped production. He wanted out and, if he could, to get back his million dollars. He was that dumb and full of himself he didn't have the sense to realise the middle of a bitter dispute with staff was not the best time to invite would-be buyers round to his office

Don MacCuish, who also had no experience of the newspaper industry, said he would consider buying the papers if I recommended the deal and if I would run the company for him. At least Don was willing to take advice from someone who knew the industry before spending his money.

I left home one Sunday morning, drove to Gatwick, caught an afternoon flight to Boston with Virgin Atlantic, arrived at 5pm American time and sat down to read the relevant documents connected with the proposed sale. I had a few hours sleep and then went to see the newspaper and meet Warren again. The information I asked for and was reluctantly given showed the whole set-up was a shambles with falling sales, little regular advertising and out-of-date equipment which needed to be replaced very soon. The silent, rubbish-strewn offices said it all.

Warren didn't have a clue, but listening to him you would have thought he was another Rupert Murdoch. It was obvious to me that when he realised what a mess he actually owned and the increasing losses he was making, he wanted a quick sale. I told Don I would not advise him to get involved even if Warren offered him $50,000 to take the papers off his hands. The fact Warren was expecting to sell for a considerable sum was staggering to my mind.

By late afternoon I had seen enough and bluntly asked Don: '*Do you want to buy a toy or do you want to make a profit?*' That was enough for Don to walk away from the deal on the table. Warren was furious. In the coming weeks he called me all the names under the sun and said I did not understand the American newspaper business. I knew enough, though, to recognise a bum deal.

To the amazement of the same air crew who had flown me into America, I caught the same plane back home the next night. I landed at Gatwick early Tuesday morning and drove back to Torquay where I was soon in bed exhausted.

Warren did eventually get some of his money back when he sold out to a large newspaper company that was able to amalgamate the *Malden News* and its sisters with existing papers in the state. There was an economy of saving which produced a profit after an expensive initial investment in new technology. There was no way Don could have afforded that.

My work since I set out on my own in 1988 has involved meeting many interesting people of all ages and titles. I have gained great satisfaction from training - at the time of writing - people who have taken up 9,000 course places. Nowadays I often bump into journalists who have been on one or other of my courses and equally often I cannot remember their names! Inevitably a few incidents stand out more than others.

An early consultancy role took me to of all places the *Birmingham Post and Mail* in the centre of the city where a few months earlier I would probably have been assaulted. I reorganised their weekly papers in Sutton Coldfield, Solihull and Walsall and did some training. Their head office in the centre of Birmingham was an incredible place because of the all-too-evident class distinction. The editorial floor had no carpet and cheap loo paper, while the management floor had expensive carpeting and top grade loo paper. The canteen was like apartheid. On one side, for management and senior personnel, there was waitress service and a good three course menu each day; on the other side of a partition were two elderly ladies who served sandwiches and anything with chips to the rest of the staff. There was an internal pub which you could use only after being invited. When Roy Hattersley did an article for *Punch* soon after the launch of the *Daily News* he contrasted the *Post and Mail's* man in top hat and long coat who greeted visitors to our '*dolly bird with coloured fingernails*'.

One night while working in Derby I joined the Editor, Mike Lowe, and his senior team at a dinner at the Midland Hotel to celebrate a growth in circulation. Those were the days! There was lots of free drink and as it flowed during the meal so tempers rose between the city news editor and the district news editor. Light-hearted banter turned nasty and after a session of trifle throwing across the table Mike told them that if they couldn't behave they should go outside and sort out their differences. As they departed for the car park they bumped into a BBC cameraman staying at the hotel who swore at them. They beat him up before settling their argument -

the ensuing fight(s) caused £5,000 worth of damage and the *Derby Telegraph* was banned from the hotel for five years.

A visit to the *Gloucestershire Echo* in Cheltenham to help them ward off an attack by one of Bullivant's recently launched but ill-fated titles saw me having to drag the Editor (who shall remain nameless) off the Managing Director when things became heated. The MD said something he shouldn't have during a long winded meeting. It clearly upset the Editor, who was keen to get back to edit his paper and was not somebody who enjoyed being in drawn-out meetings. Without any warning apart from a snarl he launched himself at his boss, grabbed him by the tie, yanked him across the desk and said a few choice words of his own. Unfortunately the MD was smoking a pipe at the time and the ash went the wrong way - down his throat. Everyone else in the room was so stunned they did not move, but I quickly intervened and persuaded the Editor to let go of the tie which was throttling his boss.

I made a number of trips to Liverpool and on one of them I had just fallen asleep while staying at the Holiday Inn when there was screaming and shouting in the corridor outside. It went on for some time so I telephoned reception to ask what was going on. '*Sorry, Mr Scott, but we have Robbie Williams staying on your floor and some girls have got through security and are trying to find his room*.' I enquired whether this was the star of the film Jumanji. When I got home my children groaned when I told them I did not know who Robbie Williams was. They soon educated me.

The most bizarre experience came when I visited Horncastle, a one-horse town if ever there was one, in Lincolnshire to do some training. I stayed at the main hotel which was really a pub with rooms on the first floor. When I went down for something to eat I sat by a large fire and got chatting about football with three guys from Swindon who were thatchers. Suddenly one of the locals came over with a pint glass in his hand and said: '*Too many foreigners hogging the fire tonight*'. The roofer next to me bristled, stood up and confronted the guy. Everything went quiet; it was one of those moments when you have to decide whose side you are on. I was definitely with the thatchers - they were big guys and looked fit. The roofer pointed to the far corner where he told the local he ought to go for the sake of his health. Amazingly, he did just that and I heaved a huge sigh of relief. A few weeks later I took a call from the newspaper where I had done the training. *'Did you notice anything unusual during your stay,'* said the Editor. *'No,'* I replied but told him the story about the near punch-up. *'Oh, it is just that the hotel's owner has been up in court today because he had peep holes into some of the bedrooms and has been watching people undress.'* A strange town I hope I never have to visit again.

For three years I did consultancy work for Northcliffe Managing Director Alec Davidson which made me at least one enemy. Alec wanted an independent view of each of Northcliffe's daily papers. Every month I would have delivered to my home one week's papers from a particular title, starting off with the *Western Morning News* based at Plymouth. *Morning News* Editor Barrie Williams did not like what I had to say about his paper and in particular my criticism of his weekly football column which featured stories about football manager Brian Clough from Barrie's time as Editor of the *Nottingham Post*. I said I did not think too many readers in the Westcountry were interested in Nottingham Forest. Barrie hit the roof when he read my report. What he did not take into account was the firm instruction I was given by Alec not to go anywhere near any of the papers I reviewed, nor speak to any of the Editors. I had no idea why Barrie wanted to educate his readers about Brian Clough. He must have had a good reason, but I wasn't allowed to know what it was.

Alec asked me to select a single week and write about what I found from a reader's viewpoint. It was important I did not know the background to the way the papers were produced. I wrote monthly reports, posted them to Alec in London and the following week travelled up by train to meet him to discuss their contents over some excellent lunches. Then I would catch a late afternoon train back to the Westcountry. Alec used my reports to try and keep the Editors on their toes and force through some changes at various papers.

Barrie and I had always got on well from my days as Editor of the *Daily News*, but for a couple of years after my report on the *Western Morning News* he snubbed me. Eventually we made it up, but I believe he never really forgave me for what I had written about his paper and Brian Clough. Other Editors took my reports in their stride: most found them constructive and used them to improve their news coverage; a few I singled out for well earned praise sent me thank you letters.

Despite our spat it didn't stop Barrie along with his fellow South West Editors from inviting me to set up a training academy for Northcliffe Newspapers based on their Plymouth, Exeter and Truro offices in 2005. This trained many young reporters until yet another recession struck in 2011. At the time of writing I still do some training within the Plymouth academy, but with spasmodic recruitment it is not as regular as it used to be.

Over the years I also always enjoyed my visits to Stoke and Swansea to run training courses. I was accommodated in good hotels where I could get a hearty breakfast and a fulsome evening meal.

One reputation I fully deserve within the newspaper industry is for getting angry with people who turn up late for any of my training courses. Nowadays most Editors warn their staffs not to be late because of this reputation. It is amazing how quickly word can spread. In 1994 I made two women from a Midlands newspaper turn around and go home when they arrived at 10 o'clock for a course that started at 8.45. I stopped them at the door, asked why they were late and when they didn't offer an apology, I said I didn't want to train them. Their only excuse was that they had overslept and '*taken a long time to get ready*'. Their mouths fell open when I told them to leave; they thought I was joking. When they realised I really meant what I said they had the difficult job of going back and explaining what had happened. While they were on their way back I telephoned their Editor and explained there was no way I could start the course all over again. He agreed. I have never had any trouble with anyone since.

Of course, there are times when people have a good reason for being late, generally because of traffic problems. When that happens they find me sympathetic if they have telephoned the hotel to explain.

One of my favourite quotes is: "*Punctuality is the politeness of kings.*" It is credited to Louis XVIII, King of France in the late 18th and early 19th century. Kings - especially before the French

Revolution - didn't need to be punctual because people would hang around waiting for them to turn up, no matter how late they were. If Louis's statement is true for kings, it is certainly true for anyone attending one of my training courses.

I think people who turn up late for meetings are bad mannered. *"Punctuality can seem like a curse because so many people today are not punctual"*, said one philosopher. I am often the first one at a meeting, one of the first people to turn up at church on a Sunday morning and definitely someone who makes sure he gets to an airport four hours before any flight - just in case there is a motorway accident. I know I annoy those around me who like to leave everything to the last minute, but I will never change. Other people routinely arrive five, ten or even 15 minutes late. They would still turn up late if the meeting time was put back 15 minutes!

Bud Bilinich wrote: *'I believe that if most people arrived promptly for meetings, they would start on time and the late comers would get the message. Being punctual displays respect for the person you are visiting. It shows that you value his or her time. It shows that you are a person who keeps commitments. If you say you'll be there at 10, he or she knows that you will be there at 10, not at 10:10 or 10:15.'* I totally agree.

In the 26 years I have trained thousands of journalists I have missed only three days' work through illness. On each occasion I lay in bed worrying about letting people down. In mid October 2013 I was running a three day pre-exam refresher course for 12 reporters at the Prince of Wales Hotel. On the second day, 30 minutes after the usual nice lunch, I started being sick. I couldn't stop retching. Fortunately, my usual trusty helper, Faith Lee, a former Editor of the *East Grinstead Courier*, was able to take over and run the afternoon session. I went to bed and for the next 18 hours travelled backwards and forwards – mainly on all fours - between bed and bathroom. I thought I had a bad case of food poisoning. The next morning I had hardly slept and felt awful, but I struggled downstairs to brief Faith who carried on where she had left off the previous day. Later, everyone told me I looked dreadful. I went back to bed and slept for two hours, but didn't feel any better. I thought that if I told a doctor I had food poisoning they would not do anything apart from tell me to drink lots of water and it would pass after 48 hours. By now I had an awful pain in my side which I thought was a pulled muscle from being sick so often. I packed up, got in my car and drove 120 miles home, the last part of which I did at a steady 60 miles an hour because I was in a lot of pain. When I got home Valerie put me straight to bed. The next day the pain was even worse. By that evening something was obviously very wrong.

Valerie telephoned the night doctors service at 10pm and was advised to take me to Newton Abbot Hospital where I had a better chance of being seen immediately. I could hardly manage to walk into the hospital. The duty doctor took one look at me and said: '*You are a very ill man. I am telephoning Torbay Hospital to admit you as an emergency.*' When we arrived a team were waiting for me at the door and I was whisked off to a cubicle so they could do blood and other tests. I was then transferred to Forrest Ward where I was to remain for seven days. Treatment started straight away, even though by now it was 1am on a Sunday. The next ten weeks were an eye-opener into what our local NHS services in South Devon can offer and have to cope with.

What I thought was food poisoning was actually severe inflammation of my gall bladder, liver and kidneys. If I had left it a few hours more, I was told, I would have been in intensive care with peritonitis. I was connected to several drips and an oxygen booster with strict instructions that I could not have any food for five days. Little did I know that I would lose 22lbs over the next few weeks! I didn't care – I felt so ill.

Eventually I was stabilised and allowed home to await an operation to remove my gall bladder. Throughout November my health deteriorated. Three times – once at night, twice during the day - I had to call a doctor to my home after suffering further kidney infections. We cancelled a holiday to Madeira and there was no way I could do any training. I felt very poorly, could not walk far and had no energy. I was beginning to despair of being called for an operation I knew I badly needed and contemplated paying £5,000 to have it done privately.

By early December I could not move out of home even to do some shopping and was suffering bouts of sickness every day. My

GP pressed for me to be treated as an emergency - the hospital responded when a cancellation became available. I received a telephone call on a Wednesday morning, met the consultant Thursday afternoon and was operated on the next day when my gall bladder was removed by keyhole surgery. I was allowed home six hours after the operation, but fell ill the next day and had to be re-admitted for three days. I received excellent care and attention from hard-working staff.

My sudden incarceration in two hospital wards did give me the chance for the first time in my life to see the NHS at work. My only other experiences had been occasional appointments at my excellent doctor's practice in St Marychurch for migraine and minor aches and pains. The loving care and attention I received from all the staff at Torbay Hospital was in stark contrast to the many national media reports about how the NHS is supposed to be crumbling and horrendous stories of how nurses in places like Staffordshire have treated some patients. What I learnt during my incarceration is that while the NHS might not be perfect in some areas, the real problem is not the doctors and nurses but some of the patients they have to deal with. Propped up in a hospital bed gave me the chance to survey what was going on around me.

One example will suffice. At 3am a man was brought to the bed opposite me. Despite being told to be quiet because other patients were asleep, he made enough noise to wake a herd of elephants. As far as he was concerned he was the only patient in the hospital. I propped myself up and heard the nurse try to get some basic information out of him: age? 48; height? five foot six; weight? 16 stone seven pounds; job? not worked for 24 years. The nurse asked how much he drank to which he replied: '*Not as much as I used to.*' She persisted. He was still not keen to reveal how much so he said: '*I have cut back recently.*' She did not give up and eventually he reluctantly revealed he drank a bottle of vodka a day and a few other spirits. After further questioning about when he had cutback he said '*last Wednesday*'. The nurse said she would get a doctor to visit him later in the day to talk about how he could reduce his alcohol intake. She warned him he was killing himself. He would have none of it.

'Don't bother,' was his response. *'I will drink what I want without you interfering.'*

Because of his lifestyle he was more poorly than I was. He had to have an immediate blood transfusion and was told not to eat or drink anything until he had had a CT scan later that morning. He was most unhappy about not being able to eat and muttered about *'his rights'*. He never stopped moaning all day. By 9am he was even more miserable about his lack of food so when the hospital shop trolley came round he bought a packet of sandwiches and a bar of chocolate while the nurse was away from the ward. Unfortunately for him she came back just as he was eating the sandwich and caught him in the act. She took it away and told him off. His CT scan had to be delayed until the afternoon.

Despite clear signs in the ward that mobile phones should not be used unless patients went to the nearby television lounge, he ignored them and spent most of the morning ringing his wife and daughter in between complaining to anybody who would listen about his *'treatment'*. I could hear every word, but studiously ignored him. So did the other two people in the small ward. He got the message after a while, but it didn't make any difference to the noise he made.

I resent paying my taxes for people like him to be treated on the NHS. If people choose to drink themselves to death and won't get the help on offer, why are the rest of us paying for it?

Different nurses remained calm in all their dealings with him - professional, polite yet firm. When he could see he was not going to get what he wanted he started verbally abusing them and at one stage tried to kick one of them. Despite being connected to various drips and a blood transfusion he got up to go to the toilet – having already said he wouldn't use a bed pan. He unplugged everything he was connected up to. Blood went all over him, the bed and the floor. Of course, it *'wasn't his fault'*. To my astonishment he claimed the nurse who had taken away his sandwich had not properly connected his drips. I wasn't having that. When everything had been cleaned up and he had been given new sheets, I got out of bed and went to find the ward manager (sister) to tell her what he had done. There was no way I was going to let the nurse take the blame. When I was discharged the next day the manager thanked me for telling her what had really happened. When I said I was annoyed money was being spent on people like him, she said: '*They rarely reach pension age.*'

It left me wondering about the cost of treating people who choose a lifestyle that will inevitably end up with them needing prolonged hospital treatment until they die. What strain are such people putting on the health service? Will the money always be there to treat more and more people who ruin their own bodies in such a way?

There were other times when I saw and heard incidents which left me feeling nothing but admiration for all staff at Torbay Hospital and, I suspect, most of the hospitals in the UK. The abuse aimed at doctors, nurses, even the ladies serving lunch was truly shocking. And through it all they kept on smiling, even at the end of 12 hour shifts. Amazing!

All but one of the reporters on the training course in Gloucestershire understood why I could not mark their mock exam papers while I was still in hospital and seriously ill. The one who didn't like me going home complained to her boss and used it as an excuse when she failed all her exams. Thankfully, she left the newspaper soon after. Everybody else on the course passed their exams.

I couldn't work for a further three months after my gall bladder was removed. I had no energy to do anything, but slowly my strength returned and I was able to carry on running my training courses round the country. It felt strange several months later when I went back to the same room at the Prince of Wales where I had been so ill.

Most reporters on my courses find them tiring and often say they flop into bed quite early. A few, however, see the opportunity away from home to have a binge. One girl had too much to drink and was in such a state she could not make the second day. Hotel staff said she had drunk a lot of port. She wanted to see me so along with a receptionist I entered her bedroom to find her slumped over the side of the bed being sick into a bucket. '*You won't tell my Editor, will you?* 'she croaked. '*Not unless he asks*, 'I replied. '*By the way, it is a pity you were not ill off bananas*'. She looked up and asked why? '*Because doctors tell me they taste exactly the same coming up as they do when they are going down.*' She didn't appreciate the humour.

One news editor had so much to drink he tumbled down the stairs on his way to breakfast, but still managed to be in the training room on time. Another was ill in his room and left it in such a mess he had to pay the hotel an extra £200 for cleaning.

The food at the Prince of Wales Hotel has been rightly praised by many of my course delegates. They get a two course cooked lunch plus ample tea, coffee, biscuits and soft drinks. In an evening most of them still manage a large three course dinner and the ones determined to make the most of what is on offer also have a full cooked breakfast. One December Giles Sheldrick from the *Oxford Mail* managed to eat three Christmas lunches straight off. Nobody has ever come close to beating that!

One memorable evening at the hotel was in May 1999 when I sat with a dozen other men round the bar to watch the European Cup final between Manchester United and Bayern Munich. One of our number was Danny Lockwood, then Editor of the *Dursley Gazette*, an avid United supporter. With five minutes to go and United losing 1-0 Danny could stand it no longer; he went to his room to watch the end of the game. In the last minute Teddy Sheringham equalised for United. The Germans were devastated as 30 minutes extra-time loomed. Danny came hurtling down the stairs from his room yelling his head off and ran out into the car park in celebration. In the meantime, and two minutes into injury time, substitute Ole Gunnar Solskjaer stuck out his foot and diverted the ball into the net for Manchester United's winner. Poor Danny never saw it live. When he came back in expecting another 30 minutes of play he was amazed - and thrilled - to know the game was over. He was in good company because George Best left the ground before the end thinking United had lost.

CHAPTER TEN

DEATH BY A THOUSAND CLOTS?

I think journalism anywhere should be based on social justice and impartiality, making contributions to society as well as taking responsibility in society. Whether you are capitalist or socialist or Marxist, journalists should have the same professional integrity --Tan Hongkai

It is easy to have rose-tinted glasses about the 'good old days', but I genuinely do believe I experienced the best years for the regional press. The golden years profit-wise were 1989 to 2005 when during this period Johnston Press became the first large newspaper company to achieve regular 30% profit margins. Trinity Mirror emulated them so the Stock Market insisted others had to do the same. The fact this was unsustainable in the long term didn't seem to bother too many managements awarding themselves fat bonuses or, in the case of one company, subsidising their failing American newspapers.

The big question today is whether print really is dead? The move to put everything on the web has not yet succeeded from a commercial viewpoint. Whether regional newspaper groups can make it work is something only time will tell. For the sake of thousands of good people whose jobs are at stake, I hope they can. Most of the big players controlling 90% of regional newspapers believe that us readers will demand our local news and advertising is served up in an instant on a smart phone by 2020. This belief is based on the fact that successive generations, who have grown up to make the best use of digital technology, will replace old dinosaurs like me who like to hold a newspaper in our hands and find reading text on a phone very difficult.

I have no argument with their moves to make the most of new technology, to offer local news on different platforms and engage with a wider readership, but the way they have neglected their print products will prove to be short sighted unless they quickly find the key to earning enough advertising revenue from their web operations. So far nobody has come up with the 'big' answer that will unlock what some believe is untold wealth – whoever does will earn a fortune in consultancy fees.

Long term it would have been far more sensible if they had invested in both the web and their print products, but in recent years long term planning for the newspaper side of their operations has not been high on the agenda of most managements more concerned with the next set of trading figures than those five years hence. How long regional newspaper companies can maintain their 20% plus profit margins if web revenues do not improve dramatically remains to be seen, because, whether they like to admit it or not, they have helped accelerate the decline of their newspapers.

Former *Derby Telegraph* Editor Neil Fowler, a fellow cricket enthusiast, wrote an excellent review of the regional press in 2012. He made eight critical points:

1.   Newspapers do not research their customer base effectively. They look at how they interact with the newspaper products themselves but did not look at how their readers' lifestyles are changing.

2.   New product development is seen as a short-term way of making more money, rather than a long-term way of possibly finding new routes for the business.

3.   Newspaper groups fail to experiment as the changing marketplace becomes apparent. Having thirteen or fourteen daily newspaper centres means that different business models could have been tried. They weren't. The sole attempt to be truly radical was by the Manchester Evening News in the mid-2000s when it launched a part-paid/part-free distribution system. Few other trials of any other radical note have ever taken place.

4.   Giving all a newspaper's output away for free on the web has been a disaster. The message that the internet would be the new rivers of gold was always false.

5.   Dreaming up new brands for newspaper websites has also been and continues to be, with a few exceptions, a disaster too. I can

buy a Mars bar in a variety of forms; I can buy Fairy detergent in different styles – but until recently if I wanted to read the *Leicester Mercury* online I had to go to thisisleicestershire website and then struggle to be sure that it actually was the same brand that had been established for well over 125 years.

6.   Politicians have believed that phone hacking on one newspaper out of twelve hundred is the real issue that bedevils the media. They are wrong and need to begin listening to the industry and, perhaps, to those who read newspapers, too. The oh-so-slow negotiations post-Leveson, where the political and judicial classes have all but ignored the needs and despairs of the local and regional press, exemplifies this.

7.   The fear of the concentration of ownership and a lack of plurality has been overblown. The Editor dancing to the tune of a power-crazed proprietor does not exist in the regions. And never has done. But still the debate goes on. Local World, the business vehicle established to take over the assets of Northcliffe Media and Iliffe Media, was subject to very detailed scrutiny over a period of six months by the Office of Fair Trading before the deal was officially allowed.

8. Newspaper groups have allowed distant ownership to become a problem, when careful management could easily have negated it.

Neil added: '*Senior executives have been viewed by their staffs, both senior and junior, as being too focused on the bottom line and not taking a longer-term view. Even in the depths of the economic decline, there were some (not many I admit) news businesses making 30 per cent margins. No one I spoke to understood how this would help the survival of brands in the future.*'

It was a well argued and thoroughly constructive piece but I have not seen any of the large groups do much to improve their newspapers since Neil's critical review of the industry. When I read his report I remembered the abuse and scorn I suffered from newspaper managements when I helped launch the *Birmingham Daily News* in 1984, when all we did was try something different. Today's newspaper industry is suffering death by a thousand clots!

It is hard to believe today that at the height of the advertising boom newspapers charged a premium on job adverts. Nowadays hospitals, councils and companies have their own web sites where they put most of their vacancies. Estate agents and car dealers advertise the same way in many towns.

Of course, changing lifestyles have played a part in circulation declines. People don't have the same affinity with the place where they choose to live after they move from where they were brought up. Once they migrate from their home town links to the area where they went to school, played football etc. break down. Their desire for strictly local news in their new home area is often very limited unless something directly affects them such as their dustbins not being emptied or poor schooling. Little or no research has been done on changing demographics or to find out what these people want from a local newspaper.

The warning signs were there in the early part of this millennium, but managements either failed to recognize them or were too complacent to do anything about them. I laugh when I see the old promotional signs 'Your town, your news, your local newspaper'. Long gone are the days when all local newspapers were at the heart of their communities, employing hundreds of local people as journalists, receptionists, sales reps, circulation managers, printers of all shapes and sizes and administrative staff. A few privately owned newspaper groups in Kent and Cumbria still do, but the majority have lost the reader loyalty they used to enjoy from employing locals.

Most regional newspapers are printed many miles away in an alien town, while their accounts are centralised elsewhere and even their switchboard can be operated by another company in another town. Adverts are made up in India or eastern Europe. What is left at a purely local level is a small team of journalists and advertising reps. Talented and committed journalists are still laboring away on their beloved papers for relatively small wages, but with fewer reporters to fill more pages, upload a set number of stories every hour to the net, produce some local video footage and keep their Twitter connections happy it is no wonder that they are often forced back on dull, easy news. Readers are not fooled. They vote with their feet!

During the 1990s and the early part of this century owning a local newspaper with a monopoly in the area where it operated was a near licence to print money. Of course it couldn't last. When the inevitable recession came along in 2008 weak, over-paid managements reacted in the only way they knew by slashing costs in order to try and keep profit margins as high as possible for as long as possible. Nobody doubted that some costs had to be slashed given the national economic situation, but the end result was too many newspapers were left with fewer badly trained staff who offered little or no customer service.

First to go were the circulation managers who dealt with newsagents and other newspaper sellers like petrol stations and corner shops. Papers were simply delivered to wholesalers who sent them out with the morning's national papers. There was nobody going round newsagents to top up supplies or get feedback on what was happening in the market. As far as managements were concerned it saved money on the wage bill and the vans could be sold.

When that wasn't enough they looked for other savings without any thought to the future and what it was doing long term to their businesses. Experienced advertising staff who had got to know their customers over many years were made redundant leaving the few that were left to simply process orders.

Next in line were the experienced Editors who, of course, were the most expensive employees. Years of loyal service and local knowledge counted for nothing as they were culled purely on the grounds of cost. A few were got rid of because they were seen as the awkward squad who dared to challenge what was happening. In 2012/13 I personally knew 37 first class Editors who were given pay-offs and told they were no longer wanted. They weren't given much choice about whether they accepted such payments. They were replaced by younger versions on half the salaries. A few of the latter have been a minor success, but too many of them now produce dull products full of press releases and awful pictures submitted by readers.

The naïve belief in what has been called 'citizen journalism' is no more than an excuse to fill the space between adverts with cheap rubbish nobody wants to pay for or read. It is a deluded short cut and it won't last all that long. When the reader content experiment fails sometime in the near future managements will claim there is no longer any market for print and close the doors on all but a handful of titles. They will never have come to terms with the simple fact that quality journalism is costly, or understand there is a market for it.

For a short time there was talk of returning local newspapers to local control where profit margins of around 10% would be good enough. That may yet happen, but so far there is no sign the large groups are willing to sell to local entrepreneurs. There have been a few successful new set-ups but nothing like the free newspaper explosion of the 1980s. Purely local blogs and web sites have come and gone – few have made any money.

The real danger for democracy is that many towns will be left with no local newspaper of any note covering their councils or courts. I have always believed one of the key roles local newspapers have fulfilled over many years is they have kept an eye on our elected representatives and been present in our courts to see that justice is done. The signs are already there that all but a few of today's regional newspaper managements either do not understand this role or don't care, even in the towns and cities served by long established titles. I often hear magistrates moan that they rarely see a local reporter.

In a few years' time when the only source of local news might be the internet I doubt whether it will offer the same news coverage. Local democracy is certain to suffer. Outside London most, but not all, councils are still held to account by a local paper, but how long can that last? When a hard pressed news editor has to choose between sending his one available reporter to a four hour meeting or keeping him/her in the office to cut and paste a dozen press releases there will only be one outcome.

So what, say the experts? That is the future. That's all well and good, but if all people will be offered by way of local news coverage is a diet of light, entertainment-based items and sanitised press releases, then society will be the worse for it. Whether the public will be prepared to sit twiddling their thumbs through a 30 second advertising video while waiting to click on to the news item they really want to see on their screen remains to be seen. What they won't find is their neighbour who has appeared in court that week or the actions and decisions of local councilors being scrutinised.

In the next chapter I reveal how in 2004/5 the then daily *Torquay Herald Express* played a major part in joining me in a campaign which exposed councillors who put up their own allowances by 62% in six months and hoped to get away with it. Without the help of the paper and its readers they would have done. How would anyone have known what was going on in the Town Hall? How could an effective campaign have been mounted over many months?

The first newspapers to undergo major change when the recession really bit from 2010 were smaller evening papers in Torquay, Exeter, Scarborough, Northampton, Peterborough, Halifax, Bath, Scunthorpe and Lincoln. They became weeklies while in Reading the long standing evening paper went to bi-weekly publication and has since closed all together when that experiment flopped. In one week alone in November 2014 Trinity Mirror closed seven weekly papers; more are expected to follow. Local newspapers are not yet dead but they are being killed by remote and irresponsible owners who care nothing for them but as a source of ready cash.

Some people claim that young people are not reading newspapers and do not want print. They claim older readers are being lost due to life's attrition. Young people have never bought newspapers and aren't we all living longer in any case? According to Neil Fowler: '*The reality is that newspaper titles have changed hands from the old family owners who saw them as a prestigious place in the local community to a small band of corporate giants totally divorced from the consumers they are trying to reach.*'

Local newspapers have been consistently starved of investment by the new breed of owners who took over in the 1990s. So long as the advertisers kept on coming back and the money still came rolling in they were happy to demand higher and higher profit margins. When things got tougher and real management was needed, they had no answers.

One of the biggest mistakes many of them made - and still do - was their decision to put all the news from their titles on the web without charging for it. They would not listen when they were told this could be suicidal. Why should anyone buy their weekly paper on a Thursday or Friday when they can get enough of it free on an on-going daily basis? We now have a generation that was given free news and won't pay for it. The hope was that advertising revenues would follow. They haven't. There is a lot of smoke and mirrors when companies report their revenues from digital – most talk in percentages; a 5% increase is not much if you are basing it on £10.

At the same time the role of Editor has been diminished. Today's regional Editors spend more time in management, marketing and other meetings than they do dictating the news agenda. Some of them have had to become experts in organising and hosting sponsored awards evenings for the tourism, food and other industries in order to replace falling circulation revenues. Others have had to tell their staffs they are expected to sell advertising as well as report the news. I have no idea how they cope with the new management speak. They sit in meetings while people who have never written a story or sold an advert talk about *'integrated content creation'* and *'ad-flighting systems'*. I suppose when these people talk about *'complete content and sales models'* they mean old fashioned newspapers full of good stories and local advertising. Who knows? And if an Editor dares challenge what is being said they are quickly shown the door and replaced by someone called a cheaper Content Editor who reports to a Group Editor looking after anything up to seven titles. It remains to be seen as to who goes to prison if the paper upsets a judge!

Despite all this there are many committed journalists still working on local newspapers and some excellent trainee reporters who battle their way through university and are prepared to accept the low pay on offer to get a foothold in the industry. I don't know how much longer the brightest and best will put up with the financial and other pressures. Many graduates spend two or three years on a local paper before moving into public relations, television, radio or working for a digital company. They have to move on if they want to buy a reasonable car or get a mortgage. They work hard on a variety of platforms, but what many of them do not do is bring in stories from local contacts. To get any job most have to move away from their home town, often hundreds of miles. They never get to know their new patch very well and have no real empathy with their readers.

Most move on before they make any relevant contacts with the public or get involved with the communities they serve. I realise I moved around, but I did do an initial three and a half years on my home town newspaper where I gained a thorough understanding of a reporter's role. It was problems at home that drove me away.

Because of the education system and the cost it places on youngsters today too many of those who do find jobs are from middle to upper class backgrounds, so local newspapers rarely employ the estate kid, the bright youngster from a poor home or the local lad. And with it they have lost local knowledge and the contacts reporters used to have from being brought up in an area where they lived, went to school, shopped, played football, went to church and had family. Inevitably such reporters do not know local history and sometimes how to spell local names. They don't know the difference between Brixton and Brixham. They make silly mistakes which are easily spotted by readers. They forget the Mayor is Jon Browne, not John Brown, or Stephen is spelt with a 'v'.

The pressure to produce as much copy as possible in any given day forces them to cut and paste unchallenged emailed press releases supplied in ever increasing numbers by the public relations industry. If you want to get a story into some regional weekly newspapers do a survey on any subject under the sun and send them a press release. I wonder how many of these surveys are actually undertaken?

In 2013 the National Council for the Training of Journalists tried to reverse this trend by pioneering old fashioned apprenticeships similar to my own in 1965. A few companies have joined in, but not enough. Managements are not interested. Editors know it is a waste of time fighting for them if they want to keep their own job.

I watched with great interest the debate about journalistic ethics which came to the fore in 2011. Unlike some of my newspaper colleagues, I didn't wear rose-tinted glasses and automatically assume that everything in the newspaper garden was rosy. In fact, I knew there was a lot of manure on the flowers. Regional newspaper reporters have always found their job more difficult when a big story breaks on their patch and national newspaper hacks throw their company's money around. Just ask local reporters in Gloucestershire about some of the problems they faced when reporting on the murders committed by Fred and Rosemary West in 1992. Neighbours held out their hands asking for payment before answering even the most simple of questions. Dog has always eaten dog in the newspaper industry with the red tops in particular employing 'heavies' to guard anyone whose story they have bought up. The poor local reporter has often been frozen out.

Occasionally, as the *Derby Telegraph* showed in 2013, with its coverage of the trial of Mick Philpott, his wife Mairead and a friend who killed six of the Philpott children in a botched arson attempt, a local paper can do a far better job than the nationals without flashing a cheque book. '*Shameless Mick*', as the paper dubbed Philpott seven years earlier, was well known to the *Telegraph*'s news room. Editor Neil White and his Managing Director Steve Hall, a former Editor, put massive resources into their coverage of the Philpott trial and its aftermath. It was local journalism at its very best. The paper still had enough reader loyalty to deliver in-depth insights and information which would have been the norm 30 years ago, but are not necessarily the case today.

When he had time to recover from masterminding what was a mammoth news room effort, Neil said: *'The paper produced 29 pages about the case – including background information – gleaned from months of interviewing those close to it.*

'For six weeks the Telegraph had at least one reporter, sometimes two, in court. It was the first time the paper had covered a trial online and in print simultaneously. Reporters in the court room sent at least 20 texts a day, which were used to update and re-headline the live story. The time of each new line was displayed throughout the article, with the latest at the top. Not a moment of courtroom action was missed as there was a two-reporter relay system in place.

'For optimum search engine optimisation each story also featured a large number of related articles links. On Twitter reporters used #philpott and #philpottstrial to tweet out each new line. The paper splashed on the Philpotts most days of the trial with between three and five pages of copy in each edition.

'Thus, organisation was paramount. One double page spread was filed during the lunch interval and another at the end of the day. The need for excellent fast shorthand was obvious. This was the most

important trial in Derby's recent history and the eyes of the world were on the Telegraph and its website.

'Equally, ethics were a consideration. On occasions salacious side-line information was presented during the trial but we made decisions not to include it. One of the reasons was that it could have sullied the reputations of those innocent parties whose names were mentioned in connection with unsubstantiated claims over sexual and physical abuse.

'The Philpott case was one of the toughest and most rewarding of my career. After its conclusion I was delighted that our coverage received praise from within Derby and outside for its thoroughness and its avoidance of sensationalism. It demonstrated the importance of all of the basic journalistic skills – accuracy, spotting the best line in a story, shorthand, time management and ethics.'

The same could not be said a year later when the Rotherham child sex abuse scandal broke. The local paper hardly knew what was going on under its nose until a national newspaper reporter investigated. I don't blame the *Rotherham Advertiser's* Editor, Andrew Mosley, who does his best with limited resources, but it took a national newspaper reporter with the time to investigate to reveal all the sordid details.

When Andrew came under fire he hit back and said: *'First of all, we didn't miss the 'Rotherham child sexual exploitation' story. It wasn't something we didn't spot on a council agenda or that was discussed in a meeting that we couldn't attend due to lack of staff. I do not know, but would surmise, that the reporter was provided with the information that led to his initial story by someone with inside knowledge who wanted to create a national splash – and it worked.'*
Fair enough, but it did expose the *Advertiser's* lack of local contacts. I would have hoped somebody would have tipped off the local paper!

I am not alone in questioning how much local papers can hold authorities and individuals to account when they are running on half the staff numbers they had only a few years ago, and to some extent are dependant financially and materially upon them. Has investigative journalism been abandoned in favour of the story count and the need to fill a set space as quickly as possible? I understand the reporter who broke the Rotherham story, Andrew Norfolk, learned his craft on the *Scarborough News* back in the days when reporters were given the time to investigate and challenge what they saw and heard. I wonder how many such reporters we will have in the future who will have what are loosely called 'old school skills'? They will need the backing of whatever media organisation they work for. Unfortunately, too many newspaper managements do not know what I am talking about. Few care; even fewer have any long term commitment towards the sort of stories readers want and would be prepared to pay to read.

New Statesman reporter Kevin Meagher commenting on newspaper coverage of the Rotherham story said: '*Local papers – certainly all the ones I've ever come across – simply lack the resources to pursue investigations of this type and break stories like Rotherham or Mid-Staffs Hospital. It's a question of having the time money and expertise to do so. That's why I'm arguing for a local scrutiny levy on public bodies to pay for accredited and ring-fenced public interest journalism so that they will be able to do so in the future.*' Nice thought, but I can't see the idea getting off the ground.

One comment posted on Holdthefrontpage at the time made me smile because it hit the right mark. The anonymous writer said: '*Have you been inside a local weekly newspaper office lately? (assuming the paper still has an office). Do you have any idea how few editorial staff are left? And how much mundane rubbish the remaining handful are forced to plough through before they can even think of tackling a proper story such as child sex grooming? The only way a typical local newspaper reporter can hope to uncover a story of this magnitude is if they do it in their own spare time, spending many hours during their evenings, weekends and annual leave working for no money. I can imagine the bean counters in charge of our industry would love that. They'd soon start insisting that all reporters work even more hours for nothing.*'

The final word on this subject goes to one senior reporter who wrote: '*If I get to Friday without anybody yelling at me or complaining to the Editor or making a legal threat, then I have failed to do my job properly - which is to stick a rod up the backside of those in charge when they are short changing the public, my readers.*' Good for him and good luck the first time he writes a story critical of a key advertiser or someone who has sponsored an awards evening!

Television has fostered the impression, which some members of the public now believe, that ALL reporters have cheque books they can flash when seeking information. A few years ago I watched in amazement as a fictitious reporter on a small Yorkshire weekly paper offered to pay someone in an episode of Emmerdale. Coronation Street and Eastenders are just as bad. Local newspaper reporters and photographers are always portrayed as nasty people whenever they crop up in a television soap or drama. The problem is that around 20 million people a week watch these programmes and too many of them believe what they see. I can imagine viewers cheering as the local reporter is either done in, beaten up or turns out to be the murderer!

It has been a fact of life for the whole of my journalistic career that policemen, government officials and others have been taking back-handers from London-based reporters. We knew it was going on behind our backs, but there was nothing we felt we could do about it. I don't think for one minute the practice will stop. I have some sympathy with a national newspaper reporter recently on trial for paying a government official who said he did not realise it was a criminal offence.

When I started my journalistic career the Press Council was the guardian of journalistic ethics followed by the Press Complaints Commission in the 1990s after newspapers were warned by one government minister they were '*drinking in the last chance saloon.*' In their lifetime both the Council and the Commission produced codes which were highly laudable, but neither had any real power to enforce their rulings which amounted to no more than a slap on the wrist. Most regional newspaper Editors tried to make the codes work and took them seriously. However, the national newspaper and press agency reporters I spoke to over the years were quite cynical about them. The general attitude was one of: *'So what if we have to correct a story and print an unfavorable adjudication months later in small type at the back of the paper as long as the original story sold more papers at the time.'*

It is too early for me to comment on whether the new Independent Press Standards Organisation (IPSO) will make any difference or have any more clout than its predecessors. Young reporters are given far more training nowadays about ethical issues, but the bottom line is that Editors will continue to make case-by-case judgements based on their own experiences and attitudes to the job.

On my training courses I show trainees the following correction published in the *Sun*: '*In an article published under the headline* **'Gollum joker killed in live rail horror'** *we incorrectly stated that Julian Brooker, 23, of Brighton, was blown into the air after accidently touching a live rail line. His parents have asked us to make clear he was not turned into a fireball, was not obsessed with the number 23 and didn't go drinking on that date every month. Julian's mother did not say during or after the inquest her son often got on all fours creeping round their house pretending to be Gollum. Also quotes from a witness at the inquest should have been attributed to Gemma Cousins, not Eva Natasha. We apologise for the stress this has caused Julian's family and friends*' This correction filled seven centimeters of space on an obscure page. The original story filled nearly a page early in the paper.

No wonder the people who have been the subject of such inaccurate national newspaper stories, like Madeleine McCann's parents and Christopher Jeffries, are among the most vociferous in calling for strict government regulation of the media. But I hope they don't forget most, if not all, local newspaper reporters and their Editors don't behave that badly and they print any corrections prominently.

The problem is that everyone in the media is tarred with the same brush. The hard-working local newspaper reporter or photographer is regarded with the same contempt as the press agency reporter who is out to sell his story for the best possible price – and often doesn't let the facts get in the way. Post the Leveson inquiry life has become much tougher for good journalists seeking to expose corruption, criminal activities and general wrong-doing, particularly by those in authority. I wonder whether the MPs' allowances scandal would be exposed today?

I am not a fan of the *Daily Mail* but in an editorial in December 2014 they said: '*Unwarranted state power flourishes where there is too little restraint on it. The weakening of the free press by the Leveson investigation has encouraged the police to behave in ways they would never have dreamt of before. Not content with employing anti-terror laws to search through journalists' phone records, they are using anti-stalker legislation to interfere with legitimate reporting. If these power-grabs succeed, we will all suffer as our society becomes less open, and scandals go unrevealed and uncorrected. The public and politicians alike should recall that newspapers, for all their faults, are one of the pillars of our liberty.*"

I could not agree more, but I am reminded we were warned what might happen if we didn't rein in the way a few – and I stress it was a few - reporters were behaving. Today's reporters, both locally and nationally, are paying the price for past behaviour which infuriated the public and has allowed politicians and others to make life far more difficult than it should be. I do not believe society is the better for it.

CHAPTER ELEVEN

LIBERAL WITH PUBLIC MONEY

A member of Parliament to Disraeli: "Sir, you will either die on the gallows or of some unspeakable disease." "That depends, sir," said Disraeli, "whether I embrace your policies or your mistress."

When I moved to Torquay I did not get involved with the local Liberal Democrats for several years. My Deputy Editor on the *Weekender*, Nick Pannell, was very active and produced most of their election literature. He became deputy leader of Torbay Council when the Lib Dems won power for the first time in the early 1990s. With a few exceptions I did not enjoy the company of the party members I met and in particular the constituency's agent, Ruth Pentney. She was not someone who encouraged me to give up my limited spare time to help the party. I was busy enough with my work and family and privately I was beginning to have my first doubts about the mess the Lib Dems might make of the country if they ever won power, given many of the barmy ideas they were now promoting and their openly hostile anti-Christian views expressed by some of the local party's senior members.

I watched from the sidelines with growing dismay at the way they behaved in meetings or at social events. It was their arrogance which held me back from getting too involved, particularly that of their councillors. Their failure to listen to either the public at large or the foot soldiers who had worked hard to get them elected did not impress me. When the party won control of Torbay Council I did not see much in common with the old Liberal Party I had supported since 1964. With the benefit of hindsight, I now believe everything changed when my old party amalgamated with the Social Democratic Party after the 1987 General Election. The two parties forged an alliance at the 1983 and 1987 General Elections – sharing the seats between them on a common programme. It didn't work.

At the 1992 General Election Torbay's Lib Dem candidate Adrian Sanders reduced the sitting Tory MP Rupert Allason's majority to 5,500, which some pundits said made Torbay a marginal seat. Up until then it was known as Tory-bay with guaranteed big five figure majorities for anyone wearing a blue rosette. The Tories didn't have to work too hard to get their man elected.

Despite several warning signs they were complacent during the 1990s and did not take note of how the demographics of the constituency were rapidly changing. Behind the sea front and the picture postcard views of Cockington and Ilsham Marine Drive there were large areas of depravation and a working population more and more dependent on a declining tourism industry. Many bread-winners could only find low paid work at local hotels and restaurants. Later, worse was to come with the collapse of the Bay's largest private employer, Nortel, in 2005. It was a massive blow to the local economy; more than five thousand well-paid jobs disappeared. This left the only reasonably paid jobs in the hands of a few private firms and public sector staff at the hospital, college and council.

At the 1997 General Election I helped with some canvassing and leaflet delivery. Nationally the Tories were well and truly thumped by a resurgent Labour Party under Tony Blair and an electorate fed up with poor economic management, rows over Europe and sleaze. Local boy Adrian beat Rupert Allason by just 12 votes after two recounts to make Torbay the most marginal parliamentary seat in the country. On election day I was working in Tunbridge Wells. I propped myself up in my hotel bed until 2am to hear the result and couldn't resist a yell of delight when the returning officer declared Adrian the winner. I hope I didn't wake up anyone!

I had high hopes of Adrian in those days, but these were to be dashed later. He worked hard on local issues but, in my opinion, he would have made a better leader of the council. The national party never saw fit to give him a front bench job, even when he became one of their longest-serving MPs. Perhaps he never sought one? He seemed happy enough working in the constituency and building up a personal vote, but I wonder if Torbay would have benefited from someone punching more weight at Westminster? His biggest achievement, and one I would not belittle, has been in helping – along with others - to get the money for a long-awaited bypass to relieve traffic congestion through Kingskerswell; a notorious local traffic bottleneck, particularly so during the summer and on Bank Holidays. It is due to open at the end of 2015.

It was obvious that after winning the seat with such a slender majority Adrian would have a tough task retaining it when he came up for re-election in 2001 or 2002. Although the Tories had been in disarray for several years prior to their 1997 defeat, it was expected they would win back some of their lost seats the next time round. Torbay was their number one target. Unfortunately for them, they selected a weak local candidate in an effort to negate what they perceived as Adrian's local boy advantage. I am sure they thought all they had to do was turn up on the day and they would win. What were 12 votes after their 1997 nadir?

To make things that bit more difficult for Adrian he had well documented problems with some of his councillors which received extensive coverage in the two local papers, the *Herald Express* and *Western Morning News*. Between 1997 and 2000 he watched with dismay as they committed a series of public relations gaffes. Public opinion counted for nothing - they appeared hell bent on undoing all the good work Adrian was engaged in at a purely local level. Typical of the small but silly decisions councillors made during this period was one to cutback spending on the beautiful flower beds along the sea front. They could not understand the outcry when the neglected beds looked a mess during successive summers. You tampered with the flower beds in Torbay at your peril!

The Lib Dems in control of the Town Hall lurched from one crisis to another and looked totally out of their depth in trying to run a unitary authority. Two councillors resigned in disgrace – one of them making it onto the front pages of the Sunday tabloids. Not surprisingly, in May 2000, the party lost control of the council; all but four councillors were rightly turfed out for incompetence. Most of them were shocked; I was surprised they were surprised. They deserved the hammering they took. I hoped it would knock some of that openly displayed arrogance out of them. It proved a vain hope! For the first time in my life I refused to help with an election campaign when asked. I had no wish to support people I did not approve of or agree with. The Tories were cock-a-hoop. They won 32 of the 36 seats. They felt the Parliamentary seat was theirs for the taking next time. Lib Dem morale could not have been any lower.

It looked odds-on that Adrian would lose his seat at the next General Election. He telephoned me a few weeks after the council election debacle to seek my advice. We agreed to meet and have a chat about what could be done over coffee at the Grand Hotel. I was surprised when he asked if I would become chairman of his re-election committee and help get the local party into some sort of shape. To make matters worse I discovered there was no money to fight the election and apparently none would be forthcoming from the national party, which already appeared to have written off Adrian's chances of being re-elected. There was even more bad news - a £4,000 debt still had to be paid off from the 1997 election! It was not the time to be thinking of penny pots and jumble sales.

I could easily have turned down the role because I was busy with a number of newspaper projects in different parts of the UK. I was also under no illusion about how difficult a task it was going to be, made even more awkward by Ruth Pentney's immediate hostility to my appointment, which in effect limited some of her power. Two days after I agreed to accept the unpaid chairman's role she dropped a bitter note through my letterbox which was full of resentment about my involvement. I wrote back and reminded her I was a volunteer while she got paid for what she did. After that we just about tolerated each other for the greater good, but I knew she would be delighted if I proved incapable of fulfilling the role Adrian had given me.

I extracted one promise from Adrian which, to his credit, he kept: I was allowed to run things my way and when Mrs Pentney inevitably complained to him he told her to grin and bear it - something that was easier said than done. The first thing I did was sit down and write a 12 month battle plan – a blueprint for victory. Once Adrian gave it his approval I set to work with Roger Stringer, the treasurer, to pay off all debts and raise enough money to fight a credible election campaign. We were fortunate the national party held their 2001 Spring Conference at Torbay's Riviera Centre which allowed Roger and I to run a couple of fund raising events. I had no time for suggestions that we should try and raise a few pounds through a tombola stall offering bottles of cheap wine or ketchup. Instead we sold raffle tickets at £1 a time and offered cash prizes totalling half of what we raised. That way we were guaranteed a healthy profit. It raised nearly £1,000 for not a lot of effort.

It was during this conference that I nearly hit the headlines for all the wrong reasons. I was trusted with the job of getting former Lib Dem leader Paddy Ashdown and his wife to a local restaurant one evening. The weather was awful - driving rain making visibility difficult. When I came to a tricky six-way junction I went straight ahead down a two lane road which was one way only – failing to see the no entry signs. Fortunately, one car managed to avoid me and I took the first turning I could onto a side street. Mr Ashdown was unfazed.

I worked hard to build an election fighting team which knew what was expected of it. I spent many hours interviewing and selecting key people who were assigned leadership roles in specialist areas eg postal votes, canvassing, leaflets, sign board making. I did not choose anyone I felt was less than 100% committed to their role. I did not have time to mess around. If anyone expressed reservations about how much time they could give, I thanked them but said I would find them another less exacting job. I did not want leaders in key positions I could not trust. When the time came for the team to be tested it performed very well.

I convinced Adrian his primary role once the campaign began should be to knock on as many doors as possible each day rather than spend time with the national media, who I knew would descend on Torbay once the election was called.

After a month's delay because of an outbreak of foot and mouth disease, Prime Minister Tony Blair announced the election would be on June 7. I was right about the national media's interest in the Torbay result. For three weeks they camped out all over the place. Newspaper and television reporters wanted to conduct time-consuming interviews or accompany Adrian on the doorstep. I said 'no' to every request. I knew that with a majority of 12 every vote would count and that Adrian needed to 'press the flesh' at every possible opportunity without time-wasting cameramen and reporters getting in the way.

Anthony Howard writing in the *Times* on April 10 said: '*I think the Liberal Democrats are in for a distinctly sticky election. They will be lucky to hold on to the seats they gained last time and that is particularly true in the Westcountry. It would be a miracle, for example, if Torbay did not revert to the Tories in eight weeks' time.*' So much for London-based experts!

I had a couple of rows with the big media boys from London when I refused to inform them where Adrian was canvassing. They tried to bully me, threatening all sorts of retribution. One even got physical and prodded me in the chest. I prodded him back, but a bit harder. When he looked me in the eye he knew I wasn't kidding. It made me even more determined to tell them where to stick their newspapers! However, when it came to the *Herald Express* I made sure things were different; they had daily contact with Adrian, but, again, not on the doorstep.

The Tories saw things differently and wasted their time conducting a vast number of interviews with all and sundry. I followed their candidate and his team manager one day and was delighted with how little hard graft they were prepared to put in on the doorstep. I never lost faith in my belief Adrian would win.

I knew my way of doing things and the management systems I introduced were on the line because during the campaign I bullied, cajoled and encouraged in equal measure to get people to work hard and do what they said they would do. The slow pace of getting anything done in Torbay was frustrating at times, as was the fact some people would not do what they agreed to do, and saw nothing wrong in not delivering their weekly batch of leaflets. I had to be right behind them every day to make sure they did the tasks I set them or they would have delivered them a week after the election. All's well that ends well though. My methods were totally vindicated when Adrian won with a 6,700 majority.

I didn't go to the count at Torquay's Riviera Centre – I was too tired. I preferred to go home, shower and have a couple of hours in front of the television watching other results come in. After the

Torbay result was declared soon after 1am everyone came back to our house to celebrate and watch the rest of what by now were early morning results. Valerie laid on lots of food and there was plenty for everyone to drink. Typically, nobody thought to thank her either on the day or later. I felt it was time for me to bow out. I had done the job Adrian asked me to do. And that might have been a happier end to the story, but a few months later in recognition of my efforts I was elected the Torbay party's President. It was a decision they soon came to regret. In order to tell what happened next I need to go back a few years.

In 1997 Torbay, which takes in the three towns of Torquay, Paignton and Brixham, became a unitary council which meant it was self sufficient and not part of Devon County Council. Only Plymouth in the south west had the same status. It was one of the smallest unitary authorities in the country and at the time many people feared it would struggle to provide an adequate quality of services. They were right. The main problem was the lack of business and management experience of nearly all councillors from both parties and the appointment of numerous senior officers on big salaries who were also not up to the job.

A council can manage if it has good councillors and poor officers, or weak councillors and good officers, but in Torbay it had **both** weak/poor councillors and officers - a fatal combination made worse by a mistaken belief in their own abilities. When the going got tough and none of them knew what to do they employed outside consultants to make decisions costing millions of pounds of council taxpayers' money. This Town Hall 'establishment' then proceeded to treat anyone outside its inner circle with contempt and often insults. If anyone showed the slightest sign of getting close to revealing their incompetence councillors and officers closed ranks in a 'you scratch my back, I will scratch yours' way of dealing with any problem or complaint. Successive surveys revealed that during the years 1999 to 2005 Torbay Council had one of the lowest residents' satisfaction ratings of any council in the country.

The May 2000 council elections swept the Conservatives into power. Unfortunately, they were just as incompetent as the previous lot of Lib Dems and they in turn were swept from power in 2003 in a reverse landslide The figures show how public opinion swung back and forth: May 2000 the Conservatives won 32 seats and the Lib Dems 4; May 2003 the Conservatives won 9 seats and the Lib Dems 27. It wasn't rocket science to see things had to change if the council was to regain a modicum of public approval.

When the Lib Dems won back control my hopes that it would be different this time were dashed within a few weeks. It didn't take a majority of Lib Dem councillors long to show they had not learned any lessons from their 2000 debacle. Their leader, Chris Harris, was the most arrogant, rude, thick-skinned man I have ever met. Once again public opinion appeared to count for nothing; one councillor even had the brass neck to tell me: *'We have four years before we face another election so we can do what we want.'*

Disillusionment across all sections of the Torbay community set in within a few months and intensified in November 2003 when councillors voted themselves a second big increase in their personal allowances in six months. This amounted to a 63% rise in the overall allowances bill at a time when the council was facing severe financial problems. It was legal, but the public were horrified.

Of course there had been no mention of this in any election literature and hence no public mandate for what I thought was an old fashioned money grab. I didn't go along with the argument that councillors were under-valued and deserved some financial recompense for the hours they put in. When the government stepped in and capped the council's spending to keep that year's council tax increase in single figures, the councillors were adamant about keeping their increase. Cuts would have to be made elsewhere. It was morally indefensible and politically suicidal.

As President of the local party I was the voice of the membership; I represented the foot soldiers who did most of the work outside the council chamber. There was widespread outrage about what the councillors had done to line their own pockets with page after page of angry letters in the *Herald Express*. It wasn't just the political damage they were causing but, for me, the moral anger I felt. I could not help thinking back to the Mayoral trip to Malden in 1979 when I paid my own air fares because I did not want the cost to fall on council taxpayers.

In November Adrian and I along with the constituency chairman and secretary tried to appeal to their sense of what was right and wrong and force a re-think. To their credit a small minority of councillors knew the increase in allowances was indefensible and a few refused to take the extra money. But the majority refused to listen to any pleas to limit any increase to the rate of inflation. They weren't in the mood to do a u-turn after benefiting from allowances which in several cases were now worth more than £20,000 a year.

The *Herald Express* and its then editor Brendan Hanrahan knew this was a story which would run and run. Its reporters did a good job of unearthing other mad Lib Dem decisions which upset the public. The row rumbled on into February 2004 with the councillors digging in their heels and becoming more and more haughty.

It split the local party with the councillors and their spouses on one side and the rest of the membership on the other. In a last desperate attempt to show the councillors they had little public support even within their own party a Lib Dem members' meeting was held at Oldway Mansion in Paignton at which the membership voted overwhelmingly to order the councillors to return the extra money they had grabbed. It made no difference - they still refused. Worse than that they told some of the people who had helped get them elected there was nothing they could do about it.

At this point the national party moved in, worried about all the adverse publicity - which by now was being featured on television - and its possible effect on the party's standing in the south west. It was agreed by all sides that North Devon MP Nick Harvey and a senior party official would arbitrate between the councillors on the one side and the Lib Dem membership on the other one Sunday afternoon in a room at the Belgrave Hotel in Torquay. The understanding was that their decision would be binding on both sides.

Adrian, myself and local party officers met for many hours on three successive days to prepare what I and a councillor who did not agree with the allowances increase would say on behalf of the members. Opposing us were the leader and deputy leader of the council. In the meantime Valerie and Robin flew to Boston to have a long planned skiing holiday with Don and Gail MacCuish and family. I was at home on my own which meant I had the time to devote to arguing the strongest possible case as to why the councillors should return most of the money they had awarded themselves.

Nick Harvey listened to what I and my councillor colleague had to say and then asked us to adjourn while he heard the councillors' case. Two hours later he called us back into the room to say he had told the councillors they should give back EVERY penny they had voted themselves since the previous June. It was unambiguous and decisive. I thought we had won.

I went back to party HQ in the centre of Torquay to tell Adrian and the constituency's officers who had gathered there what had been agreed. The council leader and his deputy went away to brief their own meeting of councillors at the hospital's social club. From there they telephoned to say they were not prepared to do what Nick Harvey proposed; there was no way they would settle on his terms. If ever there was a moment when I knew that I was dealing with people I intensely disliked, this was it. It seemed their idea of arbitration was that they would go along with it as long as the end result was totally in their favour. When it wasn't, they threw their toys out of the pram.

They were still determined to take as much money as they could get, but came up with what they thought was a generous offer: they would give back a bit of their rise to appease the Lib Dem membership and the public - a 42% rather than a 63% increase in the bill council taxpayers were expected to stomach. I am sure they thought this was very magnanimous of them.

To my amazement Adrian and the Totnes parliamentary candidate thought this was the best deal we were going to get, and most of the others agreed. They said it was time for a united face if there was not to be fatal political damage. I was furious, the more so when I realised I had just wasted an entire Sunday on a futile exercise.

People tell me that I soon calm down when I blow up and rant and rave, but that I am 'dangerous' when in a cold fury. I was the latter and more. To make matters worse I sat and listened for a few minutes as they not only caved into the councillors' offer - despite Nick Harvey's decision – but some of them talked about how they would spin this to the local press in such a way as to make out the

184

councillors had listened and were now bowing to public pressure. What rot! By now it was 9pm and I had not eaten since lunch-time. I stood up, gathered my papers and said that if they put out such a public statement I would resign and go public with what I knew. At this point Ruth Pentney made a fatal mistake - she laughed; a rare enough event in my presence and one I made her regret in the coming months.

Adrian took me on one side and said that compromise was what politics was all about. I knew he wasn't happy, but I told him it was not my idea of the way politicians should behave. I was bitterly disappointed with him that night. If he had refused to go along with what the councillors proposed I believe he would have had the backing of the local membership, the constituency officers, the national party and the public. The others in that room looked to him for leadership. For the sake of what he perceived to be the unity of the party he gave up the fight.

I left them to it with a warning that I would go public if they did not change their minds and if they put out any statement which I believed to be untrue. It was the last time I saw most of them.

When I got home my mind was racing. I got myself a meal and unsuccessfully tried to watch some television. When I went to bed I could not sleep. At 2am I got up, put on my dressing gown, sat at my computer and put down in writing everything that had happened while it was fresh in my memory. I went back to bed at 6am by now more sad than angry. Sometimes putting everything down in writing is quite therapeutic.

Later in the day Adrian telephoned to try and get me to accept the compromise decision and fall into line. I told him I had no choice but to resign as President as they were all reneging on the Nick Harvey agreement. I also reminded him that I reserved the right to put my side of the story into the public domain if the party put out any press release with which I disagreed. Later, two other local party officers telephoned to say they were uneasy too, but were not going to resign.

I don't know whether they believed me or not, or whether they even cared, but Torbay Liberal Democrats then proceeded to send a press release to the local media which, to put it mildly, I felt was a disgrace. I don't believe Adrian had anything to do with it, but whoever cobbled it together made a huge mistake.

When Brendan Hanrahan made me aware of its contents I was back in cold fury mode. I told him it was political spin at its worst and a distortion of the truth. He gave me a whole page in the next day's paper to tell the full story of what had really happened the previous Sunday, including the Nick Harvey deal. I knew what I wrote was explosive – Brendan knew he had a scoop. In putting the record straight I was happy to leave it to the public to make up their minds.

I thought some councillors might target me for character assassination and challenge what I had written, but thankfully there was not one word they could disagree with. It is hard to refute the truth. The public, however, soon let their feelings be known; the *Herald Express's* letters pages were full of angry readers letting rip for many months after.

I was glad to be no longer associated with people I had no affinity with. Nevertheless, it felt like I had just taken part in a short but very acrimonious divorce.

With the money now firmly in their pockets some Lib Dem councillors continued to stick two fingers up at public opinion and pressed ahead with further unpopular policies including closing half the public toilets in all three towns just before the summer season, taking down the cross at the crematorium in order to be perceived as politically correct (it was later put back after other faiths said they had no objection), trying to push through a 17% council tax increase and increased car parking charges. This led to calls for change – but change to what?

There was no way Torbay could reverse its unitary authority status, yet the seven years since its implementation had been disastrous. The council suffered from what I described at the time as yo-yo politics with one lot getting in, making a mess of it, being kicked out and then returning four years later when the other lot made an equal or worse mess of things. I wasn't alone in feeling it couldn't go on if Torbay was not to fall further behind its neighbours. I could have said it was no longer my problem and done nothing. It was tempting to do just that - but I didn't.

Although I was very busy running training courses all over the UK and even the Falklands, I stepped back into the public limelight in early summer of 2004 when I decided to give the people of Torbay a chance to change the way the Bay was run - a choice they didn't know they had until then. I already knew about the Local Government Act 2000 because I had studied and then included it in my journalism training course in public affairs. It gave towns the possibility of having an Elected Mayor who could bring leadership and vision to the Town Hall. The big question was whether it would be suitable for Torbay? Could it herald the start of a new era?

It was a flagship policy of the then Labour government. Although there were already 11 Elected Mayors round the country, the idea had not taken off mainly because in most towns the establishment did not want to lose power to one man, nor did they want the public (rather than a few councillors) to have the right to elect the council leader.

My research was a time consuming exercise that would have defeated anyone unfamiliar with the workings of local government who was not prepared to devote many hours to the job. In addition to reading information sent by the Office of the Deputy Prime Minister (ODPM) and the New Local Government Network (NLGN) I trawled the internet for newspaper articles and other stories.

I was helped by the late Bob Brewis from Paignton who was also very angry with the way Torbay Council was being run. Bob was a Tory, but he was just as critical of his own party as he was of the Lib Dems. We met at his home, chatted over a pot of coffee and found we had a lot in common. Ironically, as it turned out, it was Adrian Sanders who told me about Bob.

All the time I was busy doing my homework Torbay Council and its leader Chris Harris were becoming more unpopular by the day. By June Bob and I decided to see what reaction we would get from Brendan Hanrahan and his senior staff. Brendan had already attacked the council with a devastating front page which included pictures of all 36 councillors under a one word headline - 'RESIGN' - and a series of extremely strong editorials. He gave immediate, enthusiastic support and said the *Herald Express* would back the first stage of any plan I came up with to force the council to hold a Torbay-wide referendum. He did not go so far as to commit the paper to supporting the idea of an Elected Mayor, but he strongly believed it was time council taxpayers had a chance to have their say on the way Torbay was run.

In order to force a referendum on what I knew would be a reluctant group of councillors the Local Government Act stated I had to get 5,250 signatures - no easy task. But it was that meeting with Brendan which encouraged Bob and me to press ahead. In the middle of the month the referendum campaign began with page one coverage in the *Herald Express*.

Getting five per cent of the local electorate to sign a petition backing a referendum might not seem a lot at first glance. But it proved an exhausting job, mainly because the idea of an Elected Mayor was difficult for the majority of ordinary people to grasp, even though there was widespread disillusionment with the council and its councillors. Fortunately, I had done enough research to answer people's questions, but it often took five to ten minutes on each doorstep to get two signatures – even when people were in. One of the main points I made was that only a few councillors in a Town Hall room secretly appointed the all-powerful council leader, while an Elected Mayor would be democratically chosen by ordinary people at the ballot box. Other strong arguments included the need to have someone who was clearly accountable who would, hopefully, provide the quality leadership so obviously badly lacking.

The *Herald Express* printed a petition form every night for several weeks which brought in nearly a thousand signatures. The publicity the campaign generated soon attracted volunteers who came forward to collect signatures on forms I had printed and paid for out of my own pocket. One of them was JP John Kiddey, a former television investigative journalist, who provided sterling support and good advice. Each volunteer was given an instruction sheet I prepared plus information to carry with them to educate people about what having an Elected Mayor would mean for Torbay.

What really encouraged me from the outset was that the people who came forward to help were from all political parties and none and included the then UKIP Euro MP Graham Booth, several Lib Dems, the Conservative Parliamentary candidate Marcus Wood and a former Labour councillor – Vic Ellery. However, it did not take long before I suffered the first dirty tricks of the campaign with bogus telephone calls from people claiming they wanted to help gather signatures. When I arrived at the address they had given I discovered the occupants had not made any such call. It happened on at least a dozen occasions.

The more publicity the campaign attracted through my media contacts, the more questions there were to answer. I tried to educate myself and the public with calls to NGLN but they were rarely returned; the Labour government now back-tracking on its own policy after it proved unpopular with the party's council chiefs in the north of England, who feared losing their power bases.

Undeterred, I wrote and paid for a web site to be set up which enabled people to read about what we were trying to achieve. The web site had thousands of hits. Telephone calls I made to the ODPM were politely dealt with but not much real advice or help was forthcoming, particularly later in the campaign. Naively, at the outset, I thought that because the government wanted more Elected Mayors, and had previously encouraged campaigners elsewhere, that I would be able to call upon back-up advice at the very least. My hopes, and those of others who wrote to the ODPM over the next six months, were soon to be dashed. It was made very clear that we were on our own.

In order to find out how an Elected Mayor system of local governance worked on the ground and to call upon experiences so far I visited at my own expense the Mayors of Watford and Bedford, plus some of the people behind the Stoke Mayoral campaign and had a three hour meeting with Stuart Drummond, Elected Mayor of Hartlepool, when he came to Torbay. These meetings were worth the effort involved because they gave me a better understanding about what it would mean if the Torbay public opted for change in our referendum. I had a clear picture of what it would involve and began addressing local organisations on the benefits to be had.

By the autumn the campaign had attracted nearly 50 people from all shades of political opinion who were prepared to help in one way or another. In an area where partisan politics are generally the norm, it was quite an achievement to get people from the different political parties to work together and one which, given the animosity the local political parties felt towards each other – and still do - in Torbay, was unique. Not surprisingly, the Torbay Liberal Democrat party and its councillors were totally against any change in the status quo and were prepared to fight me. I was determined to stay one step ahead of them and started to address public meetings to further get the message across.

The Local Government Act 2000 gives petitioners 12 months to collect the required number of signatures from the date they first start. With the help of people like John Kiddey, Vic Ellery, Mark Dent and Tony Tostevin I reached the 5,200 mark in just under six months, but we had no way of checking whether they were valid or not. Voters' registers held at local libraries are not complete – people can have their details withheld and many choose to do so. To our amazement (and there is no way we could have known about this in advance) many people who pay their Council Tax choose not to go on the electoral register for a variety of reasons, including total disillusionment with politicians of all parties. When asked to sign my petition they reasoned that being Council Tax payers they had every right to sign anything about a council they were funding. They were wrong; for the petition to be valid only people on the register were acceptable.

Throughout the period when the petition was being gathered the Town Hall establishment attacked the Elected Mayor campaign as a 'distraction', even though it was local democracy at work. So much for the democratic part of the name Liberal Democrats! I received several nasty and one obscene telephone calls and some hate mail from writers who, of course, did not have the courage of their convictions to give their names.

Much of the information the opposition put into the public domain via newspapers, radio and leaflets was misinformed and ignorant of what an Elected Mayor could or could not do. The 'no' campaigners started off by claiming that an Elected Mayor would not have any real powers; it would be just another level of bureaucracy. They ended up by saying he or she would be a dictator with too many powers! They didn't do their homework, but what did that matter when the same story was peddled time and time again? It was the familiar tactic of throwing enough mud and hoping some of it would stick.

We handed in the petition to Torbay Council at the end of November 2004 with a few extra signatures in case anyone had signed twice. Three weeks later the council informed me that it did not meet the requirements of the Local Government Act 2000 and as such was invalid. The council engaged a top QC from London to advise them on the validity of all signatures. After taking his advice they decided to disqualify any signatures where people had signed twice (a valid reason), any signature where the writer had not included their full printed name in the box next to the signature ie they had written D.Scott instead of David Scott - even though the signature made it clear who the person was - and other signatures which they said they could not read or the writers were not on the electoral roll. This meant I was faced with finding another 1,800 valid signatures.

I informed the council I would not give up. Fortunately, I had a further six months to get new signatures. The council thought they had me on the run and tried to put the final boot in; probably hoping I would get the message that they held all the aces. I was told that even if I managed to obtain the Christian names of those who had only written their initials they would still declare such signatures invalid if I resubmitted them. They also refused to tell me why several hundred other signatures had not been accepted. Without such information I had no idea whose signature had been accepted and whose had not. I was fuming, but there was nothing I could do about it except to either call it a day or battle on. Giving in was never an option.

It made wonderful headlines for local newspapers, radio and television. Thankfully, there was a vehement public backlash. There is something wonderfully British about the way people react when they know the underdog is being roughly treated. Even thick-skinned Lib Dem councillors knew the way they were behaving was bringing them into further disrepute less than six months before a General Election. It must have made Adrian Sanders very nervous.

I had no way of knowing what was happening behind the scenes, but they finally realised they were only delaying the inevitable and the week before Christmas 2004 council leader Chris Harris announced that at the next full council meeting in March he would bow to public opinion and recommend the council call a referendum themselves without the need for me to gather any more signatures.

I wasn't bothered when the referendum would be held, but knew this was a cynical delaying tactic because the Liberal Democrats did not want a Torbay wide referendum before the May General Election. I didn't mind. It saved me tramping the streets in cold weather.

My team, the Brixham members of which were fighting at the same time for a referendum on whether that town should have a town council, decided to wait and see if the council would keep its word, although this meant we would have very little time between then and mid June if the council did another u-turn. On March 3 the council formally decided to hold both the Elected Mayor and Brixham Town Council referendums by postal ballot during the first two weeks of July. I had won round one, but fighting and winning the campaign was not going to be easy.

I formed a five strong campaign leadership team to organise volunteers. They worked hard over the next four months. The biggest problem was how to educate 130,000 people about the benefits of voting for an Elected Mayor? The councillors did some of the job for me by attracting more bad publicity, both locally and nationally, via another set of highly unpopular decisions including a £720,000 pay off for four officers made redundant.

Some of them were still totally out of touch with public opinion outside the Town Hall. Their arrogance towards anyone who dared question their authority damaged their credibility even more. They hoped blind party support and their financial clout coupled with their campaigning experience would see them to victory.

The Labour government were of no help at all during this time. There was no advice they could or were prepared to give me about how to counter the misinformation and lies propagated by the opposition. There was a concerted campaign to frighten people into voting 'no' on the grounds of the extra costs an Elected Mayor would incur. At one stage Chris Harris said Torbay's council taxpayers would have to find an extra £1 million a year if they voted 'yes'. It was an absurd figure which was never substantiated, but working on the old adage that if you say something often enough some people will believe it, I knew some damage was being done to the 'yes' campaign.

A few nervous councillors realised they ought to be more educated about what it would mean for them if I actually won. The first sign I had that they were becoming a little worried came when they spent a couple of thousand pounds of council taxpayers' money on a local government expert from De Montfort University in Leicester who ran a one day seminar in the Town Hall just for councillors and senior officers. I could have educated them for free!

An Elected Mayor at that time got a salary of around £57,000 plus expenses. I knew this would be seized upon by my opponents as a waste of money, particularly as I had campaigned for a reduction in councillors' allowances. Then I had a brainwave: how much was it costing Torbay for the role of ceremonial Mayor, the role I had undertaken in Maldon? Nobody had ever asked. I got John Kiddey to make a Freedom of Information Act request which forced the council to reveal the annual cost was a staggering £146,000 - and rising. It included a sizeable budget for entertaining, one full-time member of staff and two part-timers, one of whom did no more than accompany the Mayor and open doors. No wonder Lib Dem councillors were queuing up to do the job! I realised we could have a working Mayor rather than someone who attended dinners and fetes - and make a large saving in the process. I fed the story to the press to general public astonishment.

The referendum vote campaign took off in late May and early June. Lined up against me and determined to use everything within their power to produce a 'no' vote were all but five of the 36 Torbay councillors, the local Liberal Democrat and Labour parties, two MPs and the all-powerful Town Hall union Unison. The latter spent a considerable amount of money writing to nearly 5,000 of its members in Torbay urging them to vote against the proposal. This included all Town Hall staff, plus postal and hospital staff.

We also had problems with Torbay Council's then Chief Executive who wrote an article arguing against an Elected Mayor which filled a whole page of the *Herald Express*. So much for council officers being neutral! It surprised others who worked in local government, but we had no choice but to get on with the job of winning despite such opposition.

I appealed for the financial help I knew would be required and friends and supporters donated £1,600. This was only about a third of what was needed - the rest came from my own pocket. I was determined that we would not lose simply because of people's ignorance and wrote, produced and had printed a four page newspaper which I paid to have delivered to 46,000 of the 60,000 homes in Torbay. The other 14,000 copies were hand delivered by my team in the last two weeks of June. It was a mammoth task, some of it undertaken by elderly pensioners.

Public meetings were well attended. At several of these meetings hostile councillors turned up to take part in the question and answer sessions. At one meeting a councillor dropped his papers and eagled-eyed spectators discovered he had a briefing paper of awkward questions to ask me prepared by senior Town Hall officers. It severely embarrassed him and showed the forces at work against the 'yes' campaign. The local media were not slow to pick up on what was happening.

My main worry as the campaign reached its climax was that too many senior officials in the Town Hall were openly against an Elected Mayor, yet these same people were in charge of the postal ballot and the counting of votes. At first I was led to believe the Electoral Reform Society would count the votes, but this proved not to be the case. I was told it would be '*too expensive*'.

Nobody to this day has yet found out who ran and funded the Torbay 'no' campaign, for the simply reason the people behind it never made themselves known. It took a *Westcountry Television* programme and several investigative stories by the *Herald Express* to discover the campaign had a 'convenience' address in Paignton – an empty shop – the lease for which had been signed by two prominent Liberal Democrats. Enough said!

The Liberal Democrats claimed the 'no' campaign was being run by two people nobody had ever heard of, who never attended any meetings, or the eventual referendum count. At one stage the media were told these mystery men had business addresses in Torbay but actually came from Southend! I don't believe they ever existed. However, the opposition did produce its own leaflets and paid for an expensive full page advertisement in the *Herald Express* during the two week voting period. The fact the people behind the 'no' campaign never publicly revealed who they were added to the mystery and backfired on those concerned. Ruth Pentney (who else?) eventually revealed she was involved. At least she was honest enough to admit her involvement!

Voting took place over the first two weeks in July. Just prior to the ballot papers going out the council informed me that once voting envelopes came back they were going to open them on a daily basis to check ballot papers had been properly witnessed and they would also open the actual envelopes containing the votes '*to save time at the count*'. This set alarm bells ringing. What was to stop someone at the Town Hall getting rid of large numbers of '*yes*' votes? It would have been easy to see how the vote was going on a daily basis. I was assured this was normal practice with postal votes at local elections, but I did not believe it.

Coincidentally, the national media was full of stories about problems and possible fraudulent activities with postal votes at the recent General Election. I told the council I would somehow find £10,000, or whatever it cost, to go in front of a judge at Exeter and get a judicial review of their decision. Within 48 hours the council informed me they had changed their mind and the actual ballot papers would remain in their envelopes and thus secret.

The referendum count and result came on the evening of July 14 2005. I was nervous all day, unable to concentrate on any work or do anything meaningful. Would it be like the General Election count of February 1974? Or would it be even worse and just like the Maldon Council count the following year when I lost by one vote? It took nearly three hours to count the votes at Torquay's Riviera Centre in a setting just like General Election night. I thought we had lost at one stage. Valerie joined my team to watch the vote counting and had several nasty remarks thrown her way. I had son Timothy near me to cover my back - more than once he kept people away who he thought might threaten me. The atmosphere was hostile in some quarters.

195

The moment came when the returning officer called me forward to look at a few spoilt ballot papers and be shown the final result. As silence descended on the room, I still had no idea whether we had won or lost. Ruth Pentney stepped forward on behalf of the 'no' campaign. The council officer slipped a sheet of paper to me and I read the figures – victory for the 'yes' campaign by 18,074 votes to 14,682. It was a decisive majority in favour of an Elected Mayor and one nobody could quibble about.

After I had agreed with the figures I kept a straight face while the returning officer read out the result. It was one of the proudest moments of my life. There was also a two-one majority for a Brixham Town Council. There was an almighty roar from my supporters on one side of the hall and a sea of glum faces on the other, mostly Lib Dem councillors. The latter were as ungracious in defeat as I had expected them to be; I hate to think how vitriolic they would have been if they had beaten me.

I looked at them and remembered the laughs and taunts back in February the previous year when many of them had cravenly given in one night over the allowances row or grabbed as much money as they could.

It meant the end for council leader Chris Harris - he moved to London a few months later, although he refused to resign his council seat for 18 months. He came back by train to attend the occasional meeting so he could claim his full allowances; another shameful episode and so typical of the man. That was too much even for the Lib Dems. They had had enough of him. He quit the party and served out his final months on the council as an Independent.

Once the result was declared I was surrounded by well-wishers and the media. I gave my first interview to the *Herald Express/Western Morning News* in recognition of the support and coverage they had given me. Then it was the turn of television and radio to conduct interviews before Valerie and I left the hall soon after midnight with Trevor and Celia Bartlett to join a few friends at the Grand Hotel for a celebratory drink. As we left several councillors standing by the door made abusive comments. I told Valerie to simply walk past them - we had won! We had taken on and beaten the sitting MP, the Liberal Democrat and Labour party machines, the most powerful trade union in the Bay and the Town Hall establishment.

Another television interview followed the next day, after which exhaustion set in. I took great trouble not to gloat over the result, describing it as a victory for *'people power'* and *'the small man'*.

Within the Lib Dems the recriminations and rows continued for many months with accusations and counter accusations being bandied back and forth. They also had to pick up the bill for their leaflets and full page advertisement on behalf of the 'no' campaign. I was glad to be rid of them, yet I keenly felt the divorce. I had been an enthusiastic supporter for more than 40 years, ever since that Skipton Grammar School election. My head told me the party was not the one I had battled for through thick and thin in the 1960s and 70s, yet in my heart I wished things could have turned out differently.

The public sniping continued for some time after the referendum. I ignored most of it until I took legal action against one by now former Lib Dem councillor after he libelled me in the *Herald Express*. The paper printed an immediate apology, but the ex councillor made the fatal mistake of ignoring my letter, which asked for a private written apology and an undertaking he would not repeat the defamatory words. It angered me that he felt he could treat anyone with such disdain and had not learnt anything from previous events. I waited two weeks then contacted top libel lawyers in London. The four page letter they sent him on my behalf even frightened me! When he got it he went straight to the *Herald Express* to offer me a public apology in the next available edition – something I now demanded because of his failure to respond to what up to then I considered was a private matter. Of course, in apologising he also admitted his guilt. I wasn't after damages, but I did make him pay my £4,000 legal bill. He telephoned to say he could not afford it, but I knew that over the last few years he had received tens of thousands of pounds of public money in allowances. He paid up in instalments via my lawyer. After that there was no more sniping from any Lib Dem - at least in public.

In October Torbay's first Mayoral election was held and the Lib Dems lost that too. Ironically, the Lib Dem candidate was former *Weekender* Deputy Editor Nick Pannell. Conservative Nick Bye won but 59% of the votes were split between the 11 Independents who stood. It was a shame because I had hoped a new face outside the existing political parties would win. I am sure he or she would have if there had been only one Independent on the ballot paper because a majority were fed up with party politics in Torbay. True to my word throughout the referendum campaign, I rejected any suggestion that I would be a candidate to become Torbay's first Elected Mayor. Nobody was going to be able to say I did it for my own gain - unlike some others on Torbay Council at that time.

I was delighted when Nick brought vision and leadership to the job. Everyone knew who was in charge and who to blame if things went wrong. Critics said it was wrong to put so much power into one man's hands, but in the next six years Torbay began to recover from years of neglect, despite constant sniping and negative tactics from the Lib Dems, who never came to terms with their defeat. Nick impressed government ministers and encouraged badly needed private finance to invest in the area's infrastructure. As a result the Torbay of today has weathered the economic storms far better than most UK seaside resorts and attracts holidaymakers all year round.

An internal row within the local Conservative party in 2011 forced Nick to stand as an Independent and he narrowly lost his battle for re-election to a fellow Tory, with the Lib Dem candidate a poor third. Torbay's second Elected Mayor, who stated he would abolish the position given the chance, has not been as popular. It might well be that the area turns the clock back in a few years' time and does away with the post after another referendum. We will see! As the *Herald Express* succinctly put it: '*Only in Torbay could you elect someone for such an important job who did not believe in it!*'

In 2010 the Liberal Democrats entered into a coalition government with the Conservatives, but Adrian Sanders was not given any of the top jobs. I was not surprised. After 17 years in Parliament he seems to be a permanent fixture on the backbenches. I give him credit for being a hard working constituency MP, but cannot help thinking that he would be a good choice as Lib Dem candidate for Elected Mayor! When we meet up nowadays we always say '*hello*' and engage in friendly banter. We both know, however, that things could have been very different

CHAPTER TWELVE

FINDING GOD ALL MIGHTY

But the fruit of the Spirit is love, joy, peace, patience, kindness, goodness, faithfulness, gentleness and self-control – Galations 5 verses 22 and 23

I never felt I was part of a Christian family when I was young. My parents were not practising Christians, although they had me christened at an Anglican church in Thornton Cleveleys within three months of my birth in that dreadfully cold and snowy winter of 1947/48. Apart from a sad, short lived flirtation with the Christadelphians when my sister was dying of leukemia - in the vain hope that God would save her life - they never encouraged me to have any sort of faith. At the same time they didn't discourage it either.

The first person to have any sort of Christian influence on me was my paternal grandmother. She was in the Salvation Army and because we lived only 50 yards down the road when I was a baby she had the daunting job of singing me to sleep some days. Her favourites were 'Onward Christian Soldiers' and 'The Old Rugged Cross' with a mixture of other songs I presume the Salvation Army still sing from time to time. It was no easy task for her because I was under-fed, the result of my novice parents strictly sticking to a pre-Second World War manual which stipulated that babies should be fed at set times and not too often. I rebelled in the only way I knew and since then nobody has ever accused me of being quiet! Mercifully for the neighbours, my parents, my patient grandmother and my future health a doctor pointed out the folly of my feeding regime four months after my birth.

When we moved to Burnley we were packed off to Sunday School at a nearby Methodist Church, probably so mum and dad could have a two hour break from their four children. After we moved to Barnoldswick I joined the Boys' Brigade, but I cannot say that God touched me very much between the ages of 11 and 18. However, seeds were sown during that period and, if nothing else, I knew my way round the Bible and could sing a few hymns.

I have already related how on the first Sunday in each month Bible class was replaced by compulsory attendance at a church parade/service when we would parade round deserted streets in all weathers playing our bugles, banging our drums and waving our flags before filing into St Andrew's Methodist Church. I was a flag carrier because even at that age the two senior officers had discovered I had no musical talent. I learned how to do a slow march very well; several hundred adults in the congregation would stand and watch while I came up the aisle and handed the flag to the minister. All I can remember of the services is that his sermons were dreadfully dull but were worth putting up with because the Girls' Brigade paraded with us and they were fun.

Grammar school assemblies were dire and made no impression. Five mornings a week we stood for 15 minutes while we sang two hymns, listened to a Bible reading and did prayers at the end of which the headmaster announced who he wanted to see in his study straight afterwards to be caned. He managed the transition from preaching to whacking quite smoothly, but it didn't impress me. There was hardly a morning when some unfortunate was not publicly named and shamed and some days as many as half a dozen pupils were lined up for 'execution'. I managed to avoid the cane, but it wasn't because I prayed a lot.

I stayed with the Boys' Brigade for another year after starting working as a cub reporter during which time my parents tried everything they knew to save my sister's life, including attending church. When it didn't work, and Wendy died soon after her fourth birthday, my mother was very bitter towards God. My father, who had a deeper spiritual insight, was also angry but believed in a God. In his later years he occasionally talked about faith. My mother eventually relented and came to understand what had happened was not God's fault. But I don't think she ever truly understood why God had not saved her beautiful daughter.

And there my story might have ended but for another little girl - my own daughter, Georgina. For 20 years I rarely attended church except for weddings, funerals and the annual Remembrance Day service while I was a councillor and then Mayor of Maldon. I didn't think much about God while I was carving out a successful career as Editor of various regional weekly and daily papers.

When we moved to Barnt Green Georgina started school and befriended Julia Collins whose parents, Roger and Marilyn, attended the small Baptist church in the village. On Sundays they collected Georgina and took her to church with Julia. After a few months Valerie started going with Georgina and began to make friends with a variety of people.

The church didn't have a permanent minister and was run by a group of people from all walks of life. One Sunday I went along to see what it was like and found it totally different from what I expected. It was organised in a disorganised way and everyone was so friendly it soon disarmed me. There weren't any 'Bible bashers' as I used to call them. What I found was a group of likeable people who were good company. Soon I was playing golf with some of them, putting away the chairs after the services and eating quiche at the many social events which always involved lots of food.

By now Valerie was way ahead of me in finding God, but I tagged along, did what I could when it was required and began to realise there was a bit more to life than the materialistic world I had always sought.

In hindsight I now realise it was the sometimes chaotic but friendly way things were run on a Sunday morning which attracted me. I was Managing Director of a newspaper in Britain's second largest city - there was no way I wanted to be part of a stiff-necked church service on a Sunday morning after a tough 60 hour week. I did not need to wear a tie; I did not need to be on my knees when praying; the modern hymns were lively; and the people were some of the friendliest I had ever met. Above all, there was no hard sell. I understand it can take men four years plus to make a commitment when they first step through the doors of any church. God had me on a faster track than that.

The challenge came from an unexpected quarter - a sailing trip with a group of men from the church from Falmouth to Jersey and back. I have always been scared of drowning ever since I nearly did so in the school baths at Skipton. I have dreams which feature me under water; the thought of sailing across the channel brings me out in a cold sweat. To this day I am surprised I accepted the invitation to join four others who had sailed before, but only round England's coast. I was the novice and it showed. I couldn't find my balance the moment we moved out of the calm waters of Falmouth harbour and I kept making the crew tea with salt water. Near disaster struck the very first night when our navigation system packed up and thick fog enveloped us. We thought we were near Guernsey, but didn't really know. All we could do was heave too, drop anchor and wait for morning so we could ring the coastguard and find out where we really were. We prayed – a lot in my case because I was terrified.

There I was stuck in the middle of the English Channel with just a bit of fibre glass between me and my nightmare. The sounds all around were truly frightening. There was no chance of any sleep, so we talked, prayed and talked a bit more about God and faith for eight hours. I listened like I had never listened to any sermon before while Malcolm Weaver, our skipper, answered my questions, read bits from his Bible and, above all, got me thinking. Despite my very real fears it was as if somebody had lifted a curtain.

At 6am we were able to ring the coastguard and find out we had 'parked up' near a lighthouse. In my relief I forgot why lighthouses are there in the first place - to keep you away from rocks. We were nearer the coast of France than the Channel Islands, but Malcolm got us going in the right direction and later that day we reached St Peter Port. I have never been so relieved to get my feet on dry land. Malcolm gave me the option of flying home if I wished, but sheer pride made me carry on; that gave me five more days to do nothing but talk about God and Jesus inbetween my spells on the tiller or cooking.

The trip was still far from plain sailing. Off the coast of Jersey we were caught with the wrong sails up and the next thing I knew the boat was on its side and I was under the water. Fortunately, I was clipped in and when the boat righted itself I came up with it. Five seconds seemed like five minutes.

On the way back to Falmouth we encountered a force seven storm which kept all of us awake all night as we took one hourly turns on the tiller. At 2am I had just finished my stint and returned to the cabin to take off my wet clothes when a huge wave lifted us up and then down. I was thrown off my feet, hit my head on the cabin roof and then came crashing down on the edge of a table. Pain shot through my body; when the rest of the team had time to help they discovered I had a very bruised back. Thankfully, nothing was broken, but I was sore for many days after.

We made it back though and got to Fowey for breakfast where we all had our first shower for a week. I thanked God for getting me back to England, but I have never wanted to crew a yacht again.

The others were just as delighted as I was that we got back in one piece. Malcolm and I bonded on the trip and we remain good friends. In the following weeks I began to think about what had happened and what I had discussed with him in between battling the elements. I still had many doubts, but I started taking a greater interest in church life and attending Sunday services more regularly, particularly as Valerie was keen to be involved and the children were enjoying their Sunday mornings too.

I don't think I am any different from others who have questioned whether there can be such a thing as an almighty God. Despite all the available help from well-meaning Christian friends, I still found it a lonely place when I first started to seriously think about Christianity, faith and grace. I admire people who have the courage of their convictions to step outside their comfort zone and evangelise, but there were times in 1990 when I found them very off-putting and a bit barmy. They could do with learning how to pace their message.

I needed to take my time and think things through; there was no way I would be rushed. I knew something was happening deep inside me. I felt different and no matter how much I resisted, I couldn't escape the fact that in my private moments I was no longer just thinking about work or football 24 hours a day, seven days a week, 52 weeks of the year. I knew I had been 'zapped', but I didn't yet know whether I wanted to be. How come I was now thinking about

Jesus when I was working or watching sport? Why did the lyrics and tunes from certain hymns reverberate round my head days later while at work? Why was I thinking about something unconnected with earning more money, or being more successful, or bringing up a happy family? Why? I didn't have long to wait.

In January 1990 Valerie made her commitment and was baptised. It was an emotional service, but I still wasn't sure it was the route I wanted to take. After her baptism tea I left to drive to Torquay for the first time to undertake the media consultancy engagement which was to change everything. The three hour drive down the M5 to South Devon gave me ample time in my own little bubble to dwell on what had happened that day, but I wasn't certain if I was that committed and whether it was for me.

The following morning I left the Grand Hotel on Torquay's seafront to begin work, unaware that within six months I would be moving to the area and the rest of the family would follow a few months later. I was even more unaware that soon after that I would walk through the doors of Upton Vale Baptist Church in the town centre for the first time.

We moved from Barnt Green to Torquay the Friday before Christmas 1990 into our new large house. Two days later Valerie and the children did a 400 mile round trip back to Barnt Green for the Baptist church nativity play and carol concert, while two days after that the Collins family followed us down to spend Christmas with us amid all our unpacked boxes. The next day we all went to the Christmas Day service at Upton Vale, which was packed to the rafters. It was totally different to what we had been used to in the Midlands: much larger and far more intimidating.

A Barnt Green friend, Katherine Drake, had advised us to try Upton Vale, but I had taken some persuading because during the few months I lived in a flat in Torquay on my own while we sold our house I got to know a Paignton Baptist minister and his family. They were very kind and invited me to dinner on several occasions. I felt I owed it to them to try their church. We did visit once, but Valerie wanted us to attend a church nearer to home so the children could attend regular events and get involved. Not for the first time, she was right.

From the outside Upton Vale is quite a daunting, ugly building. I am sure that even today, until they step inside, some people find its grey external walls just as intimidating as I did in 1990. That is until they get to know how friendly the 'inhabitants' are nowadays. Unfortunately for us, and Valerie in particular, it wasn't very friendly when we first arrived. There was no warm welcome at the door or after the services. It felt very icy compared with Barnt Green.

Upton Vale had one of the largest memberships of any church in the South West at the time and was, and still is, the best supported church in Torbay, but for the first few years we felt like strangers. We tried hard to make friends, but didn't make much progress. With the exception of two couples we were never invited back to their homes by people we had to dinner. It took five years before we were 'accepted' by more than half a dozen people and in that time Valerie found it very hard going and unsettling. If I had said we were moving back to the Midlands, she would have been delighted.

One man did make a difference though. The first Sunday in January 1991 we returned as a family for the normal morning service and listened to the senior minister, the Rev Andrew Green, who 12 months before had had the unenviable task of taking over from the Rev David Coffey when he was appointed head of the Baptist Union of Great Britain.

The hard pews reminded me of the Boys' Brigade church services. There was one important difference though: the sermon was totally unlike anything I had ever heard preached before. I have a limited attention span – my mind often wanders if any speaker at a conference, meeting or wedding goes on longer than 15 minutes. If someone doesn't enthuse me, I switch off even sooner. Andrew's sermons were my 'tipping point'. He engaged my brain and my heart, explained things in a way I could readily understand, answered some of the many questions which had been puzzling me and kept my attention throughout. He continued to do so for the next 24 years. I believe God took me from Barnt Green to Torquay and plonked me in a seat where I simply could not ignore what I was being taught.

Valerie was delighted when I did nothing but chat about that first sermon all the way home and over lunch. We had just finished washing up when there was a knock on the door and there was

Andrew to introduce himself, have a quick cup of tea and make us feel welcome. I just knew there and then that this was a man who, if I had any sense, I needed to get to know and listen to. I wasn't disappointed, although there must have been times over the next few years when he was disappointed in me!

I have no hesitation in saying that Andrew Green gave my life both purpose and direction. He also challenged me to look at my lifestyle and work out what God wanted me to do, not necessarily just what I enjoyed doing.

The seeds Malcolm Weaver had sown on the sailing trip, the friendships I had forged at Barnt Green and the teaching I now received at Upton Vale all came together in one almighty (excuse the pun) rush which left me stunned. Despite the lack of warmth from the congregation I really did look forward to Sunday mornings and even went to some evening services. Within six months I wanted to be baptised and become eligible for church membership. Andrew personally did all the preparation work in Torquay, but we agreed it was better if I was baptised in Barnt Green where I was better known and my decision would have the greatest impact among non-believers.

I was genuinely excited about the faith I had discovered, but the next few years were far from easy because I quickly learned that while some of the people I got to know on a Sunday called themselves Christians, they didn't always act very Christ like. Our arrival coincided with Upton Vale experiencing a difficult time with different cliques vying to drag the church their way, generally at the expense of anyone who didn't agree with them.

On the one side were some of those members of the congregation who had been brought up in the Plymouth Brethern; on the other were lively evangelicals who some dubbed the 'happy clappy brigade'. In between were the majority who were courted by two powerful and out-spoken groups who had vastly different views about everything from the format of services, church music, mission and even whether somebody who did not wear a tie should be allowed to serve communion.

At first Andrew tried to reconcile everyone, but it was never going to work. The leaders of each faction were too entrenched in their views and too dogmatic to want to find common ground.

For three years I wondered what I had walked into – there was political in-fighting on a weekly basis and the inevitable damage to people's faith. Quarterly church meetings became a battleground; at my third such meeting I stood up and castigated those who week after week did nothing but openly and volubly criticise the Sunday services, whether it was because they didn't like the hymns, the prayers or the sermons. I told the meeting the effect it was having on me, a relatively new Christian. Afterwards a fellow member, David Voyce, came up to me and said: '*You were brave. You will have made some enemies.*'

Eventually the two warring factions left to set up their own churches and the rest of us had some peace. I was never tempted to join either of them.

At my baptismal service in Barnt Green I was given an NIV Bible. A few weeks later back in Torquay I went on my own to an evening service which included communion. At the end of my pew was a very smart elderly lady who at the close came up to me and said: '*If you think that is God's word you are very misguided. You won't go to Heaven by reading that*'. She made it clear the King James Bible was the only one for true Christians. Before I could reply she walked away with her nose in the air. I had no idea who she was and never saw her again. It was typical of some of the comments flying around after nearly every service, but nothing compared with what I later learned the church leadership at the time were enduring.

A month later I attended a weekend seminar held at Exeter University run by Ellel Ministries. Once again I was approached by a woman I did not know who asked if I spoke in tongues. There was no introduction, no greeting, no warmth – just the blunt question. When I said I didn't, she said that then I was not one of God's chosen ones and walked away.

I was fortunate Andrew always made himself available to talk through such experiences. If he hadn't been they might have had a greater impact than they did. In later life I was able to laugh off such stupid comments because of the teaching I got at Upton Vale, but at the time I was a fragile Christian and vulnerable.

Many years later I was reading my daily Bible notes and comment sent by Jeff Lucas. He said: *'I worry when people complicate the gospel. I am not talking about the apparent indifference shown towards the absolute truth claims of Christ, but whenever someone comes up with a 'new revelation' or 'deeper insights', I get nervous.*

Sometimes I meet Christians who are into bizarre expressions of worship. When questioned they insist that they have 'gone deeper' than most and, if others only had the maturity and insight they have, all would be well.

Some of this thinking pervaded the renewal movements of the 1990s. When people started to do strange things, bemused onlookers who had genuine concerns were told that they should suspend their ethical faculties and 'get in the river'.

And being enamoured with the incomprehensible is not something that only those of us from a more charismatic persuasion can be guilty of. I have been to some conferences where the speakers fascinated and bewildered their listeners in turn. Emerging from another confusing session, I was told the content was 'deep', which I think was code for: 'I don't understand a word of that'.

Andrew showed remarkable patience in dealing with my questions at a time when he was under pressure not only from the people mentioned above but in removing the last vestiges of masonic influence at the church. David Coffey had tackled this issue head-on during his time as senior pastor; Andrew had to make sure that when David left there was no revival. On the third Sunday morning we went as a family I got the masonic handshake from an elderly steward greeting people at the door. It happened again a few weeks later via another steward. It was another few years before such people either left or were not given any further chances to discover who else among the congregation was a mason.

Another practice I did not approve of was businessmen trying to forge friendships on a Sunday morning purely so they could sell me life insurance, pensions or other items they were convinced I needed. As a newcomer to the church and a new Christian I was an obvious target. In wanting to make new friends I nearly signed up to one financial package until I realised what was happening.

It made me angry. How dare these people use the church this way? The answer, of course, was that they were no different from the masons and for all I knew belonged to the same lodge. Since then I have given different work to several church friends, but only after I have approached them and not vice versa.

In 1992 Valerie and I made friends with a couple who were very much into healing and challenging satanic practices. They were good people who cared about our spiritual health, but their evangelical zeal was too over the top for us to follow the course they had prepared for us.

I did agree,however, to go with him to a Christian Men's dinner at Torquay's Riviera Centre to hear a well known American evangelist called Don Double. There were more than a hundred other men present and I enjoyed the meal until it came to the prayers between the main course and dessert. During the prayers Mr Double asked people in need of healing to raise their hands. When the prayers ended and we opened our eyes those who had raised their hands were identified and told to get up and go to the far corner of the room where they were expected to take part in a 'laying of hands.' Two people on my table were not happy at being identified, but they still got up and went.

I would have been furious if it had been me. I watched as they lined up, had a hand placed on their foreheads while someone prayed for them and were then gently pushed backwards to lie on the floor, where they stayed for ten minutes. Dessert was then served while we listened to a clever financial appeal along the lines of *'You cannot expect to leave here tonight with any money in your pocket if you are being faithful to God.'* It was the wrong message as far as I was concerned. I recognised a pitch for my wallet and responded the only way a true northerner would – by firmly planting my hands in my pockets.

When the dessert bowls had been cleared away there was another laying on of hands led by Mr Double. Everyone was exhorted to come forward. Everyone – and I really do mean everyone – but me got up. I stayed put. When the waitress came round with the coffee she looked at me and said: '*I hope you are thirsty.*' We both giggled. Mr Double stared at me. I stared back. When I did not move, he looked away. Meanwhile it was like World War Three on the floor. I never again went to any such event and I did walk out with all my money intact.

Eventually Valerie and I did make lots of friends at Upton Vale, which also provided a rich source of stories for the *Weekender*: there was the man who miraculously regained his sight; the teacher who went out to Africa to start an orphanage; the tax man who retired after 25 years; the crab fisherman who won a national award; the organist who smuggled Bibles into Romania.

I did my bit by serving at communion, doing the occasional Bible reading, organising breakfasts for local decision-makers where there was a Christian speaker, stewarding and a host of other jobs which make a successful church tick. I joined a Tuesday night house group to further my knowledge and understanding led by music leader and organist David Peacock until he moved to London.

In 1994 David asked if I would appear on the BBC's Songs of Praise when it came to Torquay for the Palm Sunday service. Presenter Pam Rhodes - a lovely, kind woman - and I did eight hours of filming in advance of the actual service for a 10 minute slot centred on my attempts to make *The Weekender* a newspaper which contained a lot of good news.

When the service was filmed at Torquay's Central Church son Robin, now aged seven, stole the show when the television cameras panned in on him singing 'Meekness and Majesty'. We had to sing some of the hymns six or seven times until the producer was happy.

The following year I accompanied Andrew Green when he was invited to be the main speaker at a Baptist Missionary Society conference near Sao Paolo, Brazil. We had two days in Sao Paolo visiting favellas (shanty towns) and seeing the excellent work missionaries do among that country's poor. We stayed with a missionary couple in a block of flats which had an armed guard at the gated entrance and visited a school where other armed guards were there to protect the children of rich parents from being kidnapped.

I had a relaxing week at the conference centre helping Andrew who was in demand from early morning until late at night by UK Baptist missionary families, many of whom were desperate for his counselling. Some of their stories were heart rending, including a minister who felt he could be murdered at any time.

We shared a twin-bedded room which contained nothing but the bare essentials. There was no television or radio in our room so I was grateful for my small pocket radio which allowed me to keep abreast of world events and the football scores.

The only luxury was the on-site swimming pool where the women had to wear one piece costumes and the men shorts, not trunks. Evening entertainment was home-made: the musicians among us – which for obvious reasons did not include me - arranged several concerts for all ages. One missionary ran a table tennis tournament which he won because he had the only good bat.

My job was to look after Andrew and ensure he took regular meals and had some sort of break each day. It wasn't the easiest of tasks because he always gives 120% to others, sometimes at his own expense. I was asked to give two talks which appeared to go down well.

When the conference finished Andrew and I flew down to Rio and had a four day break at a top hotel. It was very hot - over 100 degrees each day - but we had a great time going to the top of Sugar Loaf Mountain and taking a trip to the Christ the Redeemer monument overlooking the city. One day we sailed out of Rio on an excursion to an island. We jumped off the boat, into the sea and swam ashore where we sunbathed, read, ate lots of food and relaxed. Both of us suffered from dehydration the next day when we toured the city. Fortunately for me, Andrew spotted what was happening and made me drink a lot of water; he was less fortunate and collapsed in the hotel lift that evening. I had to watch over him all night.

Andrew retired in December 2014. I felt quite emotional at his final service when many tributes were paid to his 25 years of dedicated service. He would be embarrassed if I listed all his qualities, but he always strove to make Upton Vale accessible to newcomers: a man who was truly seeker-sensitive. He tried hard to ensure that the church's vocabulary was jargon-free, but there were times he was too intellectual for some in the congregation. His overall messages were always relevant to me. In his last few years he had the backing of a good church leadership team who worked hard to make those who were seeking after truth feel comfortable to come as they were - questions and all. To quote Jeff Lucas again: *'Sometimes we talk about people having 'found the Lord', as if in an instant they had an epic encounter with Jesus and immediately downloaded full and complete knowledge of Him. But that's not the way it is. The Christian is a seeker, gradually coming to a greater knowledge and awareness of who Christ is.'* That describes my journey. Thank goodness I met Andrew.

In recent years I have been happy to take a back seat while Valerie has been more to the fore at Upton Vale. For several years she worked two days a week in the church office as a volunteer and for 17 years she also worked on a voluntary basis in the Cottage Cafe attached to the church and was a Girls' Brigade officer. I have done regular stints on the door welcoming people on a Sunday morning, attended a house group with Valerie, organised and run quizzes from time to time and got involved when asked about legal or other matters.

Valerie and I have also run six coffee mornings/second hand book sales for a Christian charity called LINX, a dynamic and innovative Christian faith based youth work organisation that has been working with the young people of Torbay for over 15 years. It enables young people to reach their full potential through its work in secondary schools and within the local community.

I have tried, whenever the opportunity has arisen at work or play, to encourage people in their faith. I don't find this easy and it is not one of my gifts. I have had to curb my natural impetuosity and learn that God will use me in different ways; the skills I have obtained during my life will be put to His use when the occasion arises, not just when it suits me. Perhaps the best example of God using my experience of handling meetings and public speaking was when I chaired a volatile church meeting in 2010 after a senior minister left in acrimonious circumstances. I gave everyone a chance to have their say, but did not allow the meeting to get out of hand or develop into a slanging match. It was one of those nights when all my years of experience at handling meetings and people stood me, and the church, in good stead.

It is up to others who have known me a long time to judge how my faith in a risen Lord has changed me as a person. Inwardly I know I am different despite my continuing imperfections: I still don't tolerate fools gladly; I rant and rave at other drivers; I have very little time for those in our society who could work but think living off benefits is a perfectly acceptable lifestyle; I judge people by their actions as well as their words; if people ask me for an opinion I often give them too blunt an answer; I don't like marmite. The list is endless.

One item is missing, though: my faith has taught me to be much more forgiving. Every day I look at a sign I have pinned up in my office. It reads: *'The most beautiful thing a person can do is forgive'*. I don't always forgive - because I am a human being - but I do try. I look at things from the other person's viewpoint and I no longer seek revenge on those who wrong me. That wasn't always the case, particularly when I was hurt or when playing sport. I was brought up to get my retaliation in first when up against certain people.

It took time, but eventually Upton Vale Baptist Church helped Valerie and I to settle in Torbay and forge some strong, highly valued and long lasting friendships. David Jones, who is also my financial advisor, and I found we had much in common from the outset. We have been there for each other at critical times in both of our lives, which is partly what friendship is all about as far as I am concerned. We share a love of all things cricket, but agree to disagree about rugby. How can someone born in Totnes support Wales, even if they have been in the Welsh Guards?

I often catch fellow friends out when I pose the question: *'Name two people you know who have played at Wembley or for England.'* David played in the army band at Wembley, while, of course, I played football for an English Boys' Brigade team.

Valerie and I have had several short holidays with him and his wife, Beverley, while David and I spend time together during the summer watching county cricket at Taunton.

David Morey and I share a love of all things sport. We have watched football together at both Plymouth Argyle and Torquay United, which has tested our resolve on several boring occasions. Further afield we have been to Arsenal's former stadium at Highbury, the Hawthorns to watch West Bromwich Albion and Edgbaston to watch Test matches. One event we enjoy together is General Election night when he drives over from his home in Paignton to watch the results as they are announced on television. Valerie provides plenty of cake which along with ample cups of coffee keeps us going long past our normal bed times. David usually stays until around 2am. By then I am beyond sleep so I don't go to bed until 6am.

I have a lot of respect for both Davids. They are senior members at Upton Vale whose advice I have sought on numerous occasions. They have enriched my life. Long may it remain so.

CHAPTER THIRTEEN

FAMILY MATTERS MATTER

The older we get, the better we used to be – John McEnroe

One factor which has played an on-going and major part in my life is migraine. Thanks to regular medication I now have this under control and rarely get the blinding attacks I had for more than 30 years. However, even though I am now in my sixties, there are still too many days when I cannot do anything but take the medication and hope the attacks pass sooner rather than later.

I used to get annoyed when people said they had a migraine but still went about their normal daily business. Migraine sufferers know what intense pain really is. I shudder when I think of the times I drove home 300 miles from working in different parts of the country while suffering an attack and fell into bed upon my arrival. I could easily have killed myself.

For too many years my life seemed to revolve round working between attacks and spending the rest of the time in bed with a thumping headache which also made me feel sick. That was particularly the case in the 1980s when I was under pressure at the *Daily News;* Valerie had to cope with the disappointment of us cancelling social engagements on too many occasions. I cannot begin to describe the pain I used to suffer and on several occasions I would have been happy to die. I do not joke. Doctors gave me both morphine and pethidine to ease the pain during the worst attacks.

In recent years I have had arthritis in my hips and been able to bear that pain far better because it is nothing in comparison to the headaches I have suffered. Nobody has been able to tell me for certain how and why my migraine attacks started, but while working in Birmingham I did visit a hypnotist who took me back to the age of nine for my first really bad attack. My own view, for what it is worth, is that my difficult upbringing, combined with too much heading of a heavy old football when young, are partly to blame. The doctors believe it is simply down to my genes; I won't argue with that. I wonder if my real father suffered from migraine?

I am fortunate I married an understanding woman who has had to put up with a lot over the years. I cannot think of anyone more caring than Valerie. She is always there when needed by family or friends and her love for me and others has shone though even the darkest of times. She is rightly much loved by all her friends. She often tells me: *'We make a good team'*.

If anyone had told me before I was married that I would have three children I would not have believed them. At most I only wanted two and when we had Georgina and Timothy within a three year span (1981-83) I would have settled for that. Valerie would have liked six, so we compromised and Robin was duly born in 1986. It was a wise choice. I am not going to embarrass them by including too much about them in this book. They know they are much loved.

It thrills me that both my sons want to do things with me even now they are grown up and have lives of their own. One family tradition I have been able to keep going with the two boys has been an annual Christmas Eve trip to an amusement arcade in Dawlish. This started in 1991 when Valerie needed time on her own to wrap the children's Christmas presents. I took all three children to Dawlish for around four hours during which time we spent £10 at twopence a time trying to win the small toys on display. Afterwards we went to a cafe in Dawlish High Street for a late breakfast together. Georgina stopped going after a few years but the boys have always been keen to do it and apart from one year when Tim and I went down with flu, and Christmas Eve 2014 when I came out of hospital, we still go. Our record haul is 27 toys in 2007, which will take some beating! I kept them in my office for a few years until we gave them back to a surprised amusement arcade manager in 2013. Nobody had ever done that before.

I also try and separately take Tim and Robin to at least one football match a season at either West Bromwich Albion or Aston Villa. My accountant, Brian Foster, generously invited us into his executive box at West Brom for 30 years until he decided the cost was too much after the 2013/14 season. When we moved to Torquay it involved a 400 mile round trip but it gave me a chance to spend some quality time with both of them.

As a family we have had many good holidays. Trips to Boston to stay with Don and Gail MacCuish have generally involved at least a week at their second home at Killington in Vermont - which we love - as well as time with them at homes in Malden and New Hampshire. The views from their Killington apartment are spectacular and the surrounding, colourful countryside is beautiful. On one such trip we went to Lake Champlain and Lake George in Upper New York State to trace the route of the *Last of the Mohicans* and on another holiday we went to Niagara Falls. We took the children to Disneyworld in Orlando on three occasions.

In addition to the many trips to America Valerie and I have been to Tunisia, Cyprus, Corfu, Portugal, Spain, Italy, China, Kazakhstan, France, Norway, Germany, Switzerland, Austria, Denmark, Belgium and Holland.

We have had five sea cruises on the large P and O ships and two river ones on smaller boats. The longest sea cruise was from Southampton to New York - a six day crossing - and up the east coast of America, down the St Lawrence river to Quebec and home. Sailing into New York past the Statue of Liberty at seven o'clock one morning was special.

We prefer the smaller ships because on a river cruise there is more to see while sailing. They travel through lovely countryside during the day and berth for the night in major towns. The first one we did was down the River Rhone through Provence and Burgundy to Marseille; the second was down the Rhine from Antwerp to Basel in Switzerland through the Rhine gorge.

I read at least one history book a month and study both the origins of the First World War and the American Civil War for the talks I give. I have no interest in the Greeks or Romans, but I devour books on anything post 1066. Whenever I get the chance I visit European and American battlefields.

A trip to Pearl Harbour in 1987 on my way back from giving a talk in Australia was special. The Americans show off their history very well and without exception create a reverential atmosphere.

They are also prone to go a bit over the top eg somehow Pearl Harbour was not a big defeat but the start of a victory. As part of my four hour tour I watched a film of the surprise attack which really did hype me up about the infamy and treachery of the Japanese. When the lights went up 90% of the audience were Japanese, all of whom seemed very happy with what they had seen.

Two battlefields have left a major impression on me. The first is Ypres which endured four years of the most atrocious warfare between 1914 and 1918. I defy anyone not to cry if they visit the nearby Tyne Cot cemetery where 30,000 British and Empire soldiers are buried. It is only when you walk through the few trenches left today that you begin to have some understanding of the conditions that men lived, fought and died in. I have visited Ypres three times. On one occasion in 2003 I led a party of 12 men from Upton Vale which included my teenage son Robin. He christened us *'Dad's Army'* but one of our party, Alan Ridgway, was quick to retort: *'Well, that makes you Pike then!'*

The second battlefield to make a big impact is Gettysburg in Pennsylvania where the Confederate and Union armies met in July 1863. To look out from Cemetery Ridge over such beautiful countryside and understand what happened in three days of battle explains much about the American character. I have been fortunate to make two visits and I hope to go again.

I have been either best man or groomsman at nine weddings. Some were more memorable than others. I was best man when living in Maldon at Malcolm Ward's first wedding in Colchester. I say 'first' because he has been married at least three times, possibly four. Malcolm took over as the *Maldon and Burnham Standard's* Sports Editor when I was promoted to Deputy Editor. He and I were friends for many years including the time he was my deputy at the *Daily News*. However, we lost touch when he moved to the Middle East.

I was also best man when Jack Eves got married for a second time at Thaxted in Suffolk. First time round I was groomsman when he married Elizabeth, a girl from Barnoldswick I introduced him to. That partnership was always going to end in tears because her family did not like Jack and did not consider him suitable for their daughter. The wedding reception was teetotal with the two families sat well apart. Jack's brother was best man. He and I were a bit naughty because we slipped some fictitious cards into the pile to be read out - all of them from pubs. The bride's mother was not amused and even less so when I described the marquee as a tent.

I was asked to wear a dress suit for Robert Boven's marriage to Michelle on a Sunday in Manchester. The day before my sister Sandra married for the second time in Barnoldswick, so we were able to attend both ceremonies over the one weekend. This was a less formal occasion. On the Friday I put a pair of ordinary suit trousers in my trouser press, but in the rush forgot to take them with me. This meant I had to wear the dress suit for both weddings. I sat on the front row at St Andrew's Church with my mother who kept turning round to wave at people and say hello. When one guest arrived my mother shouted down the church: *'It's our David – he has left his trousers at home.'* Everyone looked to see if I was sat there in my underpants!

I was delighted to be best man when my Uncle Terry married Winifred at Burnley a few years after my aunty's death, but I dropped myself right in it when I agreed to be best man for someone who shall remain nameless. The 'happy' couple had been living together for 12 years and had three children before they decided to wed. He had several girlfriends one of whom telephoned his wife-to-be two days before the wedding to spill the beans. Despite this the wedding went ahead at Stourbridge register office. Valerie and I must have been the only two people there who did not know there had been a major row and the wedding had nearly been called off. Everything was very subdued, which in my naivety I put down to nerves. When the time came for me to give my speech at the reception I said: *'His friends are surprised he has settled down with a book when there is a circulating library'*. Afterwards one of the groom's relatives really let me have it and told me in no uncertain terms what he thought of my sense of humour. At that point somebody put me in the picture. The next day the row continued and the bride refused to go on honeymoon. He wasn't going to waste a good holiday and went on his own for two weeks. When he came back he said he had had a great time! They are still together more than 25 years on.

I have already written about three deaths which affected me deeply - my sister Wendy, Mrs Moss and my mother-in-law Ann. The older I have got, the more friends and family I have inevitably lost. My aunty died far too young; in her later years she was badly crippled with arthritis and if she had lived longer she would have been badly disabled. Both my grandmothers had reasonable life spans and while I was sad when they died I cannot say I was too upset. The same can be said for my Heybridge 'landlady' Mrs Burfoot who lived for several years after I moved out and had a reasonable life of good health until the last few months.

My mother died unexpectedly the Saturday before Christmas 2006. She was frail in her later years and was bitter that my father had not only bullied her but denied her much happiness. I saw her for the last time in August that year when I made a special trip north to show her a DVD of her grand-daughter's wedding. She cried as she watched it - I was quite moved by her response. She always gave me a big hug whenever she saw me and when my father was not around she would talk quite openly about some of the bitterness she felt. I think she knew I loved her.

I am sure she must have come quite close on several occasions to telling me the truth about my real father, but at the last minute feared my reaction. On the day she died she went shopping with my brother, Brian, watched her favourite TV programme - X Factor - and then went to bed where she died quietly in her sleep. She deserved that peaceful end. The first I knew of her death was when I came home from church and Timothy told me the news after a telephone call from my brother-in-law, John.

Two days later Roger Collins died of cancer aged only 57. He, his wife Marilyn and Valerie and I had spent many happy holidays together. When we lived in Barnt Green the Collins family always came to us on Christmas Day and our children grew up together. When we moved to Torquay Roger and Marilyn were regular visitors, either at Christmas or New Year. It was not unusual for them to visit at Easter or during the school summer holidays.

When I first set up on my own and ran my training courses at Solihull they allowed me to stay with them whenever I wanted.

Roger took early retirement from teaching as soon as he reached 55 'to enjoy life'. It was awfully sad he fell ill almost right away and could not enjoy much of his retirement.

He managed to live just long enough to see his son, Daniel, married in Denmark - a wedding we also went to in order to give him and Marilyn some support. As he and I walked through Odense I tried to encourage him, although it was obvious he was very ill and dying. '*I won't be with you this Christmas, David,*' he said, and he was right.

My mother's funeral was the Thursday before Christmas and Roger's was the week after. It left me quite morose for some weeks and unable to celebrate either Christmas or New Year. On New Year's Eve Valerie and I went to a party at the home of friends, but around 10 o'clock I said I wanted to go home and have a quiet night with Timothy and Robin. Valerie agreed. I didn't want to spoil anybody else's night.

My father never really recovered from my mother's death. He was devastated and felt very lonely. He did not keep in touch with any friends after retiring from Rolls Royce which meant my sister and brother had to try and fill the gap. He would visit Sandra most days, have a cup of tea and a chat and then walk the mile and a half back home.

He was a friendless, lonely old man who must have realised how many years he had wasted. I thought his daily walks were keeping him fit so it came as a surprise when I received a telephone call one Monday in April 2008 from Brian to say my dad had been suffering from a stomach upset for a couple of weeks and would be going into hospital for tests. Two days later I was told he had stomach, lung and other cancers and was not expected to live more than six weeks. By the Friday of the same week he had lapsed into a coma.

I was working in Tunbridge Wells at the time and got home late that night. Valerie and I had a few hours sleep and then set off for the hospital in Keighley. We arrived after a gruelling six hour journey and saw him for the last time. It was tremendously upsetting to see a man who had been so strong all his life in a coma with two drips feeding him. There was nothing we could do for him. We stayed a couple of hours, held his hand and talked in the hope he could hear us and then drove home. He died eight hours after we left, but we had the consolation of knowing that he did not suffer.

Braintree Liberal leader John Ross also died of cancer, but he was much younger - just 50. I am godfather to his youngest daughter, Jacqueline. I visited him a few months before he died and realised he did not have long to live. He, and others suffering from different cancers who I have visited, have found the chemo so debilitating. When Jacqueline was married months later I stood in for John and spoke at the reception. It was an honour.

CHAPTER FOURTEEN

CLARET AND BLUE ARMY

There is no such thing as a football hooligan. There are just hooligans. Football hooligans? Well, there are 92 club chairmen for a start. There are more hooligans in the House of Commons than at a football match – Nottingham Forest manager Brian Clough.

I enjoy watching some sports. Football, cricket, baseball and American football top the list. I am not interested in motor or horse racing and apart from the Olympics, the bi-annual Ryder Cup and the Open Golf Championship I rarely watch any other televised sport. I went to a point to point meeting in Essex in 1972 and was bored rigid. It put me off watching any other form of horse racing for life. That was eclipsed by a press trip to Dublin when on the Saturday night we were taken to a greyhound meeting at Dalymount Park; it was one visit too many. I was forced to watch under-fed dogs race round a track for 30 seconds every 30 minutes when all I wanted to do was have something to eat. I don't gamble and I am not an animal lover so I have never been tempted to take any interest in racing of any kind.

However, my weekend mood is determined by how I feel at 5pm on a Saturday when I know the football results. My love affair with Burnley Football Club began on March 1 1958 when a friend of my aunty, Sid Tennant, took me on Turf Moor to see Burnley (the Clarets) lose 2-0 to Everton. We stood behind the goal at the Bee Hole End, which was uncovered in those days, thus allowing the wind and rain to blow right down my back straight off the towering moors behind the ground. There were 19,600 on Turf Moor that day, most of them standing.

I was 10 years old and already a football fanatic, captaining the Rainhall Road school football team to a series of victories over other Barnoldswick schools. I was captivated by the big match atmosphere I experienced for the first time that day, the excitement and then disappointment as Burnley slipped to defeat. I swayed this way and that to try and get a better view and never stopped talking about the game and its star players until well into the evening when my aunty had heard enough. In my youth I always felt more comfortable talking sport with and learning from people much older than myself.

Turf Moor today is a modern 21st century all-seater stadium. The area surrounding it, however, is still full of terraced houses which on dark and dismal winter days look depressingly similar to what they were like 60 years ago when I first walked past them. I can understand why some footballers more used to the bright city lights have never enjoyed playing at Burnley. When I first started watching the Clarets half the nearby streets were still cobbled.

The next season I persuaded my father to take me with him. He was a Blackpool supporter and a big fan of Stanley Matthews, but tolerated Burnley in a half-hearted way. We travelled by Wild's buses from Barnoldswick to Burnley - a distance of only around 12 miles. The journey took nearly two hours because in those days the queue to get anywhere near the ground began two towns away in Colne.

I chatted all the way there and probably all the way back except for a brief period round 5pm when the familiar *Sports Report* music blared out from the bus radio and everyone fell silent for the scores. The bus dropped us right outside the ground, but it took another 45 minutes to get inside.

My dad used to stand with his mates on the Long Side to the right of the halfway line. Once I knew where he was stationed I was allowed to push my way to the front wall where all the lads my age gathered. There was no violence in those days unless you got clobbered by a wooden rattle the richer boys carried and waved about after a goal. About 10 minutes from the end I would make my way back up the terracing through the bellowing crowd to stand by my father and see very little of the rest of the game. He never had enough money for any food or a drink. I didn't care - I just loved being there. I wasn't to know it but this was a golden era for Burnley Football Club just prior to the days when the maximum wage came to an end and big money took over in football.

Small town Burnley, with the wizardry of inside right Jimmy McIlroy, the poise of right half Jimmy Adamson and the goalscoring abilities of future England internationals Ray Pointer and John Connelly were quite a force in English football's top division. The very first game of the 1958/59 season provided enough excitement to have me wanting to see every game I could - Burnley lost 4-3 to Manchester City after leading 3-0 at half-time. Burnley won the return 4-1 in December and the following March won seven games on the trot to finish 6th in the table and give warning they were ready to mount a serious challenge for the First Division title the following season.

Some games attracted crowds in excess of 40,000 when the surges back and forth down the terracing made it quite scary. How some people were not trampled underfoot is a mystery.

The 1959/60 season began on August 22 when Burnley won 3-2 at Leeds. It was the start of a fairy story which could not happen today when success depends on whether a club can attract a rich foreign owner prepared to 'throw away ' hundreds of millions of pounds. All that matters is money – you either have it or you don't.

Burnley followed their opening day win with a 5-2 home victory against Everton which set the tone for a spectacular season when I came away disappointed if I didn't see at least five goals per game! Seven wins in the first 10 games should have warned title favourites Wolves and Tottenham they had a serious northern rival, but the national press didn't get excited because we were conceding a lot of goals, including 4-1 defeats to Chelsea, Manchester United and Blackpool. However we continued to hammer them in at the other end.

I was present in November when Burnley beat Nottingham Forest 8-0. Inside left (a position youngsters today would not understand) Jimmy Robson got five of the goals but on the bus home some of the old timers moaned he should have had more! Burnley beat Wolves 4-1, Bolton 4-0, West Ham 5-2 (away) and Arsenal 4-2 (away).

Then came one of the best games I ever saw when we beat one of our biggest rivals, Tottenham Hotspur, 2-0 at home on a Tuesday night in February 1960. Tottenham were the London aristocrats who were expected to put these northern upstarts in their place. That night nine of their team were recognised internationals. Goal number one for Burnley came when McIlroy beat three men, got to the by-line and sent in a hard cross which Pointer dived full length to bullet head home. Ten minutes later Connelly cut in from the right and shot home from 20 yards A disastrous 6-1 away defeat to league leaders and title favourites Wolves in March seemed to end our title hopes, but then Wolves dropped points and it all came down to Burnley's last match of the season away to Manchester City on Monday May 2.

We had to win or Wolves would be champions again. My dad went to the match with his workmates from Rolls Royce, but much to my disappointment said I was too young to cope with the massive crowd; for once he was right. More than 65,000 fans crammed into Maine Road with an estimated 20,000 locked out. My dad was one of the last to get in two hours before kick-off. Burnley won 2-1 and crowds lined the streets for 30 miles waiting for the team's return. My dad didn't get home until 3am.

Winning the First Division title meant that 'little' Burnley were in the European Cup the following 1960/61 season. In those days only a country's champions qualified. In November I saw the 2-0 win over French champions Rheims who were the competition's second favourites behind Real Madrid. In the return leg in Paris Burnley lost 3-2 but went through to the next round 4-3 on aggregate.

The quarter-final tie against unbeaten German champions Hamburg, who featured most of the German World Cup team, was the first European Cup match televised live on the BBC. Burnley won a great game played on a Turf Moor mudbath 3-1, but lost 5-4 on aggregate after McIlroy hit the post from four yards out in the last minute of the return in Hamburg.

I went to every game I could persuade my father to pay for, and stood so near to the action and my heroes I felt I was part of some of the games. There was no hint of trouble inside or outside the ground, little swearing and nothing like the obscene chanting which is a feature of most games today.

The goals continued to flow in both directions: 5-0 wins over Preston and Fulham, 5-3 victories over Wolves, Newcastle and Bolton, a 5-2 win over Arsenal, 6-2 over Chelsea, two 4-4 draws with Tottenham and Chelsea, a 5-3 win over Manchester United and a 4-1 win at Blackburn plus a 6-0 defeat at Old Trafford.

Tottenham won the league and cup double but Burnley were the only team they didn't beat all season. In the 4-4 draw at White Hart Lane Spurs were 4-0 up in 35 minutes, but they still couldn't beat Burnley, while at Turf Moor the Londoners led 2-0 at half-time but still lost 4-2.

The following season brought heartbreak. Burnley finished second in the league and lost 3-1 to Tottenham in one of the best FA Cup finals ever. I didn't see it live because Barnoldswick Cricket Club had an important fixture that day and the local league's fuddy-duddy officials stupidly refused to postpone any games, despite pressure from everybody in Lancashire. I went to a dozen of the home league games and both the cup quarter-final at Sheffield United (won 1-0) and the semi-final at Villa Park, Birmingham, when Burnley drew 1-1 with Fulham and then won the replay 2-1 at Leicester's ground. At Sheffield so many people were crammed in safety barriers collapsed. My father was pushed down the terraces and suffered a cracked rib, while I just escaped being trampled on.

After that Burnley had other great teams with top class home grown talent for 14 years, but every season they had to sell some of their best players to survive in the new financial reality brought about by the abolition of the maximum wage, freedom of contract for players and spiralling transfer fees.

One of the players they sold – to Stoke City - was my favourite, Jimmy McIlroy. There was no bigger crowd pleaser on the Turf Moor stage, but chairman Bob Lord got rid of him in February 1963 after a 2-1 FA Cup defeat at Liverpool. It was a transfer that stunned both the football world and every Burnley supporter. Lord never did give any explanation and thousands of fans voted with their feet by boycotting games for the rest of that season. There were protest marches, but they had no effect on Bob Lord. In Barnoldswick furniture shop owner Billy Grace tore up his season ticket and organised a petition. He never went to Turf Moor again.

Burnley were relegated from the first division in 1971 but regained top flight status in 1973. For two seasons they played some attractive football and reached an FA Cup semi-final, but once again had to sell their best players and in 1976 they were relegated a second time. The slide into near obscurity had begun.

By the 1980s the club was in the old fourth division and gates had dropped to around 4,000. Then came near disaster when in the 1986/87 season relegation from the Football League to the Football Conference was introduced for the first time. From Christmas 1986 Burnley looked odds on to be the first team to be relegated that way - we were awful. It all depended on the last game at home when we had to beat Leyton Orient and other results go our way. Orient needed to win to get in the play-offs. More than 15,000 turned up for the wake but somehow we won 2-1 in a nail-biter and Lincoln went down. I am convinced that if we had lost that would have been the end of the club.

For the next few years Burnley held their own in the Fourth Division and even got through to the Wembley final of the Sherpa Van Trophy where they lost 2-0 to Wolves. I managed to get a ticket and met my brother Stephen by chance outside.

Promotion was achieved in the late 1990s first to the Third Division and then to the Championship. The Clarets suffered another relegation straight away but bounced back two years later. Then came the magic of a return to the top flight – now called the Premiership - in 2009 with a 1-0 play-off final win over Sheffield United at Wembley. Alas, the club were relegated straight away again but they did beat Manchester United 1-0. If our manager had not left for Bolton in the middle of January I believe we would have stayed up. I still cannot bear to mention his name, suffice it to say all true Burnley fans call him 'Judas' !

Many people thought that Burnley's one season in the top flight of English football would be their last for a long time, but to everyone's surprise they gained automatic promotion in April 2014 without the need this time of a Wembley play-off victory. At the start of the 2013/14 season national newspaper reporters marked the club down for relegation. Instead they lost only five out of 46 league games and finished eight points ahead of nearest rivals Derby County. So much for the experts!

Over the years I have found it hard to watch Burnley's games, even on television. I get too tense and suffer headaches. But I have never been tempted to change my allegiance through thick and a lot of thin. Supporting Burnley is a passion and is something only those who really care about a team and feel the hurt at 5pm on a Saturday after every loss can understand. I regularly re-read the large number of books and videos in my office which cover both the 'glory' years and the more dismal seasons.

I was fortunate enough to attend two matches during the 1966 World Cup held in England. I saw the great Pele ruthlessly chopped down and injured when Portugal beat Brazil 3-1 at Goodison Park and was in the crowd a few days later to see Brazil lose again, this time to Hungary at Old Trafford.

I watched the England v West Germany final on television at home with my father and chewed the end of a tie as the drama unfolded. When England won in extra-time I raced out onto the street to join in the fun. That night the pubs and clubs in Barnoldswick were packed as people celebrated. There was no vandalism, just unbounded joy.

Thirty years later I took son Robin to Villa Park to watch the European Championship quarter final between Czechoslovakia and Portugal and again loved the atmosphere such occasions generate. I hope my sons get tickets for a World Cup game in the future.

While living in Essex I went to a couple of England games at Wembley and also two cup finals: Tottenham v Queen's Park Rangers and Leeds v Arsenal. Both were good days out even if the matches themselves were disappointing.

Thanks to a Father's Day present from my sons Timothy and Robin I got to see the New England Patriots play a National Football League game at Wembley against the St Louis Rams in October 2012, which they won 45-7. The three of us had a great time together watching Patriots star quarterback Tom Brady throw six touchdown passes. Once again it was the atmosphere in a packed stadium which made it a memorable occasion. We got to our seats two hours before kick-off and found we were nearly the last to sit down. Timothy did well to get the tickets because there was exceptional demand. My joy was unrestrained in February 2015 when the Patriots and superstar Brady won the Super Bowl for the fourth time.

I felt the same buzz when I watched the Boston Red Sox play at their home ground of Fenway Park in 2007. The crowd was different to what I regularly experience at any soccer game in England. It was a fun day out for everyone, even when the home team lost. Mums and dads could take their offspring safe in the knowledge they would not be subjected to vile, sexually loaded chants, violent threats or an intimidating atmosphere. The antics of the peanut sellers alone were worth the admission price.

My love of watching top class cricket has grown in recent years. I have already recalled the first Test match I ever saw when England played Australia at Headingley in 1963. I saw plenty of Essex games in the early 1970s including a cup final victory at Lord's. For several years after I moved to Torquay I went to the annual Edgbaston Test match with Dave Morey who got us free tickets if we sat with his son Rob and pupils from a Leamington school. We were honorary teachers for the day.

Nearer home David Jones and I have enjoyed each other's company at county championship and one day games at Taunton. In the summer of 2013 I became a Somerset member. I could not have picked a better year weather-wise. We had three months of glorious sunshine during which I spent 18 separate days watching the cricket and eating good food, most of it consumed in the pavilion's carvery. I never failed to strike up some sort of conversation with the people I sat next to.

CHAPTER FIFTEEN

SPEAKING PERSONALLY

If you don't read the newspaper you are uninformed, if you do read the newspaper you are misinformed. -- Mark Twain

I was busy preparing to give a talk to Torquay Probus Club one Thursday morning in 2013 when I realised what interesting people I had met and the fun I had had when giving talks to such groups. It made me wonder if other local newspaper Editors, past and present, along with the friends I knew who carried out public speaking engagements, had also had similar experiences. My interest aroused, I dashed off a few emails to those I thought would soon let me know whether the idea was worth pursuing and almost immediately the answer they gave was a resounding '*yes*'.

'*If newspaper editors don't have any anecdotes, who does*? ' was a typical reply.

Encouraged by the response, I set out to unearth a treasure trove of stories which I felt deserved a wider audience. Six months later I produced my third book titled *The Joys and Terrors of Public Speaking*. **If you have read the book you can skip this chapter**. Fifty three contributors told some fascinating and often amusing stories of their public speaking experiences. It gave an insight into how difficult public speaking can be and how fraught an experience it can be for those involved – both speakers and audiences.

I encouraged contributors to tell their stories in their own words and most did. A few were happy to be interviewed. Apart from the occasional comma or full stop, I kept to the original copy they sent me. It has sold well and is a useful guide to what anyone might expect when leaving the comfort of their warm offices for draughty village halls and sometimes unforgiving audiences.

I included a list of list of do's and do nots of public speaking to which others added their own favourites. It was by no means an exhaustive list.

My own experiences as a newspaper Editor taught me that a journalist's sense of what is or is not funny is generally totally different from the public's. A joke that has the news room splitting its sides quite often falls flat when told to an outsider - as my wife often testifies. Despite this I included a glossary of jokes sent to me over the years which can be used by speakers, depending on the audience they are addressing. However, I warned readers that the art of being able to tell a joke rather that just reading it is something that only comes with experience and even then is best avoided by those who cannot pause in the right places and place emphasis on the right words.

I enjoyed putting the book together. It was good to learn that I am not alone in finding public speaking an interesting way to gain an insight into the great British public. Some of the people I asked to contribute said they didn't have any experiences worth passing on, while others told me they regarded public speaking as a chore or something that went with the job. A few admitted they took the opportunity to delegate all speaker requests to either their deputy or some other member of staff. I was fortunate to get contributions from these 'volunteers'.

A celebrity can charge a four figure fee plus travel and accommodation costs. Hillary Clinton charges $300,000 a time. I deliberately avoided such people, interesting though some, but not all, of them might be. A few well known celebrities enjoy a free cruise in lieu of any fee, although judging by the cruises I have been on there has been a reduction in the number of speakers invited to enjoy such hospitality and a definite drop in the quality of what they have to say!

I never charged a fee when I was invited to speak in my capacity as an Editor; I felt it was a duty that really did come with the job. On most such occasions I enjoyed it. Nowadays I do charge, except when invited to speak to an organisation which has me as one of its members. Any fee I get only covers basic costs such as petrol and a lunch-time meal for Valerie and I. One year I made enough for us to have a weekend break in a top class hotel.

I have been encouraged by the number of times some organisations have invited me back. I have four talks open to anyone brave enough to invite me: Life on a Local Newspaper; Was the First World War Inevitable?; The Falklands after the 1982 War; and a talk about public speaking based on the book.

A sign on my desk has always been my guide when giving a talk. It says: *'Members of the audience are always right; sometimes confused, mis-informed, rude, stubborn, changeable and even downright stupid; but never wrong.'*

I was 18 years old when I first addressed an audience of any kind. I was extremely nervous beforehand, but once I got into my stride most, but not all, of my nerves disappeared. I am just the same today despite many years of facing hostile, sometimes sceptical, but generally friendly groups assembled to hear what I have to say. The nerves are still there to a greater or lesser degree; I console myself that is a good state to be in because it means I will give my best and not take any audience for granted.

The common fear of public speaking is called glossophobia. Some people know it as "stage fright," although many people simply confuse normal nerves and anxiety with a genuine phobia.

That first step into the unknown was at a public meeting in 1966 called by those Barnoldswick Young Liberals I referred to in an earlier chapter. We were an idealistic and very naive group of young people but we scared the pants off the establishment running our small town on the border of Yorkshire and Lancashire. Barnoldswick was a 'neglected' town with a small urban council that provided the minimum of local services and contented itself with emptying the dustbins and providing work for a small group of bureaucrats. It had no chance of raising the money that would be needed to improve recreational facilities until it was absorbed into Pendle District Council in 1974, so our efforts didn't get anywhere at the time but paved the way for a future campaign which achieved its objective when a new pool was attached to the town's secondary modern school in the 1980s. I spoke for 10 minutes and tried to rouse the audience into an indignant frenzy. There was more passion than hard facts.

More importantly, as far as I was concerned, I got a taste for public speaking and telling a story. The Barnoldswick establishment got some sort of revenge on me a few months after that initial speech when I addressed the town's rotary club lunch and outlined my work as a very junior reporter. As I was leaving the town clerk took me on one side and said: '*We prefer our speakers to wear a tie that is properly knotted and a shirt where the top button is fastened.*' From that day on I have never given a talk while not wearing a tie and I would advise any male speaker who is in doubt to wear one! I learned to tie a very good Windsor knot.

In those days I listened to far more speeches than I gave. As a young reporter I attended school speech days, council meetings, public meetings and court hearings. School speech days were by far the worst. I had no choice but to listen to six of them while a pupil at Ermysted's Skipton Grammar School and not one left any impression. The school seemed to delight in inviting back ex pupils all of whom had marvellous academic achievements but few oratory skills. Attendance was compulsory and woe betide anyone who dared not turn up.

Many years later I was on the school's shortlist to be the guest speaker at the 1985 speech day when by then I was Managing Director of the *Birmingham Daily News*. But the invitation never came. I was quietly told that only those who had gone on to one of the better universities got an invitation to speak at such a prestigious event! There was no way at that time that somebody who left with seven O'Levels and chose to serve a three-and-half-year apprenticeship on a local newspaper instead of doing A Levels was going to be invited back.

I had to do my fair share of court reporting during my first 12 months as a cub reporter, but was not disappointed when I was switched to sports reporting and only went to court when the office was short of staff. Most of the cases were relatively minor – drunkeness, theft, driving offences etc – only enlivened one memorable day when the local streaker was eventually brought to trial. The defendant had run naked through a village for some months before he was spotted by a policeman. For reasons nobody could understand the streaker climbed up a tree and defied anybody to get him down. The brave policeman took off his jacket and climbed after him. In the ensuing struggle the streaker grabbed the policeman in a painful place, but was eventually brought down to earth. When the senior magistrate gave him a heavy fine he also delivered a lengthy speech about how such behaviour would not be tolerated and during it warned: *'You must learn young man that you cannot take the law into your own hands.'* The public gallery erupted in laughter, while the court officials and solicitors tried hard not to follow. The magistrate remained stony-faced. Perhaps it is a good job I did not shout out: *'What bare-faced cheek'* or I might have been brought in front of the magistrate for contempt of court.

My favourite court speech came during a Scottish trial. The accused awaited his sentence from the sheriff and feared the worst. As he stood in the dock he was surprised when the sheriff told him: *'Although I find you a fecund liar, I will not send you to prison. '* The man expressed his thanks with the words: *'Thank you, your honour, and you are a fecund good judge!'*

When I moved to Maldon I had to develop my public speaking skills very quickly because I received a variety of invitations to attend and speak at dinners, end-of-season presentations and finals nights across a wide range of sports. Naively I thought word had got around that I was an entertaining speaker until someone who had too much to drink at one football club dinner told me that by inviting me they felt they were guaranteed a picture and report in the following Thursday's paper.

At the February 1974 general election there were few public meetings. Television had taken over and political debating was mainly conducted on screen and the more serious radio programmes. If you booked a village hall you were lucky if more than half a dozen members of the public turned up along with your own supporters and a couple of people sent by the opposition to heckle you. The election count took place on the day after the election because the Braintree constituency at that time covered a huge geographical area containing many villages. I had to stand in front of a large crowd outside Braintree Town Hall early on the Friday afternoon and give what is known as the loser's speech. I was tired, disappointed I had not won and just wanted to go home and sleep. However, one's duty meant I had to cheer up my hardy band of enthusiastic supporters so I told them that the new Tory MP was keeping the seat warm for me and next time we would get him. I could not have been more wrong - he remained Braintree's MP for 23 years until being ousted by a Labour candidate in the Tory's 1997 General Election debacle.

Later in the year I was invited to give a short rallying call at the adoption meeting of a Liberal candidate who, to save his blushes, I will not name. The said candidate had three stock answers to any questions put to him at such meetings:
1.   I agree with you.
2.   Isn't that awful?
3.   I will look into that.
Unfortunately for him the meeting was better attended than most because of a hot local issue involving local schools and his three answers began to wear a bit thin. When one woman asked what he thought about stricter discipline in primary and junior schools he saw his chance to offer something different and replied that he was in favour of *'the re-introduction of capital punishment in schools'*. The woman kept a straight face and said: *'I take it from that you favour hanging five-and-six-year olds.'* He lost his deposit in the ensuing election.

After being elected to Maldon District Council I discovered that if I had a serious message I wanted to get across I needed to pepper my comments and speeches with some humour. It proved to be a great way of either disarming or infuriating my critics and helped me play a leading part within a small opposition group that challenged the ruling Tories on the council. I was the only Liberal councillor for three years but I joined forces with a handful of Independents, two Labour councillors and one renegade Conservative to have some fun with stuffy councillors who failed to enter into the spirit of things and definitely had no sense of humour. We often won the argument but not the vote!

Perhaps the moment I enjoyed best, and caused plenty of giggles among the officers and the public gallery came when the council congratulated two councillors who had claimed a cash reward for apprehending a teenager who was kicking hell out of the ladies toilet doors in a public car park late one night. The councillors were sat in a car discussing what had gone on after a planning meeting when they noticed what the young man was intent on doing, so out they leapt and frogmarched him to the nearby police station. The reward was intended for members of the public, but the councillors claimed it from their own council and donated it to charity when the teenager was convicted.

I had to put up with several minutes of public spirit/union flag waving before I stood up and said that '*as leader of the Liberal group on the council* (I was the only one*) I wished to add my congratulations to the two councillors and hoped that in the best interests of the town they would continue to hang around the ladies' toilets in the car park.*'

The committee chairman and some of his colleagues had yet another fit and sense of humour loss; one councillor was so outraged he told me I was not a gentleman!

During this time one group I addressed at least once a year to update them on council and other matters was the Heybridge Darby and Joan Club. This involved a 30 minute talk followed by questions. They were a lovely group of older citizens who helped give me a massive majority when I stood for re-election in 1979.

Public speaking had to be taken seriously during the Mayoral year and some tough lessons had to be learned. Inevitably, I got caught out more than once. Nobody told me tradition dictated that as guest speaker at the Royal Naval Association dinner I had to stay until the end because when I left the event was over. It had been a particularly tiring Saturday with Mayoral events morning, afternoon and evening and by 11pm my wife and I were ready for home. I duly did my speaking bit, chatted a while longer and even had a couple of dances but then told the chairman we would be leaving quietly. I could tell by the look on his face that something was wrong. When I discovered what was likely to happen if we left I sat down again, the band played on and we didn't leave until 1.30am.

When I became Editor of the *Banbury Guardian* I realised that while audiences like to be educated, they also want speakers to entertain them, so I started to build up a library of jokes and funny stories. I like to think that since then I have left a smile on most people's faces after one of my talks. The *Guardian's* Editor was also expected to chair any serious public meetings. My experience on Maldon Council was put to good use in controlling some quiet rowdy audiences when a funny quip often helped to defuse some heated rows.

The launch of the *Daily News* put my public speaking skills to the test on a much larger stage. I was nominated to be the public spokesman after all the senior management team spent a week in London undergoing extensive public speaking and television training. It was an experience which persuaded some of the team they would never go in front of a television camera again! I found the training invaluable, right down to what to wear and how to look at an audience. However, it did not stop me slipping up while taking part in a BBC documentary on the running of beauty competitions. The Miss Birmingham contest attracted 140 entrants via the *Daily News*. I was chairman of the panel that had to whittle that number down to 10. I was asked on camera how we decided which girls should go through to the final and without thinking said: *'I am delighted we have chosen girls you could find on any Birmingham street.'*

The traditional newspaper groups at that time were very suspicious of what we were up to and (rightly) worried about the impact it would have on their own daily newspapers. I was in great demand to speak at conferences and one occasion I came in for some tough questioning at an all-editors conference. Afterwards one of the few friendly faces came up to me and said: *'Remember, David, that the collective noun for a group of editors is an arrogance!'*

The bravest conference speech I have ever heard was delivered at a Northcliffe newspapers conference held in Bath just before the 1999 solar eclipse. One of the sessions involved editors giving a 15 minute presentation on a subject chosen for them by head office. It was a task few enjoyed and many badly stumbled over. One Cornish Editor was told to speak on the subject *'What will the eclipse in Cornwall be like for you?'* The idea was for him to outline his newspaper's plans for coverage leading up to and beyond the event. At the appointed time the Editor stepped forward holding two circular sheets of paper – one white, one black. He stood for a moment and then slowly let the black sheet move in front of and over the white sheet and then out the other side until his arms were fully crossed. His performance over, he sat down. There was stunned silence. Nobody dared laugh, although one or two shoulders were twitching. His bosses were not amused, but he had earned himself a few pints later in the evening from his fellow Editors. It did not come as a surprise when he took early retirement soon after!

In 1987 when I was asked to travel all the way to Australia to give three 35 minute talks about the *Daily News* I suffered my worst bout of nerves. Two of the talks were at Melbourne University while the third was an address to the Pacific Area Newspaper Publishers Association conference in Adelaide.

The Adelaide talk in front of more than one thousand delegates was the only time I was genuinely frightened beforehand. I don't mean the usual pre-talk nerves, but real fright. Half an hour before I was due on stage I went to my hotel room and gave myself a good talking to along the lines of ... *'You haven't come all this way to make a hash of it now!'* After I had spoken the chairman asked me to stand with him so people could come and chat about any aspect of my talk. Most people were kind and thanked me for coming such a long way, but one man hovered at the sides and I could hear him muttering ... *'not very interesting,' ' don't know why he bothered travelling that far,' 'heard better'* etc etc. I tried to ignore him but eventually I asked the chairman who he was. *'Oh! Take no notice of him,* 'he said, *'He only repeats what everyone else is saying'.* It taught me a lesson about some of the votes of thanks I received over the years.

One speaking engagement I enjoyed while editing the *Daily News* and then becoming its Managing Director was to address - on two occasions - senior boys in Rugby School's main hall on business and marketing techniques. Afterwards over a cup of tea the departmental head who had invited me said: *'You know you spoke from exactly the same spot as Sir Winston Churchill when he came here'.*

I found Devon audiences different from those in the Midlands. I soon learnt that I had to be prepared for all eventualities. One Tuesday afternoon I spoke to a Babbacombe ladies group. I was duly introduced by the chairman and was five minutes into my talk when I saw her gesticulating wildly from the back of the hall. When I stopped in mid sentence fearing a fire had broken out or even something worse, she dashed to the front and said: *'Sorry I forgot. These ladies never listen to anyone unless they have had their cup of tea and a biscuit.'* At that point they all got up and went for their tea. I sat on the edge of the stage pretending to read my notes for 20 minutes at which point the chairman said: *'Right you can continue now from where you left off.'*

I have been fortunate in that as far as I know I have only ever 'bombed' on one occasion and it was an experience I hope I will never repeat. Soon after moving to Torquay I was invited to speak at Torquay Golf Club's annual dinner. The meal seemed to take an age to be served during which time several of those present drank and drank and drank so that when the time came for me to stand up and address them all they wanted to do was bore the rest of their table with very loud conversations. To make matters worse I was given a hand microphone which meant I could not turn the pages of my speech very easily. I eventually gave up even trying and ad libbed my way through what I knew was a dreadful performance. I have rarely used a hand microphone since.

I consoled myself that two of the greatest speakers the world has ever known also experienced times when they felt they had not delivered what their audiences expected. Abraham Lincoln's two minute Gettysburg Address on November 19 1863 is now regarded as one of the greatest speeches, but was severely criticised by newspapers of that time as being totally inadequate. Lincoln took to the stage after the previous speaker's two hour effort so you would have thought his audience and the journalists present would have welcomed such brevity.

The same could be said of Martin Luther King's *'I have a dream'* speech on August 28 1963 in front of 250,000 people in Washington. He bored his audience for nine minutes as he rambled on - applause was light. If he had stopped then the speech would have been considered a monumental flop by a nationwide television audience. But as we know the next seven minutes galvanised the civil rights movement.

My bad night out was nothing compared to that of the Professional Footballers Association in 2013 when they invited black comedian Reginald D. Hunter to be the main speaker at their awards evening in London. Mr Hunter is best known for his appearances on television's Have I got News for You and Live at the Apollo. The PFA should have known what they would get. Apparently not! PFA chairman Clarke Carlisle admitted it was a *'gross error of judgement'* to invite Mr Hunter after a media storm following some of the black comedian's 'jokes'. The PFA said it was 'totally dismayed' by the *'unacceptable language'* used after making it *'absolutely clear'* beforehand that he was to avoid discussing racial issues. Hunter repeatedly used the n-word, including jokes about Liverpool player Luis Suarez who during the season had been accused of racially abusing Manchester United's Patric Evra. The incident came at the end of a season in which the PFA had been at the centre of other race storms involving John Terry, Ashley Cole, Anton Ferdinand and Rio Ferdinand.

It is amazing that somebody, somewhere didn't think that inviting Mr Hunter might be left for another season or fifty! The PFA insisted it had no inkling that the 44-year-old stand-up comic would use such language when they hired him for the event. *'He was booked on the basis of his recent television appearances,'* they said when the media storm broke around them. I can only assume that footballers are tucked up in bed between 9pm and 10pm on a Friday when Mr Hunter regularly appears on television.

I have had my own surreal moments. I gave a talk entitled *Life on a Local Newspaper* to one Probus club in Devon which was more humorous than serious. Before the meeting and over a coffee the chairman said they had a few items of business to conduct before he would call me. I sat on one side while the secretary read the minutes of the previous meeting which were like a scene from Dibley Parish Council. He spent 15 minutes explaining what had gone on at the last meeting including reference to the previous speaker who had *'enthralled and educated them'* on the subject of linear lettering and figures in the 19th century. When I eventually stood up to speak I apologised if the audience were expecting an intellectual talk, at which point a man on the front row said: *'He was bloody boring and we all feel asleep.'* I relaxed and felt at home. Moments like that make public speaking memorable.

A talk I gave to a ladies' group nearly never happened when a church hall caretaker failed to open up the building one afternoon. We stood out in the rain while the ladies group chairman telephoned his home. He obviously did not like to be disturbed because when he turned up with the keys he was in a foul mood and blamed his church committee for not keeping him informed. He grumbled and muttered and wanted everyone to know how badly he was treated until a very gentile old lady tugged him on the arm and said: *'Tell me, which charm school did you graduate from?'* It stopped him in his tracks. When I came to speak I congratulated her and said she had achieved more in 10 seconds than I would probably achieve in 40 minutes. She nodded in agreement!

One golden rule for all speakers is never to lose your temper, no matter what the trying circumstances might be. This is sometimes easier said than done, particularly when some people will insist on talking while you are addressing them. It is bad manners, but the occasional culprit is generally too long in the tooth to change the habits of a lifetime.

One of my pet hates is people who turn up late and refuse to enter the room quietly while I am speaking. I have only snapped once when giving a talk. A husband and wife duo banged the door behind them as they came in, made people stand up as they shuffled to the seats they wanted in the middle of a row and scraped their chairs as they put their coats on the back of their seats. I stopped in mid sentence, looked at them as they eventually sat down and asked: *'Is there anything I can get you? Like a watch!'* The audience loved it and afterwards the chairman told me the couple behaved exactly the same way at most meetings.

I am sure there must have been times when some organisations thought about asking me to speak, but then thought better of it. The only time I have ever been told I was simply not wanted came when I was asked if I would be the external law advisor and speaker for Leeds University's media law courses. The invitation came via a friend at the Press Association who had the awkward job of telling me some months later; *'You are the best qualified person in the*

country but they won't have you because you haven't got a degree!'
Apparently the aforementioned University of Life did not count!

I have rarely refused an invitation to speak unless it has clashed with my work, but one invitation in 2012 could have been fun, if I had gone ahead. Out of the blue Reading University sent me an email inviting me to address students on my 'exploits in space'. It said that if I could not travel to Reading personally they were prepared to arrange a video link. Some people might think I live on another planet, but I doubt whether they would want to hear about my experiences. The university had confused me with David Scott the American astronaut who was the first man to drive on the moon. I respectfully declined the invitation and while pointing out their mistake added that even my rendition of 'Fly me to the Moon' would not be worth hearing. I didn't get a response.

I have tried to get on the cruise ship speaking circuit, but so far failed. I wrote to a number of companies but failed to get any replies. I understand you have to be a 'name' or on an agency's books.

I have heard (suffered?) too many awful, cringing speeches by best men at weddings. Of course it is a necessary duty and one most people perform to support their best friend, but the audience simply want you to get up, say a few original friendly words, propose the appropriate toast and sit down. Ten minutes is the absolute maximum for any best man's speech and it is best if you remember that the bride and groom's aunts, uncles and possibly grandparents are listening to your every word. Stag night revelations are not required, nor details of schoolboy pranks. Any mention of previous girlfriends and their sexual prowess are totally taboo.

Yet time and time again I have had to sit through badly presented, sometimes totally boring, often offensive and crude speeches that would have benefited from someone using the old fashioned hook to drag the best man away. A couple of politically correct jokes are fine. Words that spell out what a wonderful couple they are go down well with the families. A bowl full of 'thank yous' are also necessary. After that sit down. Good wedding speeches should be like a mini skirt – short enough to attract attention; long enough to cover the bare essentials.

A wedding my wife and I were glad we were not invited to involved a friend who got married 'on the rebound'. One minute she was engaged to the love of her life, the next it was all off and she was going out with somebody else. Within a few months a wedding was back on to the new man in her life. At the reception her father referred to the former boyfriend as his daughter's husband rather than the groom, much to everyone's embarrassment.

Apart from my schooldays, I can only remember having to sit through two very, very boring speeches, both of which I was surprisingly looking forward to. The first was given by the then Foreign Secretary Douglas Hurd at an Editors' conference in Birmingham. Mr Hurd was a popular MP and Minister but as far as I was concerned he could bore for England. His 45-minute monotone offering was the last thing a group of Editors wanted to hear when the bar was still open. Fortunately the night was saved when I came to leave and literally bumped into Sir Stanley Matthews who had been the speaker in another room. We exchanged apologies. I would have much preferred to have heard Sir Stanley speak about his footballing days.

Another sporting hero was Sir Garfield Sobers, the great West Indian cricketer. I went to watch him tear England apart in several 1970s Test matches and also when he played county cricket. Thirty years later he spoke without notes at a Paignton Cricket Club dinner and fund-raiser at Torquay's Riviera Centre and rambled all over the place. It was quite embarrassing as he repeated himself several times and lost his way. Good fortune came to my aid that night because I won £250 in the raffle!

At least Mr Hurd and Mr Sobers did not resort to telling smutty jokes to entertain their audience. Nowadays too many after-dinner speakers liberally sprinkle dirty jokes and bad language into their offering. They believe every sentence should include the 'f' word and other obscenities which they pepper throughout their boring, repetitive discourse. They call it entertainment but only those who have had too much to drink think it entertaining – the rest find it offensive and cringe-making.

Innuendo is fine. A master of that is comedian Don Mclean whom I got to know and befriend during my time in Birmingham. He has retained the art of holding his audience's attention without resorting to the use of one bad or offensive word. It's a skill I admire.

Sadly, I cannot think of any modern politician or sportsman I feel I simply have to listen to if the opportunity arises. In most cases you can predict much of what they are going to say in advance, their efforts dulled by their attempts to survive in a media world where sound bites are needed for television in particular.

Thankfully there are people who can enthral an audience at a purely local level and they are in great demand by the hundreds of organisations which meet every week up and down the country in village halls, pubs and hotels.

I was once asked to name the three people I would have most liked to have heard give a speech and I had no hesitation in naming David Lloyd George, the Welsh windbag to his opponents, Billy Graham in his hey-day and Moses. There was much to dislike about Lloyd George, but having read his memoirs and several books about his life and times there can be little doubt he was a spellbinding speaker who at his peak held an audience in the palm of his hand. Can you say that about any British politician today? From the people I have spoken to who attended one of Billy Graham's Crusades I have no doubt he was a magnificent speaker who touched the hearts and souls of those who heard him – a special gift he used to the best of his ability. As for Moses, well anyone who at the age of 80 could lead hundreds of thousands of people for the next 40 years through a desert to their promised land must have been a gifted speaker as well as a man of action. From accounts in the Bible he had to deliver many strong speeches to keep his flock moving in the right direction.

CHAPTER SIXTEEN

FINAL REFLECTIONS

The word LISTEN contains the same letters as the word SILENT
– Alfred Brendel

Reflecting on what has happened to you, what you have done and how it might have turned out differently is no bad thing as long as you have the good sense to learn from your mistakes and never repeat them. I have led an interesting life and travelled the world. I could not have done it without the help of many people. Politics and regional newspapers have dominated my life.

At the May 2010 General Election I didn't vote for the Liberal Democrats. It was the first time I ever put my cross anywhere else than against the Lib Dem candidate's name. I still intensely disliked the 'blue-rinse brigade', but hoped Tory leader David Cameron would have the bottle to make the major changes the country and his party needed. Unfortunately, he has missed the opportunity. If he had been far more radical in his first two years he might have been able to instigate fundamental long term changes. I believe the country would have backed him. Alas, he has not proved strong enough, although some of the changes to the benefits system pushed through in 2013 by Iain Duncan Smith were long overdue. However, on immigration, Europe and same-sex marriage I disagree with the policies Cameron has pursued. I don't believe him when he says he will get the migration figures down and was not surprised in February 2015 when it was revealed the figure had risen to an annual rate of 296,000 – more than when the Coalition came to power.

It cannot go on if we are to avoid trouble in the not-too-distant future. Put bluntly, a majority don't believe Cameron's promises to introduce effective measures to limit immigration to sustainable levels. The Labour party has no credibility either. Who can forget the figures pumped at us by the Tony Blair and Gordon Brown governments? One sticks in my mind: a claim in 2004 that only 15,000 Poles would come to the UK after their country was admitted to the European Union. More than that number now reside in Southampton alone!

Our economy needs sensible immigration. It is nonsense to suggest we should put up the barricades and keep out every foreigner. We need skilled migrants and should welcome those who can contribute something to our country and earn a better living for themselves and their families. A majority don't want the current open doors policy forced on us by Europe.

What upsets ordinary people like me going about their everyday business is the belief we have been lied to and the fact we have been far too generous in handing over taxpayers' money to foreigners who have seen us as a soft touch. Proper integration has not taken place or been encouraged. Integration with the resident population is difficult when large numbers from another country settle in one area. In my lifetime successive governments have never made a serious effort to tackle the effects and drawbacks of mass immigration into some of our towns and cities. This is not racist propaganda, but reality.

Some people argue that we need the present level of immigration to fuel the low income economy. But they don't take into account the strain such large numbers who have come into this country in the last 15 years have put on the NHS, schools and a scarce housing stock. Cheap migrant labour has undercut wages for all and led to the public becoming very cynical about what politicians tell them.

In a damning indictment of the UK's current and past policies on immigration, Sir Trevor Phillips, former head of the Equalities Commission, revealed in a television documentary in March 2015 how he and others had got it awfully wrong. Only time will tell whether the damage can be undone. I have my doubts!

Many people think the government has been reducing our debt since 2010 after years of Labour mis-managing the economy. What the majority still don't realise is that all we have done is reduce the amount we are borrowing and over-spending each year. The national debt is growing. We are still spending money we don't have. Future generations will not forgive us for landing them with the bills when large amounts have to be paid back.

The last General Election result was the worst one possible for the Lib Dems because they were forced into a coalition with the Conservatives which was bound to anger those on the left. They had no option really because Labour had made such a mess of the economy and Gordon Brown was an awful Prime Minister. After years of advocating consensus politics they could hardly turn their backs on playing their part in government when the chance came, yet it exposed them to the realities of power.

Many of my worst fears about how they would respond were realised, not helped by several of their MPs becoming embroiled in sex scandals and criminal activities. Surprisingly, the coalition has held together despite the occasional blip. I think the next General Election in May 2015 will not be a happy one for them and they could well lose more than half their seats to both Labour and the Conservatives. If the opinion polls are right the party could be reduced to only a handful of MPs.

Deep down in my heart from the mid 1980s onwards I worried that once placed in power the Lib Dems would be useless; up to then they could be all things to all men and an attractive home for those wanting an alternative to Labour and the Tories. At the 2010 General Election they made the fatal mistake of promising silly things they could never deliver including a disastrous claim they would not support any rise in students' tuition fees - which were duly increased within a few months of the election. Party leader Nick Clegg was 'toast' from that moment.

This hadn't been a problem before, because they had never had to carry through their policies, but when they joined the coalition and became part of government they were rumbled. If the opinion polls are to be believed the public has deserted them in droves. Monthly ratings have been lower than the dark days of the mid 1970s. I fear they will be in the political wilderness for many years to come.

The old Liberal Party I supported from my teens no longer exists. It joined forces with the short-lived SDP at the end of the 1980s and changed in the process. I regained my old political flair during the 2001 General Election campaign, but the honeymoon did not last long and well before my well recorded fallout with Torbay Lib Dems in 2004/5 I had seen enough of the party, its supporters and its MPs to realise I no longer belonged and, perhaps more importantly, did not support many of its policies.

I do not agree with giving votes to prisoners, or the under 18s; I do not support equality policies that encourage gay marriage and I certainly do not support the current Human Rights Act which allows dangerous terrorists and criminals to both stay in this country and pick up full benefits.

I have also become very disenchanted with the continued expansion of the European Union. How can you support an organisation whose auditors have refused to sign off the accounts for 13 years running because billions of pounds cannot be accounted for? There is no check on where huge sums of money go. In 1975 I - along with many others of my age - voted for a Common Market, not a United States of Europe! I don't believe that coming out of the European Union would damage our economy, but the scaremongers will claim that it would and they will probably frighten people to vote to stay in when we do eventually get a referendum. Unless, of course, after the next election another promise is broken! I find it amazing our politicians have allowed the European Parliament to pass a large number of laws which the majority of people of this country do not want.

Perhaps I was too idealistic in my youth but I was a Liberal because I regarded the Conservatives as the establishment and reactionary, while Labour was dominated by militant unions. I saw enough of the latter while working in Chelmsford and whilst an Editor to understand how they were dragging the country down and down. They didn't care about pensioners or anyone who was not a member of their union. The middle ground, centred round doing my best for ordinary people, fighting for the underdog and those genuinely in need either through poor health or unemployment was where I felt most comfortable. In the sixties and seventies I could never have supported a party in hock to either big business or the most powerful unions.

My generation has a lot to answer for, particularly in allowing vast swathes of the population to believe that benefits are theirs as a way of life rather than a safety net. Why should any youngster bother with a job when they can collect £100 a week plus other benefits for staying in bed all morning and doing nothing? The more enterprising do a few jobs on the side for cash in hand. Why should people save to buy a house when they can get so much housing benefit? We now have second and third generations who don't want to work because they have seen how mother, father and older brother live off benefits. It must be soul destroying for good teachers when they hear a 13-year old say: '*Why should I work hard at school and pass exams. I will be happy never to work.*'

In March 2012 I trained a young girl who went to Churston Grammar School and was working on the *Plymouth Herald* on a trainee reporter's salary of £15,000 a year. She told me that out of 12 female classmates, eight now had children and only two were working. However, all the benefit claimants could afford to spend more on their Saturday night's out than she could. It cannot be right. How have we come to such a state?

Every week new figures come out showing how we have allowed a situation to develop which economically is unsustainable. More than 80,000 people say they cannot work because of obesity and claim full benefits, while disability benefits are abused by those who say they suffer from back pain or stress. I feel genuinely sorry for anyone who falls on hard times through poor health or lack of work opportunities, but far too many people permanently out of work have chosen a lifestyle never intended for them when the welfare state came into being after the Second World War.

The welfare state appears to be doing the opposite of what it was intended to do. Far from giving people a route out of poverty, or providing some temporary help, it has created a culture of dependency and with it an inevitable underclass.

It is interesting to listen to my sons, Timothy and Robin, who pay their taxes and feel angry that people they know refuse to work but can still afford to buy alcohol or have a good holiday. There are many young people who do work hard – the majority. The politicians better watch out because they will rebel one day.

Torbay, while not alone, is a microcosm of all that is wrong. Too many people of all ages hang around the town centres. They are not actively looking for work. One day we will have to tell these people: '*If you haven't paid anything in, you can't take anything out*'. The bill will only get worse as more people live longer. Future generations will have to pay it.

That should not mean we don't have compassion for the genuinely poor, the man or woman who has fallen on hard times through no fault of their own, the ill or the mentally disadvantaged. Instead we should be directing even more effort their way. However, the state should not be expected to do everything. I see much good work done by churches and charities, despite successive governments over the last 25 years actively discouraging Christians in particular from dealing with many of society's problems. I pray nearly every day for a reversal and a realisation that if we are to look after the needy we do need Christian values in this country to prevail.

In 2013 and 2014 I spent 12 months helping out at the Living Room run by St Mary Magdalene Church in the centre of Torquay. They asked Upton Vale Baptist Church if they would provide a team to run a community cafe in the main church on Fridays. Their own volunteers run it on Wednesdays and Thursdays. It caters for the homeless, ex offenders, people undergoing drug or alcohol rehabilitation, or anyone who just needs a safe haven for a few hours. Team leader was Rachel Kiddey, wife of John who had played a big part in the Elected Mayor campaign.

I was asked to run a Job Club aimed at getting people back into work and helped a dozen people of all ages with CVs, interview techniques and general job advice. The problem was that few of the people who turned up for the free food wanted to work, although many of them were quite capable of doing so. We served free bacon baps, cake and drinks and within a few months had brought in housing association managers, the *Big Issue's* south west organiser, council support staff and credit union expertise to help us. The police gave excellent support, but this created some tensions, particularly when it was discovered the Living Room attracted drug dealers who were happy to find many of their clients under one roof every Friday.

When the Prince's Trust came to have a look at what we were doing, they asked if I would be prepared to become one of their volunteer business mentors helping people aged 18-30 find work or start their own businesses. I underwent their training programme in Plymouth and started helping in Torbay in March 2014.

Working in the Living Room was quite an eye-opener into the problems society faces. I talked to and helped several people who were actively seeking a way to come off benefits and lead a normal life. They were prepared to listen to the expertise we had available and work out their best route to normality. However, far too many people I chatted to each Friday were not only happy to live off the welfare state for the rest of their lives, but as far as I could see had their priorities very wrong. When they received their weekly money their must-have purchases - in no particular order - were topping up their mobile phones, drugs and alcohol. Food was fourth on their shopping list. I doubt the founders of the welfare state would approve of the way quite a bit of public money is spent today.

In July 2014 St Mary Magdalene decided they no longer wanted the one-stop shop we had created with the various agencies and reverted to running the Living Room as a straight forward community cafe with their own team of volunteers. Upton Vale relinquished their involvement at that point.

I rarely see an Asian face in Torbay unless I visit the hospital or go to an opticians. It is a different story, however, when I make the occasional visit north to see family in the Pendle Council district covering towns like Nelson and Brierfield. All but a very small percentage of Muslims are law-abiding and hard working people wanting to make the best of the opportunities available. They appear to share a common loathing of terrorism. But until recently the country has been sleep-walking with regard to the spread of Islam and terrorism within the UK. If you dared criticise Muslim extremism you were called a racist, especially by the people I call the 'Notting Hill set' whose ultra liberal views are out of touch with reality elsewhere. A recent report which revealed London is the centre for radicalising Muslims who go on to commit terror acts should be a wake-up call.

We got it awfully wrong in the 1980s and 1990s when governments failed to implement policies that would have made a success of multiculturalism. The Labour Party cynically knows it owes some of its seats in Parliament to the Muslim vote. I fear it will take something really shocking to make us do something about the problems we now face. I have no sympathy with right-wing extremists, but they do attract support – and it will grow – because the main political parties won't tackle this issue.

There were growing signs in 2014 that the majority have had enough of mere platitudes and want real action – not mealy-mouthed words. It's difficult to disagree with the 72-year-old man who wrote this letter to both David Cameron and Ed Miliband. He did not get a reply.

'Dear Sirs, You BOTH worry me! In fact, both of your political parties worry me. Over the last three years, you both have been turning this country into a place that I no longer feel at home in, or feel part of. I watch you in Parliament sneering at each other and acting like children. If you were my children, I would be ashamed of you.

Although you would like us all to believe that you are putting the needs of this country first, everyone knows that neither of you are doing that. You are more interested in scoring points off each other. Do you somehow think that will impress people and get you votes next year?

What is achieved by all those shenanigans in Parliamen is denigrating our once-great nation in the eyes of the world. You would never see German politicians doing that. They have recovered so wonderfully from WW2 by hard work and image - being careful never to run down their own country in public.

People have come here from other countries, for a better life, for more years than I have been alive. Pre and post- war immigrants came for a better life, settled in and became wonderful contributors to this country. They have contributed to the rich diversity of Britain and many have fought for this country. They were glad to become UK citizens and they had no handouts.

I have never before had a problem with immigrants, but I do now. Please tell me why there are some areas where the police are afraid to go? Please tell me why we can no longer have religion in schools for fear of "offending" someone?

Please tell me why Christmas celebration is no longer allowed in some schools for fear of offending someone? Please tell me how Christmas decorations in stores might offend someone? Please tell me why we have to have segregated days in public swimming pools for fear of offending someone? Please tell me why we allow radical Muslim clerics to demand Sharia Law? Please tell me why our laws need to be changed so as not to offend someone?

Please tell me why we must not wear a bike helmet if we go into a bank and yet it is OK to wear a Burka, covering the whole of the face? We even have a British born "radical," who states that Britain will become a Muslim country under Sharia Law, and that we had "better get used to it ".

Will both of you grow up and start sticking up for this country and its people? '

I could not have put it any better.

In May 2010 I realised I had to make a decision with regard to how much longer I wanted to be away from home every week running training courses. This coincided with a downturn in regional newspaper profits and the start of a massive cull of 'expensive' Editors, photographers and reporters. For a while recruitment dried up until managements realised they had cut too far and had to start taking on staff again, some of whom they had given redundancy money only a few months earlier!

Suddenly, there were fewer junior reporters to train and many of the Editors whom I had got to know, and had given me a lot of work, found themselves out of their well-paid jobs. Out of the door with them went local knowledge and experience. Inevitably, quality suffered and readers deserted their local papers in droves. When sales nose-dived the internet was blamed for all the industry's ills in a collective amnesia to put the blame at every door but at the one where it should have been placed. I can't say I was surprised, having watched how greedy some managements with no real feel for the business had been over the previous 10 years, along with their failure to invest in their printed products.

However, it meant coping with a major change of lifestyle. The only saving grace was that I had put aside enough money over the years to see Valerie and I through to December 2012 when I turned 65 and started to receive both state and private pension income.

I knew I had had enough of living in hotels two or three nights every week; it had lost its appeal. I was beginning to strongly resist regularly travelling long distances by car and train in all weathers and not getting home until very late on Friday nights. I knew it was time to re-think what I wanted to really do when one Tuesday lunch-time I was waiting at Newton Abbot railway station for a train to take me to Kent for four days. I wanted to cry. I felt so lonely and knew then it was time to re-evaluate what I wanted from the rest of my life.

Thankfully, the decision was partly taken out of my hands. Some of the newspapers I worked for cutback training – a few cut their entire budgets - and their decline accelerated.

I thought my work might dry up all together; for the first time I had no work at all some months. To my initial surprise I enjoyed being at home and doing what I wanted to do, particularly during the summer. When it came to a toss up between watching cricket at Taunton or running a training course in a once thriving, but now half-empty, office there was only one winner.

In the last two years I have had more work than I expected and been more than happy with my lot. I believe I have found the right balance. A few nights away from home each month have been bearable. Mentally I have adjusted and not let the state of the newspaper industry worry me.

On reflection, I realise I was fortunate to have plenty of work during the years I most needed it. If the recession and print decline had come 10 years earlier it would have been devastating. As it was, we had only a small mortgage after moving out of Ferndene in 2006 and down-sizing. I paid it off in June 2012 – another landmark for someone of my generation. By then all three children were through university and not living at home which meant Valerie and I could significantly reduce our overheads and enjoy a comfortable lifestyle. Praise God!

I hope my Polish father would be proud of me – if he only knew!

INDEX

Hutchings, Dennis, 62

Idi Amin, 75
Inmates pop group, 22, 41
IPSO, 173

Jack, David and Eve, 85, 96
Jackson, Warren, 148, 149
Jeffries, Chris, 173
Jehovah's Witnesses, 80, 81
Job interview tips, 73
Jones, David, 213, 214, 230
Johnston Press, 160

Kay, Richard, 46
Keeler, Christine, 20
Kelly, Terry and Irene, 3, 10-12, 48, 88
Kennedy, Nigel, 122
Kent and Sussex Courier, 144
Kiddey, John and Rachel, 188, 190, 193
Kidderminster Times, 115
Kinnock, Neil, 138
Korean War, 6, 7
Kyle, Keith, 66, 68

Laker, Freddie, 92
Lamont, Norman, 138
Land, Barbara, 47
Langley, Bill, 46
Laurie, Peter, 50, 64
Lawrence, Marcia and Amanda, 86
Lawson. Nigel, budget, 138, 139
Lawson, Stan, 25, 36
Laycock's buses, 16
Lee, Faith, 154
Leeds-Liverpool canal, 20
Leeds University, 242
Leicester Mercury, 111, 162
Levy, Harry, 101, 102

*Romford Recorder,*71, 76
Ross, John, Dianna, Jacqueline, 65, 67, 222
Rotherham Advertiser, 170
Rowntree Trust, 84
Rugby School, 239
Russell, Sir Bob, 40, 46, 50

Sadds CC, 63
Salvation Army, 6, 199
Samuel, Brian, 46
Sanders, Adrian, 175-187, 191, 198
San Diego Chargers, 95
Savage, John, 66
Saxton, John, 78, 91, 101, 103-105, 144
Saye and Sele, Lord, 110
Scarborough New, 171
Scott, Annie, 5, 6
Scott, Brian, 3, 6, 13, 24, 223
Scott Ernest (father), 2, 4-10, 17, 89, 223
Scott Ernest senior, 5, 6
Scott, Georgina, 111, 116, 142, 201, 216
Scott Robin, 124, 142, 183, 210, 216, 218, 223, 229
Scott, Sandra (see Taylor), 1-3, 6, 11, 219, 223
Scott Stephen, 3, 13, 24
Scott Timothy, 124, 134, 142, 195, 216, 223, 228, 229
Scott Valerie, 1-2, 86-89, 91-96, 103-105, 116, 124, 125, 141-143, 148, 155, 183, 196, 201, 204, 205, 215, 216, 254, 255
Scott Violet, 2, 4-10, 220, 223
Scott Wendy, 31, 32, 220
Searle, Keith, 44,
Sevenoaks Chronicle, 144
Shalford CC, 59, 63
Shah, Eddy, 70, 101
Sheldrick, Giles, 159
Sheffield Morning Telegraph, 49, 58
Sheffield United FC, 227
Sheringham, Teddy, 159
Silentnight, 16, 33
Skipton Hospital, 17
Smith, Cyril, 66
Smith, George, 18
Smith Norman, 53, 56

14153125R00153

Printed in Great Britain
by Amazon.co.uk, Ltd.,
Marston Gate.